american daughter

american daughter

•

ERA BELL THOMPSON

Minnesota Historical Society Press • St. Paul • 1986

Borealis Books are high-quality paperback reprints of books chosen by the Minnesota Historical Society Press for their importance as enduring historical sources and their value as enjoyable accounts of life in the Upper Midwest.

Minnesota Historical Society Press, St. Paul 55101

Copyright © 1946 by The University of Chicago Press
Reprinted 1967 by Follett Publishing Company

Reprinted 1986 by arrangement with The University of Chicago Press
New material copyright © 1986 by the Minnesota Historical Society

International Standard Book Number 0-87351-201-4
Manufactured in the United States of America
10   9   8   7   6   5   4   3   2   1

Library of Congress Cataloging-in-Publication Data

Thompson, Era Bell, 1907-
  American daughter.

  Reprint. Originally published: Chicago: University of Chicago Press.
  1. Thompson, Era Bell, 1907-   2. Afro-
Americans — Biography. 3. Afro-Americans — North
Dakota — Social life and customs. 4. North Dakota —
Social life and customs. I. Title.
E185.97.T53A3   1986   978.4'00496073'0924 [B] 86-12786
ISBN 0-87351-201-4

*To the memory of
my Mother and Father*

PUBLISHER'S NOTE

"Ever since I left the state in 1931," Era Bell Thompson later remembered, "people have asked, 'where is North Dakota' and 'what in the world was a nice Negro girl like you doing in that godforsaken country in the first place?'" In 1945, living in Chicago but filled with pride in North Dakota, Thompson applied to The Newberry Library for a fellowship to answer the first question with a book "differentiating between the two Dakotas and denying that they are overrun by buffaloes and Indians." The Newberry committee, however, was more interested in the second question. She was awarded a Fellowship in Midwestern Studies to support the writing of her autobiography, *American Daughter*, which was published the next year by the University of Chicago Press to generally favorable reviews. The *Christian Science Monitor* called it "one of the most delightful books in a long time"; *Current History* thought the work "a rattling good story of [Thompson's] family and her own life, with a keen sense of humor"; *Library Journal* found her story "moving, human, positive, triumphant."[1]

As Thompson explained in her preface to the 1967 edition of this book, "Usually an autobiography is written near the end of a long and distinguished career, but not taking any chances, I wrote mine first, then began to live." After the publication of her autobiography, Thompson became associate editor of *Ebony* magazine, then newly established by

[1] Thompson, "What's a Nice Girl Like You Doing in a Place Like That," *North Dakota Horizons* 3 (Spring 1973): 26; *Book Review Digest, 1946*, p. 817-18. See also Kathie Ryckman Anderson, "Era Bell Thompson: A North Dakota Daughter," *North Dakota History* 49 (Fall 1982): 11-18; interview by Larry Sprunk, September 16, 1975, State Historical Society of North Dakota, Bismarck; and interview by Marcia M. Greenlee, March 6 and 10, 1978, Black Women's Oral History Project, Schlesinger Library, Radcliffe College, Cambridge.

the Johnson Publishing Company. She was *Ebony*'s co-managing editor from 1951 to 1964, when she became international editor for Johnson Publishing, a position she still held in 1986, although she was semiretired. She has written many articles and a book, *Africa, Land of My Fathers* (New York: Doubleday and Co., 1954). She also co-edited *White on Black: The Views of Twenty-Two White Americans on the Negro* (Chicago: Johnson Publishing Co., 1963).

In 1969 Thompson was awarded an honorary doctoral degree from the University of North Dakota; ten years later that university's Black Cultural Center was renamed in her honor, and in 1981 she was inducted into the university's Athletic Hall of Fame. She received North Dakota's Theodore Roosevelt Roughrider Award, the state's highest honor, in 1976, and her portrait hangs in the Roughrider Hall of Fame in the state's Capitol. In 1978 she participated in the Black Women's Oral History Project, sponsored by the Schlesinger Library at Radcliffe College, which produced interviews of women seventy years of age or older who had made "significant contributions to the lives of black people and to the development of American society"; her photograph is included in *Women of Courage: An Exhibition of Photographs by Judith Sedwick* (Cambridge, Mass.: Radcliffe College, 1984), which was based on the project.

In 1986 Thompson lived in Chicago and volunteered her time at a hospital and a library nearby. She made occasional trips to North Dakota, where, she remembered, "You can go all day long without saying anything. Even if you have somebody with you, you don't talk a lot, but you think a lot. My brothers didn't like it. I got there just in time—at just the right age—to love it. I would go back now and live there if it weren't for the winters. It's just like going home."

CONTENTS

american
daughter

1) GO WEST, BLACK MAN

"My Lord, it's a girl!" Pop stumbled blindly out into the kitchen, slumped into a chair, and again said, "Oh, my Lord!"

Now, my Lord had heretofore been very good to my father, for he had three sons: Tom, Dick and, Harry.

There had been another girl a long time before, a girl with fair skin and blonde hair. My father and mother said she "took back." Our white neighbors were taken aback, too. They didn't blame the iceman, exactly, but they strongly suspected there was something in the Thompson woodpile besides a Negro—and there was.

In Father's mulatto veins flowed also the blood of a Dutchman, a Frenchman, and a couple of Indians. Pop had to claim two Indians to make up for the Cherokee chief who was my mother's grandfather, and to cover up that touch of Chinese he couldn't account for.

He, too, had had fair hair when he was a little boy down on the Old Thompson plantation in Virginia, for his mother, a freed woman, was a servant in the Big House, and his father was Old Thompson's son. Though not a slave, he was still a Negro, with all of his blonde hair, and, as such, could not attend school; but his white half sisters taught him from their books, and by the time he was ten he was teaching grown men and women how to read and write. When his father was killed in the Civil War, his mother was free to marry Evans, a colored man, father of her son, John, and the three little girls. After Emancipation the family did not wait for the "mule and forty acres." They set out on foot for the great Northwest. Father ran away at the first stop and became a stableboy at a roadside inn, but the others moved on.

Twenty years passed before he found his people, and during that time he did many things to earn a livelihood. In Terre Haute he was the best-dressed and fastest waiter in town; he cooked for racehorse men throughout Kentucky and Maryland, was chef on the private dining car of the general manager of the Baltimore and Ohio, and was waiter, cook, or proprietor of eateries from New York's Hole in the Wall, to the notorious Bucket of Blood in New Orleans. The large oval picture that hung on our living room wall was the bust and apron strings of Pop. The starched white cap sat at a rakish angle, the small black moustache didn't quite cover the confident smile, and the bright eyes twinkled mischievously. A much larger edition of the same picture graced the side of an Illinois hotel in the town where he married my mother, a nursemaid for a wealthy family and also a Virginian. Of his first two wives I know very little, for he had learned, by the time I was born, to let bygones be bygones—especially female bygones.

In 1899 Father located John, then a coal miner in Iowa. Ever restless, always venturesome, Pop took Mother and Baby Dick to join his half brother. Father was disappointed. The sooty cap of the miner was a far cry from that of a cook, and then, too, there was Ann. Ann Evans was white—white and

Irish. Father couldn't quite forgive his brother for marrying a white woman—and Ann never forgot. When the Evanses and their two children moved on to a North Dakota homestead, Father again felt the call of the kitchen and went to Des Moines, where Tom and Harry were born, and where the little girl was born and later died, still blonde, still white.

So when they told him he was again the father of a girl, he began to worry. He needn't have. When I lost the newborn pallor, I began taking on racial traits so quickly and decidedly that Mother became alarmed. They had worried about Tom, too. He startled everybody with his tight, red hair and his yellow, freckled nose. Pop would look hard at Tom and shake his head. "You'd better go 'way from here with that red stuff, boy, and come back lookin' like one of us." But now, at eight, Tom's hair was brown, and his freckles and complexion were one.

Colored storks are notoriously inconsistent.

We Thompsons were a constant surprise to the good people of Des Moines. Ours was the first Negro family to move into the little East Side community, and whatever fears the neighbors may have had about property devaluation were soon dispelled by the continuous improvements that went on about our home. Pop planted flowers and shrubbery; he built a neat white fence around the yard and painted the house. When he sodded the lawn, even the policeman who lived on the hill came down to watch and stayed to help. By the time I was born, we owned the little cottage on the bank of the lake, and my father was a community leader and proprietor of a thriving restaurant.

There were brief, but lucrative, intermissions into Iowa politics that relieved the monotony of cooking. Pop was given the colored babies to kiss and a job in the senate as cloakroom attendant. He was a good speaker, and he loved to talk, but every time he appeared on our school program, Tom and Dick were conspicuously absent.

Our Sunday mornings were spent in the Sunday school across the lake, but the greater part of the day and much of the night found Trustee Thompson in the center of things religious

15

at Colored Baptist downtown. Colored Baptist could be very exciting. I can still remember one of the more successful "unchurchings," one aimed at the dear Elder himself. He was a little reluctant about giving up his position in the church, but, with the aid of three policemen, they eventually got him into a patrol wagon, and he was not alone.

It was also the duty of a trustee to visit the sick and console the lonely. There was one very lonely widow in the congregation whom Mother called a hussy, so, when Mom couldn't go to the church, she dressed me in my ruffled best and admonished me to stick with Pop. I didn't mind, for I worshipped my father. That the ladies made a fuss over me only when I was with him didn't really matter.

The lodge of which Pop was Most Noble Grand something or other was a secret organization, but their goings-on sometimes leaked out. When meeting nights became too frequent, I was again put on detail. Pop balked. If I was old enough to follow him around, I was old enough to go to school, where I could really learn something. So, long before I should have, I was following my three brothers to the brick schoolhouse down on the corner.

My education had a propitious beginning—I flunked kindergarten. The curriculum wasn't difficult; I ate the smooth white paste in the glass jars and was stand-in for a mamma doll when the children wanted to play real rough. My parents were so busy with the boys that they had little time to worry about my I.Q. They went to school, by request, at least once a week in behalf of the two older boys, and I became the family carrier pigeon, bringing home notes when Dick didn't go to school and notes when Tom did.

Tom was an inveterate fighter at the age of eight, but as he grew older and stronger the fights had serious results. During a recess quarrel a boy swung at Tom's head with a baseball bat. Tom ducked and the boy ran, but not fast enough.

"We've got to do something about these boys," Mother said when they brought him home, "or they'll both be expelled."

16

"If they're old enough to get into trouble, they're old enough to work, Mary. They got to have somethin' to do to use up all that energy."

Putting action to words, Father promptly got paper routes for his sons and bicycles for the paper routes. Dick ran amuck with a Scott Street trolley, and the streetcar won. That canceled one route. With a wheel, Tom got around faster, saw more people, and had more fights.

My father tried competition. He brought home a billy goat, which led the neighborhood a merry chase and us right out of Iowa.

"If trouble's what they want," Pop said, breathing heavily, "this here gentleman's willin' and ready."

Pop had made good time en route. Billy was replete with green wagon and harness, but the master of the house preferred to lead him quietly home. The tempo increased, however, when a certain goatlike pressure was brought to bear, and my father's sprinting ability stood him in good stead. The last lap of the journey, according to public opinion, was a thing of beauty, and Father set a precedent Billy never forgot. During the next three months, Pop spent more and more time out in front.

Again the neighbors came to gaze, but they didn't come very close. Billy was lean and white, with a sharp Vandyke beard and long, menacing horns. He had Tom's combative instincts, Dick's fleetness, and everybody's respect. The goat had no inhibitions, and, even if he had, Mother wouldn't have liked him. On a clear day one could see far across the lake into Gilbertown. It was just such a day that Mom looked up from her washing and saw Billy streaking over the bridge, hell-bent for home. She never bothered to close the door; she jumped right into the tub, clothes, suds, and all.

After that the goat had to go. There was a three-day period of frustration, but on the fourth day we crated him after he was in the baggage car, and shipped him on to North Dakota and Uncle John. The community once more settled down to comparative peace and quiet.

17

When Uncle John saw the goat, he sent for the rest of us. He wrote glowingly of the boundless prairies, the new land of plenty where a man's fortune was measured by the number of his sons, and a farm could be had even without money. Father wasn't immediately impressed; he wasn't ever sold on the soil. Space was all right for John and that white wife of his, but, according to the spiritual, "There was plenty good room in the Father's Kingdom," and he, for one, could wait.

Remembering John's other appeal—and its results—Mother wasn't sure.

Pop had one more ace to play: he started a garden, a co-operative venture. Maybe the soil was the solution, after all. My brothers lacked proper enthusiasm, however, and Father was forced to resort to chain-gang tactics to get the work done; but done it was, and the crop was good and bountiful. It was probably that touch of gardening that put farming in Father's blood; if so, it was later a touch of farming that took it out.

The garden also did something to Dick's sensitive soul, and we lost him in the middle of the potato debugging, when the Paris green ran out. The killing had proceeded by hand, but Dick wasn't the killer type. A week later my mother got an SOS from St. Louis which read: "Please send twenty dollars. Your loving son, Dick." That telegram, with upward monetary revisions, was the pattern of many more to come. Later, as the family grew less susceptible and time between receiving and remitting lengthened, Dick added: "Am in (a) danger, (b) hospital, (c) jail." But the first telegram from the firstborn brought tears of relief to my distracted mother. To cover up his troubled mind, Pop pitched a mulatto breeze.

"That rascal! Let him git back the way he got there. Let him walk!" My father was in a beautiful rage. "And me," this was the real issue, "with all them potato bugs!"

Pop didn't know it then, but Dick hadn't walked; he had pawned Father's revolver. For several evenings I went visiting with Mother as she secretly borrowed the money from friends.

We didn't kill the fatted calf when Dick returned, but

some mighty healthy chickens met an untimely death. My father just happened to feel like getting into the kitchen that day, and Mom put on the white tablecloth, because the old red-checked one was soiled. Father asked his Sunday blessing, the embodiment of the regular Baptist grace, with deviations and original supplications to fit the occasion. He told the Lord many of the things he couldn't bring himself to tell Dick, and I hope the Lord understood, because Dick wasn't listening. It was his first square meal in two weeks.

The next day the family went on a picnic. When the last potato had been dug, Pop took every boy in the neighborhood on a weekend fishing trip up the Des Moines River.

As soon as finances warranted it, Mother bought a piano—a square ugly thing, with shiny veneer finish; but to us it was beautiful. It gave the family a new social status, but that wasn't Mom's real motive. What Father failed to accomplish with goats, gardens, and the willow switch, she attempted with music: an appeal to our aesthetic sense, if any.

She engaged for us one P. Fauntleroy White, professor of music and conductor of the Little Seraphim Choir at Colored Baptist, who also gave recitals when he wasn't too busy at the Drake Hotel, where he was better known as Bellhop Number Four. A petite man, was P. F. W., with pince-nez glasses and thin, expressive hands. Professor White's name was somewhat misleading, but his vitality was good. When he gave a music lesson he became animated, activated, inspired; the stiff pompadour reared back from his perspiring temples in well-oiled unity, and the veins of his bony arms rippled for want of muscles. "One, two, three!" he'd scream, and musical scales were born—a bit deformed, perhaps, and often belabored, but born.

Dick responded to the piano at once. I had progressed to the "First Waltz" on page six, and Harry was catching up with me before Mother and the Professor cornered Tom. During their second encounter, Professor P. Fauntleroy White made a slight error. Tom, slow and thorough, had mastered "one" and was improvising on "two," while the Professor stood, arm suspended, at "three." Suddenly the little man's baton came down across Tom's thick knuckles.

There was a crash.

Mother and I again visited friends, and secretly she paid a consolation fee and purchased a new pair of pince-nez. The musical careers of the Thompson family ceased abruptly, and I was stuck with the "First Waltz" for the rest of my life.

Sometimes, after supper, Mother would sit down at the deserted piano and play slow, sad things. She never played from music—I doubt if she ever had lessons—but, as she played, her eyes had a faraway look, her small fingers responding to the song in her soul. She taught me some of the melodies of her childhood; one, a somber song, was about a "downward road." I associated the song with a scene in the "devil book," for beyond the red-tailed demons and the fiery furnace was a picture of a long, winding line of white-robed "souls" marching slowly towards the Angel Gabriel. The devil book lay on the lower shelf of the library table beside the family Bible, its graphic pictures of eternal hellfire, brimstone, and pitchforks keeping me closer to the paths of righteousness than the promises of God or the faith of my parents.

Mother was playing the piano one night when the phone rang. It was the police. They had Tom. Pop brought my tough brother home a little before midnight, trying hard to conceal his pride. Tom had the build and strength of a stevedore.

"I always told you," Pop kept repeating, "don't take back-water from nobody. Did that boy hit you first?"

"Yes, sir."

"How many times you hit him?"

"Oncet."

Pop was incredulous. "Great Scott! What you hit him with?"

The ball bat incident wasn't entirely forgotten. All this happened down on the lake bank, near the bridge, and Tom could have used anything from a tree trunk to a catfish.

"Nothing; just my hand."

20

"Umph!" Pop grunted in unveiled admiration and shook his head. "I always told you to protect yourself, but I ain't never told you to go fightin' no policeman."

Tom was silent.

"What you have to hit him for?"

"He pushed me."

"Hard?" Father was doing his best to justify the second fight.

"Kinda."

Pop stopped pacing the floor and looked straight at Tom. "Out? Boy, you knock that big man out?"

"Uh huh." Tom pulled aimlessly at his suspenders. The cop was begging for it, had been bullying the gang for months. All the boys were laying for him.

"Go to bed," Pop said at last. "I want to think."

"Maybe," he told Mother later, "we'd better take the boys to Dakota, like John says. They're getting big now. Should be workin', anyhow. Paper route's no kind of job for boys their age. Can't force 'em to like the restaurant; nothin' for colored boys to get in this town but porter work, washin' spittoons. They need to grow and develop, live where there's less prejudice and more opportunity."

Mother didn't answer right away. She hated to bring it up. "Dick hasn't been to school for a week."

"Where's he been? I give him carfare every day. He comes down to the place at four-thirty as usual."

"I don't know, Tony," she said, "but the truant officer was here."

"Great Scott!" he said mildly. "What'd he want?" Pop wasn't getting too excited about Dick. He would run away or play hookey, sure; but he wouldn't fight, couldn't knock a policeman down like Tom."

"He and some more boys set fire to a field. I think he's been seeing that Davis girl again, too," said Mother, thinking of another kind of fire.

"I distinctly forbid him . . . ," Father began.

21

"He's nearly fifteen," Mother reminded him.

"Yes," Father answered wearily. "We'll have to take them away from here; city's no place for growing boys, specially colored boys. I'm tired of the city, too, Mary. We worked hard and got this home, but we can work for another one, a real home this time, out in God's country."

Mother's silence was consent.

"I'll write John," Pop continued; "yes, sir, I'll write John tomorrow." Already his enthusiasm was rising.

I awoke one morning not long after, and my brother was screaming. The screams came from under my bed, and were mixed with Father's heavy breathing and the muffled sound of hard scuffling. Dick was getting too large for Pop to whip with any degree of dignity. He usually maneuvered the battle into close quarters or around breakable furniture, so that the clatter of splintering wood and shattering glass would bring Mother to the rescue. Rolling under the bed was even better, for every time Pop raised up to strike, he bumped his bald head mercilessly against the steel springs, so Dick screamed and Father took the punishment.

It was Pop's farewell message to Dick and warning to Harry and me. He and Tom left in the cold gray of morning, left for far-off North Dakota to find a new home in the wide open spaces, where there was freedom and equal opportunity for a man with three sons. Three sons and a daughter.

2)   GOD'S COUNTRY

It was a strange and beautiful country my father had come to, so big and boundless he could look for miles and miles out over the golden prairies and follow the unbroken horizon where the midday blue met the bare peaks of the distant hills. No tree or bush to break the view, miles and miles of grass, acre after acre of waving grain, and, up above, God and that fiery chariot which beat remorsely down upon a parching earth.

The evenings, bringing relief, brought also a greater, lonelier beauty. A crimson blur in the west marked the waning of the sun, the purple haze of the hills crept down to pursue the retreating glow, and the whole new world was hushed in peace.

Now and then the silence was broken by the clear notes of a meadowlark on a nearby fence or the weird honk of wild geese far, far above, winging their way south.

This was God's country. There was something in the vast

stillness that spoke to Pop's soul, and he loved it.

But not the first day.

John Evans, taking precious time out from his threshing to meet Father and Tom, drove them to the farm and whisked them out to the field as soon as they had changed their clothes.

Father was disappointed in his brother's house—a low, colorless shanty squatting down among the lesser sheds in awe of the big hood-shaped barn, whose silver lightning rods and bright red paint could be seen for miles. He was soon to learn that, in this country, livestock came first, man second.

He hardly recognized Ann. She was very fat now—fat and white. Bossy white. He was shocked all over again by the sight of her, again resented her whiteness. Ann was effusive in her greeting. She kissed him twice, and he was ashamed of his thoughts of her, hoped they could learn to get along.

Clad in straw hats and faded overalls, Pop and Tom clung hard to the sides of the big grain wagon as it lumbered out across the rough stubble fields towards a funnel of smoke and the chug of an engine.

"All this yours?" Father was impressed.

"All this as far as eye can see," said the wiry little man, with a munificent sweep of his hand, "is my land, Tony." He drew up in front of the busy threshing machine. "All this machinery is mine, an' all these men work for me." John was on his favorite topic; he swelled visibly as he hooked his rough, brown fingers in his suspenders and waited for his brother's gasp.

"My Lord, John! You own all this? You must be rich, rich, man!" There was pride and awe in Father's voice, and the last sentence was mingled with a new personal hope.

"Sue! O Sue!" John shouted.

A pretty, buxom girl of fifteen tumbled down from the top of the separator and ran towards them. Her sloppy overalls ill concealed the fast developing curves of her healthy body.

"So this is Uncle Tony." She wrung his hand until he winced.

24

"Tom," called Pop. "Where's that boy? Tom, come meet your cousin!"

But Tom had vanished among the bundle-wagons. Drawn by the magic of machinery, he found himself staring up into the cabin of the big, hot engine, staring at a boy his own age, a boy with white skin and sandy hair. When Sue guided Pop to the noisy engine, Tom was in the cab with his cousin, Ben, and they were already fast friends.

The tour ended, John assigned father and son to a bundle rack, and they were on their own. The prairie sun hung suspended in the white-hot sky, its lambent flame playing upon their tender necks and arms. The slick, round handle of the pitchfork galled their city hands as they staggered under the burden of the golden bundles; prickly beards of wheat worked down their shirts and into their bodies to torture them; dry stubble cut through thin city soles. Other threshers passed them going to the machine with full loads, passed them returning in empty racks, while Pop and Tom struggled in sweat and silence.

"Hey there, Tony!" yelled John from the top of the separator. "What's the matter with you city fellas? You've missed three turns." John laughed loudly as he sauntered towards them.

"John," said Pop, hot and aggravated, "you know I ain't used to no hard work like this."

"You'll git used to it out here. Do you good, eh, Tom?" John winked broadly. He was enjoying himself; he wanted to see his brother sweat, wanted to see if he could take it. This was his country, his land. He was sure of himself with the soil, scornful of those who had never slaved for the bare essentials of life. While light-skinned Tony cooked in fine hotels and served the rich, he, dark-skinned John, had swung the anvils, shoveled the coal, hoed the corn. Two broken ribs from a mining mule, a broken leg from a Washington mountain slide, a missing finger from the sharp blade of a metal shear were his souvenirs. And all this—the acres of land, the stock, the expensive machinery, and the crew of thirty hands—had come gradually, slowly, after years of struggle with the stubborn earth, after long, frozen winters, self-denial, and personal deprivations for himself and his family. Tony, too, should learn. There was little mercy left in John Evans. He laughed with his men and goaded his brother on.

The next morning when the big, bad Dakota sun sent its golden feelers up over the rim of the earth, Pop's urban bones creaked and rattled, and when Old Sol emerged from his lair, red and ready, every part of Pop rebelled. John relented and made him handyman around the machine, responsible for the stray bundles that missed or overflowed the jaws of the separator—a job reserved for old men, cripples, or the mentally disturbed. That morning Pop was all three.

Tom took the bundle-wagon out alone. He was already a man.

Late that fall Father sent for us. Harry and I were excited, for at last we were going to fight the Indians, and ride the range in search of buffalo—we hoped. Sadly Mother sold the house and turned back the shiny veneer piano. All through the last day, white and colored neighbors came with gifts of parting and words of sympathy; for them our destiny was an untimely death in the frozen wilds of Dakota. Smiling through her tears, Mother packed our things, and at last we were on our way.

As the train sped along through amber fields of corn dotted with yellow pumpkins and bright orange squash, through the mellow haze of an Iowa autumn, Harry and I sat glued to the windows, entranced by the passing panorama, enthralled by the miracle of locomotion. Leaving Minneapolis and the wide Mississippi River the next morning, the scenery gradually grew gray and hushed; trees, baring their limbs, looked sad and forlorn; the last flowers were withering and dying, and with them went some of the glamor of the journey. Past Fargo and the Red River Valley came the barren prairies of North Dakota—vast, level, gray-brown country, treeless and desolate.

Suddenly there was snow—miles and miles of dull, white

26

snow, stretching out to meet the heavy, gray sky; deep banks of snow drifted against wooden snow fences along the railroad right-of-way. And with the snow went our dreams of Indians, for somehow they did not fit into this strange white world. We could sense the cold wind without feeling it, without hearing it. Here and there was a tiny cluster of buildings, a windmill or silo towering above the snow-covered roofs; strawstacks sheltering thick-coated horses and cows that had eaten their way deep into the sides of the stacks away from the wind and the snow. Occasionally we passed through tiny country towns with their inevitable grain elevators, one-room, dull red depots, and companion section houses.

All day long we rode through the silent fields of snow, a cold depression spreading over us. I looked at Mother. She tried to smile, but there were new tears in her eyes. She was thinking of the green hills of Virginia, thinking, too, of the lush valleys of Iowa. All these things, these friendly things that she knew and loved, were far behind her now. I think she knew then that she would never come that way again.

Weary and hungry, we arrived at last at Driscoll. I tumbled down the steps of the train into the outstretched arms of my father, hidden in the collar of a huge sheepskin coat, his face buried in the folds of a wool muffler, only the merry eyes visible. Pop was beside himself with joy. He and Uncle John loaded us into the straw-covered bed of a big sled and covered us with horse blankets. I was so thoroughly bundled and so firmly lodged between my mother and father that I could see very little, but I could smell the clean, fresh odor of straw and feel the sideways jolt of the runners as they bumped into rocks underneath the snow. The steady, rhythmic beat of horses' hoofs sounded pleasantly beneath my uncle's constant chatter.

"But aren't there any colored people here?" asked Mother incredulously.

"Lord, no!" said Father.

"What'd you want with colored folks, Mary? Didn't you come up here to get away from 'em? Me, I could do without 'em for the rest of my days." Uncle John laughed. "There's a couple of colored families over north of Steele, about thirty miles from here—Williams brothers, Ted and Mack. Both of 'em got kids; got right nice farms, too. A little gal there about your age, too, Dick." Uncle John looked at my brother and winked.

All too soon we arrived at the house. Ann's "Hello there!" boomed out above the barking of the dogs and the general din of welcome. It was good to see Tom again. He didn't take on like the others—just patted my head as I leaned against his sturdy legs. Soon the Thompson and Evans clans were gathered around a bountiful feast, as Ann prided herself on setting a good table.

"We ain't got nothin' fancy, but we always got enough fer everybody. If you folks can put up with what we got, you're welcome. We've took many a one in in our time, divided everything we had with 'em, and didn't even git thanks." She was talking on and on in a singsong fashion. "John's too easy; he's always doin' fer others, but you don't see nobody doin' nothin' fer him. There's them Murdocks. John took 'em food and grain and even give 'em the clothes off his back."

"Oh, for Christ's sake, Ma! Ya gonna go over that again?"

"Ben, you shut your face!" Ann's martyrlike voice vanished as she lashed out at her son.

"This is for your benefit, folks." Ben grinned maliciously. "Anything you get out of the Evanses you earn."

"The clothes we give away can't nobody wear," chimed in Sue.

"They're better'n they had." Ann was on the defensive now.

"Go on, Ma, tell 'em what they did for us, tell 'em." Ben's eyes sparkled as he egged her on.

"What'd they ever do? Tell me that. What'd they ever do fer us?"

"Remember all that grain Murdock hauled? Remember that calf he saved?" Ben's eyes became crafty, his speech slow and deliberate. "Remember those three stacks of hay we stole?"

"Ben!" shouted John. "You shut your damned mouth!"

28

Ann's placid, white face turned fiery red, and a big blood vessel in the center of her forehead throbbed with her mounting anger. "We never stole a dern thing! That hay was rightfully our'n!"

"Benjamin, you're a liar," Sue announced happily.

"Sue's right," barked John.

"Sue's always right, everything she says is right; but every time Ben opens his mouth you're ready to cuss him out."

"Oh, for Christ's sake!" Ben threw down his fork and left the table.

"Now see what you've done," said Ann triumphantly.

"His feelings ain't hurt. He's just getting out of cleaning up all that food on his plate," said Sue knowingly.

The Murdocks and the hay were forgotten, as father and daughter lined up against mother and son. It was a familiar pattern, as old as family life itself; but this alliance was accentuated, maybe motivated by another division: Ben was as white as Ann, his sandy hair straight, his eyes gray; only his features gave slight indication of mixed heritage. Sue was sallow, with big brown eyes and brown freckles, her reddish-brown hair a mass of heavy curls. She was a far cry from John's copper color, but not so far as Ben.

"I'm sorry you folks had to listen in on a family row the first meal," Ann apologized, still bristling.

"They might as well get used to our wrangling, gonna hear it from now on." John's good nature was already restored. He looked at my mother and laughed. "What's the matter, Mary? Scared?"

Mother smiled uneasily; Pop grunted. We Thompsons sat that one out.

Mother, Father, and I took Sue's tiny room with its magazine pictures pasted on the walls and embroidered shams over the pillows, a cozy, little-girl room, not large enough for a big girl, let alone the three of us. My aunt and uncle slept on the wooden folding bed that let out in the living room beside Sue's cot, and the boys were billeted on pallets on the floor, a sheet separating them from the beds. Ten of us in a three-room house was crowded, but not stuffy. The heater in the center of the room offered little competition to the cold north wind that whipped around the corners of the building and in through its many cracks and crevices. Manure banked around the outside of the house kept out some of the drafts, and each night Ann put old rugs against the threshold and chinked up the windows with rags, before she blew out the lamp.

Mother and Father talked far into the night. "Tony, I don't like it here. All this fussing and crowding."

"I know, I know, but we've got to put up with it somehow, until spring anyway, when we can get a place of our own. You'll like the country in the spring, Mary, when the snow is gone."

"Let's go back to Iowa."

"Can't go back. Cost money to go back, and besides, our home's gone. What'd we do when we got back?"

"You've got some money, haven't you? Where's the money you and Tom made working this fall?"

"Time we paid John back for train fare and clothes and things, we didn't have nothin' comin'. It's like Ben said tonight, John always gets his. Time he got through figuring, we owed *him* money.

"But Ann, is she always like that?"

"Old Brother Satan hisself couldn't get along with that old white woman. Lord, honey, she's . . . ." Pop's Christianity was making it difficult to find a word. He searched, failed, put his religion aside. "She's a bitch."

"Tony!" screamed Mother, sitting bolt upright in bed. "What's that? Wolves?" A long, weird howl pierced the night. It was followed by short, sharp yelps.

Father pulled Mother back down on the pillow. "Them's coyotes; them ain't wolves. Them rascals howl like that all night."

"They—they sound so close."

"They just up the hill there a piece. The dogs keep 'em away. Jepp, the big dog, he's part coyote hisself. Lord! Lord!

30

Dogs and coyotes chasin' each other up and down the hills all night long."

Suddenly Mother remembered all the stories she had heard about timber wolves and early pioneers, how a young couple overtaken by wolves, threw their only baby to the animals to save themselves. "Tony, what'd you bring me and my children out to this place for? We'll all be froze to death or eaten up alive!"

"Now, now," soothed Father. "They can't get in here, and ain't nobody been et up by them things recently. You'll get used to 'em by and by. Yes, Lord." Father continued without much conviction. "You'll get used to 'em, maybe, but God knows I won't!"

The Monday after our arrival, Harry and I were bundled off to our first day of rural schooling. Ben, like many farm youths, had quit school early, so my parents, remembering what they went through in Iowa, most eagerly excused Tom and Dick. In the gray-white cold of early morning, with the temperature hovering around thirty-five below, Harry, Sue, and I climbed into the big sled, John whipped up the horses, and we bounded off in a flurry of snow.

Driscoll was a typical small North Dakota town, population about one hundred. Main Street, a broad, snow-packed road, was lined on both sides with frame store buildings, and its few homes were scattered out to the west of Main and south towards the Lutheran and Protestant cemeteries. A four-room consolidated school sat up on a hill, midway between the cemeteries and town.

A canvas-covered school rig was pulling away as we drew up to the gate. Sue herded us into the tiny entrance hall and up the three shallow steps to the first floor, where a short, red-haired woman gasped in disbelief.

"Good morning, Miss Breen," said Sue perfunctorily. "These are my cousins; they're both in your room."

Miss Breen had spent most of her three years at Driscoll trying to classify the Evans' offspring. They weren't white and they weren't black. Some of the children, drawing their own

31

reckless conclusions, had called them "skunks" and fought it out. Miss Breen didn't know what it was the mulattoes objected to: the skunk's predominance of black fur over white or its more distinctive qualities. Now, suddenly, without warning, here were two studies in brown, not quite like the pictures in the geography or funny papers, but near enough to be identified. They were the first bona fide Negro children she or the pupils had ever seen.

We left our wraps and overshoes in the cloakroom and, still stiff with cold, joined the other children by the big tin drum which surrounded the stove. Every eye was upon us. One or two little girls snickered; a boy pushed another against me and grinned. Miss Breen rang a little handbell, and the eighteen children marched reluctantly to their seats. Summoning Harry and me to her desk, she plied us with questions—questions far from educational lines, questions about our parents, what they did in Des Moines, where they were born, about the South. She questioned us until my mouth began to quiver, and I had to blink hard to keep back the tears. Finally she led me to an empty seat in the fourth grade section and took Harry to the sixth grade on the opposite side of the room. The two middle rows were filled with disappointed fifth graders who felt left out of this new thing that was happening to them and the community.

A girl seated across the aisle from me, delicately featured, and with long, flaxen curls, smiled. The girl directly in front of me turned around. "Hello," she whispered. "My name's Ollie Koch." She laid her open reader on my desk. "You can use my book." There was method in her kindness. Without a book she was free to sit in the next aisle with her cousin, Tillie. Tillie made a face at me and buried her head in her arms laughing silently. I didn't like her; I wanted to go home.

At recess the blonde girl came to my seat. "I'm Jewel Nordland," she said. Her name was like a poem, and her voice was like music. I liked her.

At noon the children gathered around the stove to eat lunch from their round syrup cans and their tin tobacco baskets. It was like a picnic back in Iowa when it rained. I choked a little when I thought of Iowa, and ate my half-frozen sandwiches in silence. One of Sue's friends put her arm around me and felt of my hair; Tillie stared at the white palms of my hands, and I closed my fists tight until they hurt. For the first time I began to wonder about that and about the soles of my feet and my pink toes, and I was glad she couldn't see my feet where the color ran out. Long before four o'clock I had had enough school.

Mother, standing in the yard that night waiting for us, clasped me in her arms, hugging me as though she had never expected to see me again, and I soon forgot about the soles of my feet and the palms of my hands.

On those frigid winter evenings after our homework was done, we joined the others in games of checkers and dominoes or listened to the hard-to-believe tales of Uncle John's pioneers and Pop's ghosts. Then Ben would bring out his harmonica and play far into the night. As he played the songs of the prairies the tempo became slower and the music saddened. I liked the sad cowboy laments best, for they were a part of the whistling winds and the lone prairies.

Sunday afternoons, curious but friendly neighbors stopped by to visit the Evanses and welcome the Thompsons. They wanted to see for themselves if the family was white or black, and the brownness of us was a surprise.

The monotony of the long winter days and the increased bickering and quarreling between the two families made Father's short temper shorter. The friction with Ann increased in the narrow confines of the little house, and he and Mother spent more and more time in their room, talking in low, bitter tones.

"It won't last always," Mother would say. It was she, now, who mollified him. "Try not to say things to aggravate Ann. You know how she is."

"I tell you, Mary, I'm goin' to forgit myself one of these days and hit that woman, so help me!"

The first open break came one morning at breakfast when Aunt Ann set before me a warmed-over plate of codfish balls and a half-eaten biscuit—my supper from the night before. "You eat that up before you git any more, young lady. We ain't got food to waste around here."

I looked at Mother. There was a hurt look in her soft brown eyes, her lips tightly closed. I looked at Pop, and got the green light. His thin, yellow nostrils were quivering, his blue-black eyes like slits of steel. I drew a deep breath and began to howl. Aunt Ann hovered by the table, alert and waiting, like a big polar bear. Ann was fast tiring of her husband's relatives.

Pop pushed my plate roughly aside. "She don't have to eat leftovers!"

"It's her own plate. I make my kids clean up their plates; she ain't no better'n them."

"Ann, I've seen you give better'n that to the dogs. I've seen you give 'em buttered biscuits right off the stove. My children's as good as your dogs!"

"Sure I feed our dogs. Dogs got to eat same as you, but they don't waste it. Nobody's gonna waste food around here, as hard as John has to work fer it!"

Pop jumped to his feet. He was cold with fury, his words measured, brittle. "You white, Irish devil, you!" I stopped crying to listen. "You can take your food and . . ."

"Tony!" Mother was beside him. "Tony," she pleaded, taking him by the arm. "Don't say anything more. You're angry now. Come." She led him from the table into the bedroom and shut the door.

Ann was pallid, and her hands trembled. Suddenly she threw a coat over her head and rushed from the house in search of Uncle John. Left alone at the table, I helped myself to fried mush and, for the first time, got enough Karo syrup.

Before the week was up, John gave Sue a whipping—a noisy, farcical affair with a lot of unhelpful coaching from the sidelines. I was so greatly impressed that I told the kids at school.

"You're going to get it!" Sue hissed in my ear at recess time. "You told on me!"

The rest of the day I suffered as only a guilty nine-year-old can suffer. By four I was terrified. All the way home I waited for her to tell Uncle John, but she said nothing. When both families gathered at the supper table, I was sick with apprehension; still Sue was silent, biding her time. In that satisfied and satiated lull that precedes dessert, she spoke.

"Papa," she said dramatically, "do you know what happened today?"

"No. What?"

"Sissy told. She told everybody in school that you beat me. I was never so mortified!"

All eyes turned towards me. John carefully laid down his knife and fork. "Did you repeat at school what happened in the sanctity of this house?"

I nodded my head, not trusting myself to speak.

"What made you do it?"

"Yes, dear, you knew it was wrong." Mother took the play away from John.

Ben grinned. "She didn't have to tell 'em. They could hear her, all the hollerin' and screamin' she was doin'. Lord, you coulda . . ."

"You shut your face, Ben Evans," snapped Sue, forgetting her look of martyrdom. "I didn't holler any more than you do."

"Did you hear that, Dick?"

"Did I! Man, oh, man! I was down at the other end of the lane . . ."

"You stop that lie," Pop silenced him. Tom and Harry were convulsed with laughter.

"What'd you think it was, boy—a train whistle or that old sow with the little pigs?"

"Papa!" wailed Sue.

"Shut up now, all of you!" bellowed Uncle John. "And I don't want to ever hear of anyone telling tales outside of this house again. Not anyone."

It would have come anyway—the end, I mean. The old axiom about the one roof was never more true. Things were nearing a climax. Ann and Pop weren't speaking, the Thompsons were eating alone—after the Evanses—and even Ben's harmonica couldn't fill in the long silences.

So I broke the emery wheel. I was forbidden to touch anything in my uncle's toolshed, but the foot-propelled emery wheel was irresistible. I sneaked out to the shed, mounted the machine, and began to pedal. The chain snapped, and the pedals went limp. Sue walked in.

Uncle John said he was going to whip me. Pop didn't say anything; he just hitched up a team and drove into Driscoll. When he returned, we piled all our belongings into the big sled and moved to the empty hotel on the edge of town.

The hotel was an old, eighteen-room barn of a building, bare and cold, but we set up living quarters in the spacious kitchen, and that night Pop made southern hoecake on top of the gigantic range and fried thick steaks in butter. The tightness was gone from the corners of his eyes as he threw his head back and sang:

"I'm so glad, trouble don't last alway,
Oh, I'm so glad, trouble don't last alway!"

Chef's cap tilted, eyes shining, Pop shouted above the roaring stove and the sizzling steak, "Sing it, Mary; sing it, chillun! 'Oh, I'm so glad!'"

We all joined in, loud, off-key maybe, but united, together again, a whole hotel in which to sing and play and fight.

The food we ate that night was purchased on credit from Old Lady Anderson's store across the street. "Yah, yah," she had said, "I give you credit, you farm soon. Little ones must eat." And Pop borrowed twenty-five dollars from the bank on our furniture to buy coal and the little things we needed. Debt was no disgrace in North Dakota; everybody was in debt, everything was mortgaged—that's why they didn't need money out there.

At night the family sat around the big range and played checkers or got out the old Baptist hymnal that somehow followed us and sang the old songs in a setting the old folks never

36

knew. For the first time, the folks didn't have to worry about the whereabouts of the boys.

One night I came in from school to find a Norwegian couple and a colored missionary woman visiting us. I stared rudely, not at the couple, but at the colored woman. Aside from my mother, I hadn't seen one since we left Des Moines. They stayed for dinner, a meal freely interspersed with "Amens," "Hallelujahs," and "Word-of-Gods." Hallelujah, coming between bites of boiled pig's feet, was too much for Dick. He choked and left the table, Tom and Harry following.

After supper Mother, Father, and I accompanied these new and voluble friends home. For twenty miles we drove over the silvery, moon-swept snow, the runners of the sled singing out in the harsh cold. The unabated conversation of five newly met people who had just found a common ground—religion—went eagerly on, unmindful of the distance and the cold.

The man, Oscar Olson, spoke fervently in broken English. Twenty-five years before, he had left his native land and come to America to get rich. His first wife was dead ten years before he married the loquacious Scotch widow and mail-order bride, who, one soon gathered, was not very popular with her half-grown stepchildren.

The missionary woman was a little off the heathen trail, but still preaching the Gospel to all who would listen—and contribute to the price of a railroad ticket towards a warmer land. Just how the plump little woman got that far out into the sparsely settled country was a mistake she never explained. "All I wants to do, praise God, is to get back to Kansas, hallelujah, and preach the Word, yes, Jesus!" That was her problem.

When I awoke, Father was carrying me into a big warm kitchen. Fresh coffee was boiling on the stove, and the whole Olson household was waiting up to greet us. A big girl, with wide blue eyes and the smell of clean milk about her, took me gently from my father's arms and deftly removed the many layers of wraps around me. A younger girl, a thin, pale child,

37

with white pigtails bouncing about her sharp shoulders, hurried back and forth from pantry to table with butter and cheese and fresh coffee cake. The task completed, she stood before me, gazing solemnly and silently. The older boy was defiant and sullen, openly hating his stepmother; but the other one teased everybody, laughed at everything. The "Hallelujahs" had a hard time maintaining their sacred intonations in his presence. Pop, a little out of practice, a long time out of church, caught himself grinning with the boy, cast a furtive glance at Mother, and dropped his head.

Those three pleasant days with the Olsons were the first of many such weekends and the beginning of a strong and lasting friendship, one wrought with prayer and much drinking of coffee.

Several weeks passed before Uncle John came to see us. "Blood's thicker than marriage," he said. "If Ann could learn to keep her darned mouth shut, you folks would still be with us."

"No," Pop demurred, "it's better this way. We'll get along somehow."

"Anything I can do for you? Have you got enough to eat?"

"No, John; no, thanks. We're doin' all right. The Lord will provide."

"He won't provide no horses." John winked at Mother. "That colt, Major, that I promised the boys, he's still theirs."

"Yes, John. Thanks. If you can just keep him till spring, till I can find a farm, I'll be mighty grateful." Pop didn't believe Major would live until spring. He was about to die when John became philanthropic, but somehow he survived and grew into a scrawny, hump-backed horse.

After that visit Sue occasionally came home with me at noon, and Ben came often, but Ann never lightened our door.

Diligently Father searched for a suitable farm to rent, one on which we could gain experience and make enough money for a down payment on a farm of our own. Just before the spring thaws, he heard about the Old Hansmeyer place, two and a half miles west of Driscoll.

38

Hank Hansmeyer, owner of the local blacksmith shop, was tight and shrewd. The rock-ridden quarter section had never made a living for anyone, but a man with three sturdy sons, a man who didn't know wheat from barley, Hank reasoned, would make a good tenant, wouldn't be too choosy or too demanding. He drove my parents out to the farm one Sunday and with pleasant generalities and heavy emphasis upon the hidden possibilities of the soil (hidden two feet under the snow) explained his terms. He, Hank, party of the first part, would furnish the land, the buildings, and the horses, if we, parties of the second part, would furnish the seed, do the work, and give him half the profits. The sod-covered barn leaned heavily to the south, and the corral fence was broken down in many places, but the house looked pleasant and bright in its once-white paint. The small frustrated grove of stunted willows gave faint hope of living things. My parents were impressed.

"Now, where are the horses?" Pop asked.

"Oh, yes," said Hank and drove out towards the open range. Half an hour later he sighted them, eight or ten broncos far to the north, galloping across the snow like streaks of flame, their long manes and tails shining in the cold sun. "There they are. Now you just get them in the barn and feed them up a little, and you've got fine horses, good working horses."

"Umm umph!" Pop squinted. "How you tell them wild things your horses—ten miles away?"

"Oh, they're mine, all right. I know all of my horses. Let 'em run the range every winter—saves feed, makes 'em self-reliant."

"You say, put 'em in the barn. Who's gonna git them rascals in a barn when you can't even git close enough to read the brand—if they got a brand? Tell me that."

Hank Hansmeyer laughed tolerantly. "When the snow begins to thaw, they'll come closer in. They're not wild horses; they've been broke, had harness on."

Pop liked horses, thought he knew horseflesh, all the time he'd spent with racehorse men. "Them's the wildest tame horses

I ever see. But ain't no horse livin' I can't handle. No, siree. Ain't no horse livin'." Hank looked straight ahead; Mother looked at Pop and crossed her fingers. Pop looked back at the fleeing horses. "Ummm umph!" There was admiration and excitement in his grunt. "It's a deal."

Hank Hansmeyer stopped the team and pulled out a prepared contract. "Sign right here," he said, trying to appear casual.

Right there in the middle of the prairie, Pop pulled off his glove and, with fingers numb with cold, shaking with emotion, signed his name. "Lord, today!" he said with a start. "I'm a farmer, Mary, I'm a farmer."

3) TESTING GROUND

By the end of March we were firmly ensconced on the Hansmeyer place, but without my brother Dick. His faith in Father's agricultural instincts was still a bit shaken, so he hired out to Charley Koch, nearer town and convenient to the pool hall. And we were short one hand.

High winds and the tepid spring sun sent the snow scurrying down hillsides in tiny rivulets, honeycombing the scattered drifts that clung to the shady sides of the knolls until they slowly crumbled and disappeared into the ever-thirsty soil, revealing the Hansmeyer farm, rough, rocky, and recalcitrant.

Everywhere there were rocks, millions of rocks pimpling the drab prairie: large blue-gray boulders, free and bold in their shallow pockets; long, narrow slits of rocks surfacing the soil like huge cetacean monsters; sharp stone peaks jutting from the horny earth. Pale gray sage and dull buffalo grass flecked the fields, and here and there were red-brown patches of stiff buck-brush sheltering a coyote's den. In the slough at the north end of the pasture was long, dry marsh grass, flat from the recent weight of snow. Purple crocuses blossomed reluctantly on thick, furry stems among the rocks and boulders.

We watched the transformation with heavy hearts.

"Well," Pop said sadly, "we ain't never gonna want for no tombstones."

Major, still lank and scrawny but surprisingly swift, munched hungrily around the big yard, our only bit of animal life and our sole means of transportation. Uncle John agreed to take Harry and me to school, providing we met him on the road a mile to the south. Tom delivered us to the meeting place, Harry behind him, hanging onto his middle, and me in front of him, astride Major's thin neck, arms flying helplessly as he galloped the horse over snow and ice, through puddles of mud and water, unmindful of my tearful pleas and the scrambled food inside the dinner buckets. John never waited for us; most of the time we overtook him like cowboys in a Western thriller, only there were no Indians—six months and still no Indians.

Father and Tom spent the early spring days mending fences, repairing the windmill, and trying to prop up the sagging barn, while Mother scrubbed the little house until it was clean and bright. Every day Tom rode out over the range in search of the Hansmeyer horses, but it was April before he sighted them, and ten days later when he brought them charging into the corral. All but two got away.

Mother watched Tom lure the horses into the barn, follow them, and carefully close the door, while Pop took a safe position outside the barn window—club in hand.

"Tony!" she screamed. "Don't let that boy go in there alone; he'll be killed!"

"He ain't alone, Mary; I'm takin' care of him. You better go in the house." Pop was breathing hard, his knees were rigid, and he was having trouble with his bloods. The Dutch said, "Go inside"; the Indian said, "Stand still." The other bloods raced up and down his veins and said, "Lord! Lord! There's no hidin' place out here!"

From within came a high shrill whinny, the thudding sound of bodies, splintering stalls. The old barn moved ominously.

"Tom, Tom," called Mother weakly.

Pop took a quick peek inside, and covered his face. All he could see was flying hoofs. There was another commotion, and the door flew open. A small sorrel mare, eyes glazed, ears back, nostrils distended, charged out into the corral. She stood on her hind legs and pawed freedom's air. Pop dropped his club and disappeared around the side of the barn—the far side. Instinct was more reliable than blood.

Tom went for Old Gus, the drunken bachelor who lived below the hill. Together they got the mare back into the barn, harnessed both horses and hitched them to a dilapidated buggy, Tom holding the bridles while Gus climbed in and gathered up the reins.

"Let 'er go!" called Gus, through his whiskey.

Tom released the broncos and jumped to one side. "Yippee!" he cried and swung on as the buggy lurched by. The horses made a new gate through the yard fence and tore down the muddy road on a dead gallop, as Gus sat waving his bottle and yelling in Norwegian. Tom took the reins and guided the horses up a big hill. For two hours they raced up and down the hills, in and out of rutty roads, the buggy groaning and creaking as it bounced off rocks, out of holes. Tired and panting, bodies steaming and covered with lather, Tom brought the erring horses home. The buggy was a shambles, Gus was stone sober, but we had a team.

The reputation of Hansmeyer's broncos and the fame of Tom's horsemanship (thanks to Gus) brought people from near and far. Every Sunday the yard was filled with the wagons and buggies of those who came to watch and help us break our horses. In the house jolly farm women opened baskets of food, while Mother made pot after pot of strong coffee for the in-

43

evitable lunch that followed the show.

Pop's equestrianism was manifested in various safe ways, such as naming the horses after racehorses he had known. His favorite team was Buck, a handsome buckskin devil with a dark brown seam running down the center of his back, and Dixie, a fat, little dapple ball of hell. Pop made his maiden trip into town without mishap. An hour later the horses returned on a dead run, heads up, heels flying, a picture of rhythmic beauty. Turning in the gate on two wheels, they stopped only when the buggy lodged in the barn door. Pop and one seat were missing. By being careful, he had got them into town and tied to the iron railing at the bank. While he was negotiating a loan for more feed and equipment, Buck worked his way free and rammed his head under Dixie's chin, breaking her halter rope. Pop and the banker ran out in time to see them racing down Main Street.

"And you'll need another buggy," the banker said, without emotion.

"Yes," Father sighed, "another buggy. But, man, did you see them rascals run?"

There were few people, thereafter, who didn't see them, for Thompson runaways became legendary.

Mother couldn't keep me from the horses after Harry learned to ride. I fell off or was thrown off with disconcerting regularity, but backed the jittery broncs up against wagon wheels and fences and climbed back on until I was able to race with my brothers, no favors asked.

The farm people were kind and friendly to us, encouraging and advising, offering the use of their tools and machinery, even bringing a pig or chicken to help us get started. Old Gus offered fresh milk. The first time Harry and I went after it, we found him lying on a pile of dirty quilts, his bottle and pipe beside him. A huge stack of cold pancakes lay on the back of the cookstove, more pancakes than we had ever seen, even in the heyday of Pop's cookery, and certainly never such large, sturdy ones.

Gus laughed. "You want some pannie cakes?"

We shook our heads and edged towards the door.

"You never see so many, yah? Aye make pannie cakes for whole week. Aye no like to cook." Gus spat out, but not quite clear of the bed. He looked at our tight brown faces and roared. "You take tandy, maybe? Come, aye give you tandy." He reached for a dirty tin box near the bed. "Come, little Tovey Gustus." He held the sticky peppermint towards me. I fled out the door and up the hill, but the name followed, and I became "Tovey Guts" to my brothers the rest of my life.

Jewel's parents, Nell and August Nordland felt close to us, for they, too, had come from Iowa. The Nordland farm, some five miles away, was a prosperous place, with a roomy house and one of the largest and most modern barns in the township. Tow-headed Skippy became Harry's pal, and the friendship between Jewel and me blossomed with that of our parents. When I visited their farm, I rode their ponies and played in the mammoth loft of the big barn, rolling down mounds of hay, sliding through floor chutes into the mangers of startled horses, admiring—at a safe distance—the beautiful tan stallion who chafed and fretted in a private box stall. There was always homemade ice cream and cake with thick frosting for dinner, and, when I spent the night with Jewel, I wore her pretty nightgowns and slept in a soft bed between real linen sheets. I could never ask Jewel to stay at our house. There wasn't room.

Father heard it first. "Mary, Mary!" he cried. "Did you hear that?" Mother ran out the door into the early morning sun. Pop shaded his eyes with his hand, as he peered around the yard. From a fence post across the road came the clear, unmistakable notes of a meadowlark. "Shush, you all, don't scare that bird!" We stood at the door, scarcely breathing. The bird sang out again, then flew away. "Reminds me of Virginia. Never knew I'd be so glad to hear a little bird sing." Pop looked towards the dying grove. "Wonder what he do for trees?"

There were more meadowlarks, and later there were robins. Droves of raucous crows sometimes blackened the sky, and white-winged sea gulls swooped gracefully overhead. Pop won-

45

dered what they did for sea, but didn't ask. It was indeed a strange country. We gazed with awe upon the prairie rose, a delicate pink flower growing close to the ground, whose thorny stem belied its tender beauty. As the wild rose was the official state flower, so was the gopher, commonly called the flickertail, its namesake. Since these little, squirrellike animals destroyed grain, a bounty was placed upon them. Tom and Harry got a couple of rusty traps from Gus and hunted with fairly profitable results, considering the bounty was only three cents a tail. Sometimes Skippy brought his .22 over, and the boys picked them off as fast as they stuck their heads out of their holes. Tom was intrigued. He worried Pop for a shotgun, but he didn't get far until we saw the timber wolf while we were eating breakfast one morning. He came from behind the barn, trotted close under the window, and went calmly down the road. Pop froze in his chair.

My first pet was a puppy Dick brought home on one of his casual visits and asked me to keep for him. Sport was beautiful, with long, tawny hair that turned blonde with the snow and deepened to bronze in the summer sun. His snowy white chest and white-trimmed face were the markings of a collie, but Sport was part shepherd, part coyote. He was a companion dog, not one for herding cattle or flushing game, but a dog I could love and trust.

The frost was barely out of the ground when Pop took the boys out to the field to show them how to handle a plow. He made the first row in something like record time, the plowshares occasionally digging into the ground, but more often scooting over the top, miraculously dodging the rocks. My father was too involved with reins and the business of remaining upright to manipulate the lever. The speed of the horses increased with the commotion from behind, and Tom and Harry rolled over on the ground howling with laughter as our father disappeared over the hill. Tom finished the plowing.

Home from school at night, Harry and I changed our

clothes and hurried out into the field to watch the shining shares slide along beneath the stubborn sod, turning over long rows of damp, blackish earth like unending dusky curls. We walked behind the plow in the shallow, trenchlike furrows, watching for earthworms, or sat on the velvety, upturned soil and let its warm earthiness seep up into our bodies.

Sometimes Harry took the plow. He was thirteen now, growing straight and tall, growing away from me and my child's world, seeking the companionship of Father and Tom, and I found it increasingly difficult to tag along.

Mother, too, began to make demands upon my time. She found tasks inside the house—little-girl tasks like setting the table, doing dishes, sewing my clothes, or endless pounding on the clabber in the stone churn until fine flakes of gold appeared around the cover and gathered inside, forming a floating isle of butter. My dislike for housework often brought me into violent conflict with Mother. As I grew, the oak table, with its four sturdy legs, began to fail me as a place of refuge, and Mother reached some part of my anatomy no matter how I squirmed.

I emerged one day from one of those skirmishes burning and humiliated. With Sport at my heels, I went to my hide-away on the sunny side of the haystack behind the barn. "Damn," I whispered. Nothing happened; lightning did not strike me dead. "Damn it!" I said aloud. Sport looked at me curiously, then looked away with that quiet indifference dogs possess. For a long time I stared off into the distant hills; I'd go there some day. I'd run away from these colored folks and live with the Indians. I watched a white fluff of cloud drift slowly across the sky, then another and another, forming the head of an angel, a horse with horns, an ethereal castle edged in gold. On and on they came, swifter now, darker and closer together, crossing between me and the sun, casting dark shadows on the prairies. Suddenly there was a flash of lightning and a clap of thunder that brought Sport and me to our feet. The rain caught us before we reached the house. I buried my head in my mother's apron, while Sport lay quivering beneath the bed. It was the first

47

storm of spring, the one that wakes the snakes. The rain ceased as quickly as it had begun, the sun came out, and, when I opened my eyes, Mother pointed to a giant rainbow. All the way across the sky, from horizon to horizon, stretched the shining ribbon of colors, both ends resting firmly on the ground. There was no pot of gold. "Damn!" I said softly, under my breath, and another illusion was destroyed.

Suddenly it was warm, alive spring. The sting was gone from the morning air, and the thin layers of ice disappeared from the water trough; the two chickens were cackling and laying unfertile eggs, the prairie grass took on a greenish hue, and my heavy winter coat felt like a suit of armor.

Father borrowed more money. Now he borrowed money on the things he had borrowed money for, on the things that did not yet exist—the crop yet unplanted. This time the money was for seed and a new seeder. Tom had done all he could, handicapped as he was by inexperience, poor machinery, poorer land, and horses that ran away every morning and collapsed every night. And Pop—he wasn't much help either.

Somehow we buried the funny little seeds in the rebellious earth, and great was our joy when the first scared shoots escaped from the stubborn soil and fought for a place among the rocks and weeds. The garden lagged. Sweet potato and cantaloupe seeds that Pop so hopefully planted—against the neighbor's protests—lay still in their strange, cold beds and died. Only the potatoes prospered.

Under the two hens Mother placed the eggs our friends had given us, and in due time strange things came from the nests. Besides the downy yellow chicks came noisy little ducks and scrawny, speckled baby turkeys. The mortality rate was high, more than one dying from handling, but some lived and grew into ugly half-naked things that ran chirping and peeping in shrill monotones about the yard, and I no longer loved them.

On Sundays Mother and Father walked arm in arm through the pasture to the grain fields to sit on the sunny slopes

48

and dream and plan for the farm that some day would be ours. We did not go to church, for there was none except the little Lutheran church in Driscoll. It must have been hard for them, my parents, to give up their worship. We still sang the old hymns and said the long prayers over the food, but the boys scoffed at the family Bible reading and grew cynical of Pop's religion, critical of his leadership on the farm. Father felt himself slowly losing his position as head of the house. Tom's strength, Tom's ideas, Tom's plan of work was sturdy, sound; always in the end his way was best. On major issues Pop stormed and commanded, then withdrew. Tom said nothing, went on with his plan. Succeeded. Mother stood as a buffer between them; it was she and Tom who signed the last mortgage while Father sulked.

For the program that marked the close of the school year, I was to give all eight stanzas of "The Village Blacksmith," dressed in white. Mother mended and starched my white eyelet dress and took the ribbon from her wedding gown to make a sash and bows for the end of my short braids, but my lingerie consisted solely of black sateen bloomers. Mother ripped open a flour sack and made a remarkable pair of straight-legged drawers. Somehow Harry got them before I did, and for a while it looked as though the Blacksmith and the Chestnut Tree were going to be stood up.

"Tovey flour-britches," said Harry. "Old Lady Pillsbury's gonna say, 'Who dat in my sack?'"

Clouds gathered in my eyes.

"Umm umph!" Tom joined in. "You gonna look just like a fly in a glass of buttermilk."

"Mamma!" I wailed. There was no response. I turned to Father for help, but he looked at me in all of my whiteness, his face worked oddly, and suddenly he bolted for the barn.

The Smithy got two and a half stanzas that night. "You can hear him swing his heavy sledge." I swung my dark arms to the right. "With measured beat and slow." I pivoted far to the left. Too far. The "bury" began to separate from "Pills," and I retired

49

before the audience became fully aware of a sudden disunity in the garment industry.

Anxiously we scanned the sky for clouds, watched them slowly gather, disappear, gather, come closer, then skirt our dry fields, drop their white curtains of rain on some distant prairie. And when the precious drops did come to us, we waited for the cold that brought the hail that would beat down the growing grain, mercilessly pounding out the half-ripe kernels. Usually hail came in regular paths, hail belts, and farmers living in these areas protected themselves with hail insurance—if they could afford it—or waited and watched and cursed God when it came. We waited and watched and praised God, for to us it did not come.

Spring faded into hot summer. A rain now, followed by the burning sun, meant black rust, those little dark specks of blight that rotted the stocks of the grain. It rained and the sun came out, and our spring wheat was beautifully blighted.

Then there were days and weeks when no rain fell, no clouds appeared. A dry, hot wind seared the crops, scorched the earth, and dried up the little slough until stiff alkaline rings formed a chalky mosaic in its hard, cracked bed. The heat increased. There were still days, silent, hot, motionless days when not a blade of grass stirred, not a stalk of grain moved. You didn't talk much then; you hated to break the prairie silence, the magic of its stillness, for you had that understanding with Nature, that treaty with God. There was no need for words. The silence wore hard on those who did not belong.

The twenty-acre strip of flax clung stubbornly to its greenness as the short, tough stems swayed in the hot July wind; then overnight the whole field burst into delicate blue flowers, miniature stars against the yellow mustard blooms that clutched at their throat and strangled their growth. The blue flowers disappeared as quickly as they had come, and tiny bulbs of seed began to form in their place, to brown and ripen too quickly in the searing wind.

50

Only the potato vines remained green, and, but for watering they, too, would have withered, for when the wind did blow and the windmill turned, we caught the tepid water in barrels and hauled it to the garden. In the quick coolness that came with the dusk, the thirsty plants drank the water and, like the potato bugs, survived. Passing farmers shook their heads. Nobody but a greenhorn would water potatoes.

Haying time, to me, was the happiest time of the year. As soon as Tom got in a few days with the mower, our whole family took to the field. We arose early, while the air was still fresh and cool, before the sun was up, and drove to the hayland we had rented—through the courtesy of the bank. Harry drove the rake, making long windrows, while Tom followed with the wooden-toothed buckrake, gathering up the hay into little doodles. As stacker man, Pop was in his glory, again head of his family. The first few loads he rounded and packed to form the bed of the stack, then began the building, the piling-on, the spreading-out, the tramping-down. It was a creative thing, this building a stack, rising higher and higher in the sky, above earthly things. He was master of all he surveyed up there, in his grassy chariot, rising nearer to the Glory Road, closer to the Golden Stairs. He took Mother with him sometimes, and together they would stand in silence and look away over the prairies. Away over Jordan.

My first job was driving a horse that was hitched to a device called a stacker. This implement lifted the hay up to the stack. When I had mastered this task, I was taught to drive the hayrake. I couldn't manage the buckrake because it took weight and strength to bear down on the teeth and accuracy to deposit the hay on the carrier of the stacker. Hidden rocks were an ever-present danger to the buckrake as well as to the blade of the mower. They didn't let me drive that either.

At noon we unhitched the horses, fed them, and sat down under the shade of the rack to eat. It wasn't much of a meal: hard slices of summer sausage, potato salad, soupy with vinegar, hard-boiled eggs, bread, and buttermilk. Sometimes cookies.

Brushing aside the flies that suddenly came out of nowhere, we ate steadily, silently, leaving nothing.

Afternoons were hardest, for then we fought the heat and hay-needles and horseflies and the mosquitoes and the droves of flying ants—those schools of black devils that descended upon us and crawled through our clothing and down our necks, biting and stinging. When they were very bad—the mosquitoes and the ants—we made smudges of oily rags or dampened hay. From old gunnysacks the boys rigged up bizarre fly nets for the horses and put straw hats on them, tying fringed rags around their noses to keep the botflies from depositing their wormy eggs. They made sport of our poverty. With bandannas hanging under their battered straw hats, raggedy shirttails flying, sleeves shredded to the armpits, they looked like something right from the Fijis, and it was little wonder the horses ran away.

The coming-home on a load of hay in the warm silence of twilight—the slow rhythm of tired horses, the muffled rattle of the harness on those tied behind, the hayrack creaking under its burden as we moved slowly across the prairie in the shallow road of our making—had a sacredness about it that filled us with the inner happiness that comes of a day's work well done.

Having no produce to sell, we were without the small cash income which tides the dirt farmer over the lean summer months, and our borrowed funds again gave out, our food and credit with it. The gay pastoral picture changed. It wasn't much fun haying when you were hungry. The boys became irritable, and high haystacks made Pop's head swim. Secretly each one of us wished for a rain that would send us in from the field for a few days' respite, but no rain came, so Harry broke the mower wheel, which was just as effective.

The second day we were home, Mother set the dinner table out in the yard to escape the heat of the cookstove and scraped the bottom of the flour bin to make the thin milk gravy for the boiled potatoes. We had no more bread, and no meat. We gathered around the table, not eager, but curious to see what she could find to put into the dishes. At breakfast we had tried the porridge made from flax seed, but it was a sorry mess, far worse than the hand-ground oats and fruits of earlier experimentation.

"What'd I wash my hands for?" demanded Harry. "We ain't got nothing to eat."

Tom studied his brother's hands carefully. "Look at those bear claws, son. What makes you think you washed?"

"They're cleaner'n yours. You can't talk."

"Why, son," Tom spread his short fingers out against the patched tablecloth, blew at an imaginary speck of dust on his grimy, broken nails, "look at my lily-white hands; there's simply no comparison."

"What you call that black stuff—pigment?"

"Them's veins, blue veins where flows the blood of potentates."

"You all stop that crazy talk an' eat." Pop started the potatoes down the table.

"I pass," said Tom.

"Me too," said Harry.

I pushed my plate away. "I want bread and jelly; I'm tired of potatoes."

"Where'd you see any jelly? In the catalog?" Harry was sarcastic.

"Listen, children. Eat your dinner. It's all we have. It's the last of the flour and lard, sugar's gone, too. Maybe we can have some mustard greens tonight, maybe I can find some not too strong," said Mother hopefully.

Tom looked accusingly at Father. "Why don't you go to town and get some food? We've got to eat. We can't sit here and starve."

"What am I goin' to git food with, tell me that? I've borrowed, I've mortgaged everything we got—things we ain't got. Banker won't let me have no more money. Store won't give me no more credit, not with everything burnin' up."

"What about Uncle John?" asked Harry. There was silence.

"I'd rather starve than ask him. I've done the best I can; somehow the Lord will provide."

"And in the meantime we go hungry!" Tom was bitter now.

Pop stood up, his plate untouched. Defeat was written in the lines of his face.

"Sit down, Tony, someone's going by." Mother pulled him down as two spirited horses, hitched to a fine black buggy, came dashing up the road, slowed down at our gate and turned in.

"Hello, there!" a voice boomed out. "I'm Carl Brendel, your neighbor—don't git up. I yust stop by to see how you git along."

Pop went over to the buggy and shook his hand. He recognized him now; it was Big Carl, the German widower who lived in the tiny speck of a farm far to the northeast. "This is a surprise, neighbor. Won't you have some dinner?" Father was embarrassed.

"Yes," said Mother, "Won't you get out and join us?"

Carl Brendel tried not to look at the bare table. "Nein," he said, "I yust et. On my vay to town; thought maybe I bring you somet'ings."

"Thanks, much obliged, but we ain't needin' nothin' jest now." Pop shifted his feet and looked out over the prairie.

"Yah, yah," said Carl. "I go now." He picked up the reins, the horses whirled, and he was gone.

That evening Brendel returned. He was lifting the sacks out of his buggy when Pop came up from the barn. "I bring you some little t'ings I t'ink you need," he explained, resting a hundred-pound sack of flour against the house, beside the big sack of sugar.

"God bless you!" said Pop, tears running down his face. "God bless you, man! Mary, Mary! he cried, "come here an' see what the good Lord has brought us; jest come an' looka here!"

Mother clutched my father's arm; she could not speak. I came in from the yard, Sport close on my heels, and stood beside the pretty horses, watching the big man with the red hairs on his hands as he set more food on the ground. There were canned goods and staples, meat and lard. Carl Brendel smiled as he worked, not looking at Father and Mother. When he had finished he pulled a little sack from his pocket and held it out to me.

"Here, little girl, here iss candy for you. I bring dis all for you."

I looked at Mother. She nodded her head, and I took the sack, mumbling my thanks. The big man smiled and climbed into his buggy.

Pop moved then; he grabbed Brendel's arm. "Mister, I've got no money; I can't pay you now. God knows we need this food . . ."

"Nein, nein! I no vant money. Ven you git it you pay me if you vant. I got money, I your neighbor, I help you. Dot iss all."

He whipped up the horses and drove away.

Far down the road he looked back. The man and woman were still there in the yard where he had left them, but they were kneeling now, praying and thanking their God.

That night was Christmas—Christmas in the middle of August. Harry washed both of his hands, and I brought my jelly beans to the table and lined them up in a colorful circle in front of my plate. There wasn't a potato in sight. Once more the plates were hopefully stacked in front of Father, who beamed as he passed them out, laden with good food.

"Oh, I tell you, children, the good Lord will provide!"

"Yes, man!" grinned Tom. "Him and Mister Brendel."

We were still waiting for the new mower wheel when Harry ran into the house shouting, "Fire, prairie fire!" Three miles away was a vast cloud of smoke, now and then the blaze showing through, red and angry. Swiftly it moved northward, towards the square black house on the top of the hill, towards the Widow Weiss—and our hayfields. Starting at the railroad tracks, where section men were burning off the right-of-way, it had spread rapidly over the dry grass, gathering momentum as it went, leaving behind it a smoldering path of blackened prairie.

We stood in the yard, stunned, sick with dread. Old Gus came thundering up through the pasture, his horses on a dead run. "Fire!" he screamed. "It's headed for da Widow Weiss! Hurry, man, hurry! Git in my wagon, aye take you!" Pop started for the barn, turned, started for Gus's wagon, went to the house for his hat. "Git sack, blanket, git somet'ing to fight wit," yelled Gus, pulling hard on the nervous horses.

Tom disappeared into the granary, came out with an armful of sacks. Harry ran to help him. I clung to my Mother's dress. The wind increased as we stood there, fanning the fire closer to the house. Another wagon dashed by headed for the fire; across the field more wagons joined in the procession.

Pop ran out of the house with his hat, handed it to Mother, then jumped into the wagon beside Gus. "Don't git excited!" he shouted. "Don't nobody git excited!" Mother reached for Harry as he ran towards the wagon, but he eluded her and jumped in on top of the sacks and blankets, tumbling down among the barrels and buckets of water as the team started off.

"Tom!" called Pop. "Where's Tom?"

Tom came charging out of the barn astride Major. They took the corral fence in one leap, cut down through our pasture and hurtled the gate, Major's thin yellow legs stretching out into long, even strides. They disappeared beneath the hill, the clatter of the wagon behind them, shot up over the next hill and the next like greased lightning, growing smaller and smaller, farther and farther ahead of Pop and Gus and Harry, catching up, passing others.

Mother and I could make out the moving forms now, see them running about like tiny figurines, now silhouetted against the blaze, now enveloped by the smoke. The Weiss house vanished from view. Mother covered her face with her hands. Big, black columns of smoke arose as the men frantically beat the flames with wet sacks.

"Look!" I cried. "The house is still there. There it is, Mom!"

She opened her eyes. "Thank God," she breathed. But our precious hayland and our menfolk were still in danger.

Jumping the firebreak, the head-fire went within half a mile of our hayfield, then burned itself out at an old slough bed.

They fought the side fires until late in the evening. They had saved the widow's house and most of her stock, but the other buildings, the grain, a few chickens, an old sow—all were destroyed.

Slowly the wagons began to trickle back towards home. Tom came first, smudged and scorched from head to foot. Major's tail was much shorter; he held it high and carefully now. Gus let Harry off at the gate, and right behind came Uncle John and Pop. Side by side they had fought, and somewhere in the smoke and flame, they had also fought their differences and buried the hatchet. Uncle John stayed for dinner.

"You'd better git that firebreak plowed, Tony, an' right away," he said, smearing a piece of hot cornbread with yellow butter.

"Yes," said Father, "first thing in the mornin'. You hear that, Tom?"

"Now, in the old days," John continued, "we'd catch a big steer, split 'im in two, an' tie the bloody halves between two horses an' drag it through the flames to put out a fire."

Mother winced. I pushed my Jello aside and left the table.

"Musta been big fires them days," ventured Pop, trying to get away from the blood-and-guts trend.

"Yes, siree!" John held his cup for more coffee. "All this country's been burnt up sometime or 'nother. That's what makes the land good. After a big fire—a fire say twenty miles wide, hundred miles long—the prairie was full of dead buffalo, stampeded and burned to a crisp. Bones make good fertilizer." He grinned at Pop's scowling face.

We half-expected her. It was a hoping, dreading expectancy that hung over us following the new brotherhood, yet, when "Miss Ann" drove up in a cloud of dust, Pop couldn't find the olive branch. She sat, big and belligerent, on the hot buggy seat, deaf to Mom's entreaties, waiting for Pop to hoist the white flag. Both my brothers were strangely out of sight.

"Tony," called Mother, "come out here; we've got company."

"He knows I'm here!" said Ann scathingly. "He could have the decency to come out without bein' called."

Pop dashed from the house, his arms full of clattering buckets, his brimless straw hat smashed down over his forehead. He glanced at Ann and scowled. "Good afternoon," he said shortly, and sailed on by.

"Well!" Ann began to swell, her face red with anger. "Well, I'll be derned if I'll stay where I'm not welcome!" She lashed the horses with the whip and thundered out of the yard.

Halfway to the barn Pop stopped to watch the buggy as it bumped down the road. He put his hands on his hips and grinned. "Now, who," he said aloud, "do she think she is?"

As fall drew near, the intense heat subsided. There were quiet, silent days when the grainfields were hills of whispering gold, undulating ever so softly in the bated breeze. So warm, so tranquil was the spell that one stretched out on the brown, dry earth, whose dead, tufted prairie grasses made the lying hard, but put even the breeze above you. The sun alone stood between you and the blue sky of your God.

Time stood still.

By harvest time the heat had done its damage, the rust taken its toll—it was a bad year for farmers. Our crop was no better, no worse, than that of thousands of others far more experienced than we. Borrowing Gus's binder, Tom and Harry harvested our meager crop, then Gus hired the whole family to do his shocking—that is, all except Father, who suddenly developed rheumatism.

There is an art in shocking grain, just as there is an art in cooking or catching rivets or shooting a basketball through the net. Tom and Gus walked along tossing the bundles together, setting them up like tenpins, with quick, precise strokes, while the rest of us staggered awkwardly under our burdens, unable to make the shocks stand still. But, for all the sweat and strain, we loved it. There was something clean and sweet about the harvest, something Biblical about the reaper and the golden sheaves of grain.

A couple of days in the hot sun, and Mother willingly retired to the house to cook for the menfolk. I wasn't much good either, but I tagged along behind the others and made two dollars a day. It was my first job.

Gus liked having us there. "Aye no drink a t'ing now," he assured Mother. "Aye only drink ven aye lonesome, but now I have party like in ole country. Yah, yah, you cook lots of t'ings; I pay for dem, have like party, yah?"

Later in the day Mother heard his cracked voice ringing out over the fields as he sang the songs of his native land, stopping now and then to bellow with glee at Tom and Harry's absurd imitations.

In 1915 a growing rebellion against "big business" and the "city fellers" resulted in the formation of the Nonpartisan League, a political organization composed entirely of farmers. The League swept the country like a prairie fire. In 1916 it was ready to take control of the state. My father was cheered by this odd turn of events. When he left politics back in Des Moines, a rock-bound farm in the middle of North Dakota was the last place in the world he expected to find it again; but there it was, all about him, on the tongues of everyone, for the farmers were up in arms, drunk with sudden power.

"We join da 'Nonpartition' League," said Gus. "Big business dey take our money, dey cheat us wid our grain. Ve do dere verk; dey sit behind big desk an' smoke big cigar wid our money. Dey dirty t'ings!"

"But what you 'spect a bunch of green farmers to do in office?" asked Pop.

"Dey can yust be 'onest!" shouted Gus, all six feet of him rising in anger. "Dat's vot dey can do!"

That Saturday Pop went to Steele with Gus and Oscar Olson and August Nordland for a political rally at the Farmers'

Union hall. Something about Townley, the dynamic little organizer, inspired Pop, set him to thinking. Two weeks later, when Lynn J. Frazier, the League's gubernatorial candidate, came through Driscoll campaigning, Pop was the first to shake his hand.

"Remember me, Governor, when you get to the capital. I'm Tony Thompson." The big, pleasant-faced man smiled.

That night Pop wrote a letter.

Fall was the time of threshing, of hunting, and of cold, drizzling rains. As the sloughs and ditches filled, wild game flying out of the North paused to feed in the fields and swim in the muddy water. There were little brown-flecked teals and big green-necked mallard ducks with their gray coats and white dickies; in the grain and high grass were prairie chickens, fat, meaty birds, close kin to the grouse and the pheasant; and far, far up in the blue heavens came the melancholy cry of the wild geese, kings of the sky, flying like silver-arrowed squadrons on their pilgrimage to the Southland.

Each dawn found Tom lying motionless in the weeds at the edge of the slough and heard his old shotgun explode noisily in the crisp morning air. Tom's shooting was good, considering his weapon, which had a habit of dividing into four parts every time a shot was fired. He swore he killed the first duck with the barrel of the gun; said it flew into the air and knocked the mallard in the head. There were no bullet holes in the duck, but the general consensus was that it died from natural causes. Mother refused to cook it.

The next one resembled a sieve.

"Just lay the dressin' outside the body," Pop advised Mother. "It gonna come right out them portholes anyhow. Son," he continued, "never mind what I told you 'bout the whites of their eye. Next time, you back up off that duck an' then shoot. This here gravy is plump full of buckshot."

As soon as the rains ceased and fields dried, the threshing season began. Pop engaged his brother; then, with difficulty, broke the news to the family. "A man couldn't hire somebody else when his own brother had a outfit, the biggest outfit 'round here. What else could I do?"

"You won't have nothin' left time you pay him," Tom warned. "You know how he charges. That brother stuff don't mean a thing to Uncle John when it comes down to business. You ought to know."

"But what must I do? Somebody got to thresh the grain!"

"Kill the fatted calf, get out the velvet carpet, and bend low, chillun," shouted Harry from the window, "cause here comes Massa John now!"

A thin string of smoke moved slowly over the prairies as John pulled his crew out of the Knudtson's field, heading for us. Suddenly Sue rode up out of nowhere and ran into the house. "Hello, Aunt Mary, Uncle Tony, kids. Papa sent me to tell you to get ready. We're movin' over now. About thirty men'll be here for supper. Papa told me to tell you. She patted my cheek, gave a poke at Tom, and was on her horse and gone.

"Tonight," wailed Mother. "Tony, you said next week they'd be here; you said John told you next week. What will we feed them?"

"Oh, my Lord! Oh, my soul! Comin' here this time of night, with all them hungry men. John know better'n that. Whyn't he stay where he was till mornin'?"

Tom rode into town on Major and brought home a gunny-sack full of groceries. There was a preponderance of pork and beans not included in the list Mother had given him, but Tom loved pork and beans.

Uncle John presided at the first table. He quickly scanned the food, then used his short grace, the Methodist one about the nourishments of the body—if he could be permitted to call cold baloney nourishment. Food at the second table showed decided evidences of having been tampered with, stretched. But hungry threshers never did expect too much in the way of "vittles" from new folks, especially city folks.

I don't think my mother and father got any sleep that night. They peeled vegetables, baked bread and cakes, and set the

61

table up for five o'clock breakfast. I was up before dawn with the rest of them, thrilled and excited by so many people, in everybody's way. Breakfast over, Pop and Harry took the wagon into town and got enough food for three more meals. There was less than a day's work, everything going all right. But everything didn't.

At ten o'clock the engine broke down. The men came in from the field and sat around the yard until it was repaired, then on the first round Slim's pitchfork went into the separator. John swore and raved, and the men came back to the house to pitch horseshoes until supper. Slim was an I.W.W.

The next day broke cold and cloudy. It began to rain at breakfast—a hard, driving rain, tapering off to a slow, chilly drizzle that lasted throughout the day. Pop bought more food for the men. Pop bought more oats for the horses. Tom and Harry went out into the rain and hauled in more of our precious hay.

"I'm goin' home," said Ben. "It's a damned shame, all of us hangin' round here eatin' you folks out of house and home, Uncle Tony."

There was true love in Pop's eyes as he waved good-bye to his nephew.

John soon followed, taking some of the men with him. The farmers in the crew, those who lived near by, also went home, but we still had thirteen pie-hungry hoboes. Tom and Gus went hunting, and that night there was roast duck and dressing and sweet potato pie. The men sat around on the floor after supper, telling stories and singing until late into the night.

Mother's heart went out to those men, some mere youngsters, away from home for the first time. A tall, clean-faced kid, not much older than Harry, a kid from somewhere in Ohio, helped her with the supper dishes. He asked to help. He didn't talk much, just wiped the dishes, then sat watching Mom work down the bread and set the rolls for morning. After a while she gave him pencil and paper, and, while she peeled potatoes, he leaned over the kitchen table and wrote a letter to his mother in Ohio, telling her he'd be home soon—in time for school. Even among the older men there was a feeling of fellowship, a natural affinity to us and our pathetic efforts at hospitality. Pop, who hadn't smiled since the threshers descended upon us, joined in the storytelling that night. Slim taught me the signs of the hobo language, and I hitched my wagon to the open road and gave the Indians a rest.

By noon of the third day, the rain ceased and the sun came out. Uncle John finished our threshing.

What little of our share of oats was left after the men had fed their horses, we stored in the granary; the rye, the flax, and the blighted wheat, went into town to be sold and divided with Hank Hansmeyer. The few dollars we realized from the year's work were outnumbered by creditors three to one. To Carl Brendel went the first check and Harry's services (gratis) for as long as he was needed. Because we had to eat and because we had to—Old Lady Anderson and Uncle John were paid in full. With newly-borrowed money, we paid the interest on the mortgages and then gave the banker a new note covering the purchase of a couple of cows. We were still broke and further in debt than ever. There was nothing left to buy a farm of our own, not even money for clothing and food to tide us over the dreaded winter; so, with a definite lack of enthusiasm on Pop's part, it was decided that he and Tom finish the season with John's crew. A man and team could earn seven dollars a day, and there was nearly a month's work left.

Mother filled two gunnysack mattresses with fresh straw and rolled up the heavy quilts inside them for the cold nights on the frosted ground. Arrayed in new harness and hitched to the smallest rack, Dixie and Buck bore Pop proudly off into the cold dawn, Tom following close behind.

Four days later Pop came home, Dixie and Buck preceding him by fully an hour. Pop was limping noticeably, elaborately. He was home to stay.

Every Saturday night we waited for Tom. "He's coming, Tom's coming!" we cried when we heard the faint rumble of his wagon far away over the prairies. As it grew louder, came

63

closer, Harry and I raced down the road to meet him. We wouldn't eat on Saturday nights until Tom came home; then we sat in the kitchen around the warm range, eating hot rolls and butter, drinking the thick, freshly churned buttermilk, and listening to Tom's tall tales of threshing.

The catalog is the farmer's Bible, his literature, and when it has passed its usefulness in that capacity, when it is no longer current, it becomes an accessory to the outdoor plumbing, where it is further and more deliberately perused. On Sundays, with Tom home, we gathered around the table after dinner and made out the fall and winter order, each one making out his own lists, selecting his clothes and Christmas gifts from the slick, colorful pages. My lists invariably included a saddle and bridle, but I settled for a box of chocolate bars—without almonds—and things like woolen sweaters and long, fleece-lined underwear which lost its fleece at the first washing.

Everyone helped on the food order. It was fun for us, buying in such large quantities; but to Pop the cook it was the old restaurant routine, old and dear to his heart. We picked out choice cans of fruit, favorite vegetables, and always the little wooden buckets of white fish. The fish had to be thawed and soaked to remove the salt, but the brine was good for Father's feet, so we ate white fish steadily for four years.

Tom gave half of his threshing money to the house; the other half he spent on his secret list, laboring arduously and mysteriously over the order blank, throwing out strange hints, asking odd questions. Long after dark, Mom and Pop reworked the lists, cutting down, substituting not quite so good for good, fitting the order to our limited budget, and preparing for the terrible winter days ahead.

Mother and Father shuddered at the thought of the approaching winter, those days and weeks and months when we would be marooned from the world by an arctic wall of ice and snow. Twice they put a heater on the list, and twice they replaced it with food and clothing.

"We can git along with the stove we got for one winter," said Pop.

"But, Tony," Mother protested, "it's only a laundry stove, a two-hole laundry stove. We can't heat this old house with a laundry stove."

"What's the reason we can't? I won't have nothin' to do all winter but keep it goin'. Besides, we got the range in the kitchen."

"All right, then, but remember they burn lignite here, not Iowa hard coal. You know what a time the Evanses had with that stuff last winter."

"I told you I'd make it burn, didn't I? Never saw no coal yet I couldn't make burn."

"Tony, if we can survive this winter, we'll make it; I know we will. Next year we'll have a bigger and better crop, and we can buy that land across from the Widow Weiss."

"That'll make a good farm, Mary. It's high and smooth like a baby's skin. Ain't much rock on it either; I been all over it on foot. I want that land, Mary. We been through one year out here, and we ain't none the worse off—'cept for a few more debts. If we can just make it through this winter, we'll belong here. Lord, we'll be farmers, sure 'nuff!"

4) BLIZZARD-BOUND

The tumbling tumbleweeds heralded the coming of winter. Huge Russian thistles, ugly and brittle now, free of their moorings, rolled across the prairie like silent, gray ghosts, catching in fence corners, piling up in low places, herded and driven mercilessly by the cold wind that whistled down from the far North. Days grew gray and worried, gray and colder, erasing the boundaries that separated them from night.

We began to dig in for the winter with the tense fearfulness of approaching doom: for my parents a worried, apprehensive fear; for us children a delicious, exciting fear that welcomed the storm and the cold and the unknown.

Came time to dig the potatoes, and the crop was prodigious. "My Lord, what's that?" Pop exclaimed as the plow went down the long row. "Must be rocks; can't no potato be that big. But they were potatoes, and they became bigger and bigger as the digging progressed.

"Now, ain't this somethin'," said Tom. "We should of watered the grain, too."

Remembering our summer diet, Harry got a little sick at his stomach, but the thin-skinned Early Ohios continued to emerge from the chilly earth and lay thick and cumbersome at our feet. For two weeks we plowed and hauled potatoes, for which there was no market—everybody had them. Pop took six of the largest, six that filled a bushel basket, and put them on exhibition at the bank. Market or no market, he was proud of his tubers.

The potato crop in, the boys hauled hay from the field, stacking it in a long fortress around the old barn and back behind the chicken coop and granary, then began hauling ties—the discarded railroad logs which section men left along the tracks. They were the only source of wood in the treeless country, and one needed wood to coax the stubborn lignite, native coal from North Dakota's shallow mines, which stewed and simmered and, if you didn't watch it, put the fire out.

The winds settled down to their blowing, to long steady blowing, unbroken by gusts and blasts. Perpendicularly down across the vast gray plains they swept, increasing in intensity and coldness, howling and shrieking in fiendish anger until the very prairies echoed their savage refrain. The tumbling tumbleweeds were lifted high in the air and dashed to the ground, while the winds rushed on.

Heavy storm windows were nailed into place, and the one storm door was hung at the south entrance, the other entrance nailed closed. Manure was banked around the base of the house and barns, and a fifty-gallon tank of kerosene was stored in the granary for the lamps and lanterns. In the barnyard, animals put on their thick, furry overcoats that swirled and spiraled in the wind, and the few chickens and ducks that reached maturity walked stiff-legged and sideways, tails up against the wind, fearing to venture far from the shelter of the sheds. The seven turkeys took to the air.

Pop stood in the yard one morning, hands on his hips, eyes

squinted upwards. "Ducks and geese goin' south all fall, timber wolf run past my window, tumbleweed rollin' 'cross the prairie, but this," he shook his head sadly, "is somethin' I ain't never seen in all my born days. Turkeys we raise from chicks done got up in the air and flew right on 'way from here like black angels. Do Jesus! Have mercy!"

While Father philosophized, Tom got his gun. "Where you goin', Daniel Boone," called Harry, "or is it Mister Alden?"

"What's the Pilgrims got that I ain't gonna git?" Tom asked.

Pop eyed him passively. "They went thata way," he said, nodding towards the pasture. "Stun 'em, Son; don't mutilate 'em!" Mom's pin money was about to turn into pinfeathers, but before she could intervene there was a loud bang.

We had six Thanksgiving dinners that year. The gobbler surrendered.

When Pop won the bid on the school route, he invited the Olsons, the Nordlands, and Old Gus over for a big Sunday dinner, and by five o'clock we had a brand-new, canvas-topped school rig. Jewel and Skippy drove to our farm in their cart, leaving the pony in the barn, and went on to Driscoll with us. For that we were paid an additional fee by Sterling Township.

Snow began to fall the middle of October—big, dry flakes, light and feathery. It snowed for three days, snowed until the world was white and even, then the weather grew bitterly cold, the mercury dropping to thirty below, thirty-five during the nights. Our windows were frozen over solidly, casting a white, cold glare over the taut house; snow seeped in through the cracks around the windows and under the frosted threshold, forming little white rows. The wind whistled along the floor, and the thin house creaked with the cold. There was snow on the boys' bed upstairs, and a thin coat of ice covered the north wall of the living room behind the couch where I slept with Mom and Pop. True to his promise, Pop kept the belly of the laundry stove red with fire, and the long length of pipe that ran through the ceiling to the attic room was also red from the prodded coals; yet, as our faces stung from its heat, our backs were cold. We could see our breath beside the stove. Although the fire in the range never went out, water froze in the water bucket on the kitchen table and canned fruit froze and burst in the cupboard nearby. We slept in long, fleece-lined underwear and in our heavy stockings, the beds piled high with coats and sweaters. Bathing was a precarious business—a choice between cleanliness and pneumonia. The tin tub was filled with water and placed behind the stove, blankets were spread over surrounding chairs, and we prayed for a warm night, one in the twenties.

More snow fell, fine snow, driven hard by a northeast wind. For days it fell, packing solidly enough to hold up a team of horses, drifting as high as the roof. We shoveled hard and fast to keep the well cleared, the doors of the buildings free, and we built fires in the venthole to thaw out the pump and chopped openings in the ice-caked trough so the stock could drink. On the long drives to and from school, our feet sought the heated bricks in the bottom of the rig, and, with heavy blankets wrapped tightly around our legs, we talked through frozen breath above the singing runners and ate frozen sandwiches left from lunch. The kitchen oven held more feet that winter than it did food.

Just before Christmas we had our first blizzard. Two days and nights of heavy snowfall, then the short lull when the sun came out bright and cold and the wind abated, shifted from northeast to northwest. Loose snow began to creep over the shiny surface of deep-packed snow. Faster and faster it traveled. At forty miles an hour the gale was picking up the virgin snow, whirling it about, obliterating the sun. Then the storm began to close in, forming a blurry whiteness, an opaque haze that blotted out the distant farms, enveloped first our barns, then the windmill, closed in upon the house. Still the wind increased, churning the snow about in all directions now. Fifty, sixty miles an hour it roared in with all its fury.

All night the blizzard raged. Father sat up with the fires, and the rest of us retired fully dressed. Morning was a vague, dull lightness. When Tom forced open the kitchen door, wind and snow rushed at him like angry beasts. A drift as high as the house stood two feet away, but the wind had eddied out a small foyer at the doorstep, as clean and smooth as a marble hall.

"Man, oh, man!" he shouted, slamming his weight against the door. "This is a blizzard which am a blizzard!"

"No school today, Tovey!" Harry was jubilant.

Both of us were filled with the excitement of the storm, the ecstasy of an unexpected holiday; but Mother and Father looked grim and worried. We ate breakfast crowded around the open oven door of the kitchen stove. Midmorning, and still the storm showed no signs of subsiding. Tom put on his sheepskin coat, pulled the collar high around his head, and taking Mother's clothesline, ventured outside. He tied one end of the rope to the big thermometer hook at the northeast corner of the house and, taking the other end, started in the direction of the barns. When the rope ran out at the corral fence, he tied it to a post and followed the barbed wire to a large drift blocking the barn door. Climbing on the top of the manure pile, he crawled in through the window, fed the stock, gave up the idea of watering them, and slowly made his way back to the house, covered with snow, eyebrows and lashes plastered white.

All that day we sat close to the fire. Sport, making the most of his brief stay indoors, romped around the table, howling foolishly back at the gale. Towards evening the wind went down a little. When we could again see the buildings in the yard, Tom went back to look after the stock and milk the cows. After supper we made ice cream with syrup and snow. Pop would have none of it.

"It ain't enough with all that snow outside," he observed ruefully; "you all got to bring it in the house and put it inside you."

The following morning broke still and gray. But cold. A bitter, aching cold that hurt your forehead, stiffened your face, made you speak low, lest you shatter the brittle algidity.

"Must be fifty below out there," Pop predicted.

"A hundred and fifty!" amended Harry. "Too cold to go to

70

school. Too cold for the horses."

"Since when'd you start worryin' about the horses?" asked Tom. "I say it's forty-five. What do you say, Mom?"

"I don't know, Tom. Whatever it is, can't get no colder. Go see what it says. I don't think the children ought to go to school today. What do you think, Tony?"

"If Nordland sends his kids, then we hafta go," he answered gloomily; "but I'm most sure he won't. Roads all drifted over bad by now."

Tom and Sport went out to the thermometer and came back in a hurry. "Why, man, it's hot out there. Come on, Harry, let's go swimming."

"Stop your foolishness. What'd it say?" Pop demanded.

"Only forty-one. Shucks, I thought it was cold."

"Whoopee! That does it!" Harry threw his cap in the air, and Sport pounced upon it. Around the table they went. Tom stuck his foot out, and Harry and the dog piled on the floor.

Pop began to laugh. He didn't really want to laugh, out there facing slow death at the mercy of the elements, but laughing made him feel better. "Boy," he said, "all them indispensable legs of yours. You gonna break your neck one of these days."

"Gonna have to tunnel our way to the barn," said Tom. "The whole Rocky Mountains moved in durin' the night."

"Is it that bad?" Pop sobered.

"All I can say, said Tom, "is that we're gonna have a white Christmas."

A week later Pop brought home a big box and a small wooden keg, Tom's special Christmas order from Sears. There was cider written all over the keg, but we couldn't persuade Tom to open the box. Mother and Father sat up late Christmas Eve, hoping Dick would come home to his family, but he did not come.

Christmas morning I ran to my long, ribbed stocking on the doorknob to find a solitary orange and a little red apple and a red cardboard house. Nothing else. I knew we were poor, and for a long time now I had known there was no Santa Claus, but

71

it was Christmas. I stared at the stocking, tears blinding my eyes.

"There, there," soothed Mother. "Christmas means more than store gifts. You must be thankful for the gift of health, thankful to be alive this awful winter, and thankful for your family. Even," Mother faltered, "even if we're not all here."

I threw down the red house and began to cry. Pop went upstairs to his trunk and came back with a little pair of gold scissors. "Here, take this, Baby. They belonged to your grandmother. She give them to me when I was a boy down in Virginia. Take care of 'em. They're yours now."

"Come here, Tovey," Tom beckoned.

I went to him, holding tight to the scissors. He whispered in my ear, and together we bounded upstairs to get the mysterious box. I was laughing when we tugged it down. Even Pop crowded around as I cut the strings with the little gold scissors, revealing two five-pound and seven one-pound boxes of expensive chocolates.

"Do Jesus!" moaned Pop. "We all gonna be sick as dogs. Boy, what'd you spend all your money on that rich stuff for? Here, let me taste it, see if it's fit to eat."

We were seated at the breakfast table, heads bowed, when a horse galloped into the yard. Pop stopped praying.

"It's Dick!" I yelled. "Dick's here, Mom!"

"Thank you, Jesus!" breathed Pop.

I scooted from the table and out the door. When I came back Dick had me by the hand, the nearest he had ever come to showing any affection for me. Dick hated things like that.

Mother was, oh, so happy; you could see it in her eyes, hear it in her voice. "We were hoping you'd come," she said. "Christmas wouldn't be Christmas without you."

"Welcome, Son." Pop was trying hard to be casual, but his voice was singing. "You just in time for breakfast."

"Merry Christmas," said Dick. "Thought I was never gonna make it. Had to borrow one of Koch's horses."

"The Williamses—those colored folks over by Steele—

asked Evanses and us over there for dinner. Would you like to go? We didn't promise," Mother added hastily. "We can have dinner here just as well."

"Evanses ain't goin'," Pop said triumphantly.

"Sure, I'll go along. Like to meet 'em."

Mom and Pop were relieved. Dick was in one of his rare moods.

By eight o'clock, Sport and the whole family were bundled up in blankets and bedded down in the straw in the big sled. The farther we went, the bigger the farms, the farther apart. Rising up out of the snow were large, prosperous houses and barns, many of them flanked by sturdy groves of cottonwoods, straight, symmetrical rows that served as windbreaks. Trees! We could hardly believe it, and real houses that did not need to be reinforced by manure.

It was late afternoon when we came in sight of the Williams farm. Sport leaped over the side of the sled and joined the barking dogs that came running down the road to meet us.

"Merry Christmas, and welcome!" bellowed Mack Williams, as we pulled up in front of his door.

"Merry Christmas to you, sir." Pop climbed out of the sled and gave him the Odd Fellows' grip.

"Brother Thompson. Bro—ther Thompson!" Mack jumped up and down, his big body shaking, smiles wreathing his dark face.

"You must be starved," said Mrs. Williams. "Dinner's ready. We've been waiting for two hours. Afraid you'd got lost."

Circulation slowly returned to our numbed limbs. Under the warmness of welcome, our tongues loosened, and soon everybody was talking, laughing, shouting like old friends. Mrs. Williams hugged Mother, and somebody kissed me squarely in the mouth before I could fight my way out of the wool muffler.

Half an hour later we were seated at a table groaning with food. We ate and talked, ate and rested, then started all over again, as an unending stream of food flowed from kitchen to table. Food was urged upon us, pushed off on our plates against first mild, then vigorous, protests. Near the end of the meal we sat back dawdling with the food. Slumping down with the weight of it, I mournfully watched the mound of ice cream melt before my very eyes, melt faster than I could eat. No one scolded for half-empty plates. Mack raised his mighty voice in laughter as, one by one, we children grudgingly withdrew.

"I like to see the young 'uns eat," he said. "Look at my brood; fat as hogs every one of 'em. Fat, black and sassy." Mack Williams was proud of his blackness.

While the grown-ups were still sitting around the table, Ted Williams, Mack's brother, and his family arrived. Ted was shorter and lighter than Mack. He spoke in short, precise sentences, and I had a feeling that something over which he had no control was holding him in. Just when he was about to enjoy himself, something inside of him stopped. Maybe it was Mrs. Ted, the Maryland schoolteacher. She was nice—reserved and nice. Fifteen years, two children, and Mrs. Ted still made noises like a schoolmarm. It even showed in her fourteen-year-old daughter, who was full of "Yes, mamma," and "No, mamma," instead of turkey and ice cream.

Now there were fifteen of us, four percent of the state's entire Negro population. Out there in the middle of nowhere, laughing and talking and thanking God for this new world of freedom and opportunity, there was a feeling of brotherhood, of race consciousness, and of family solidarity. For the last time in my life, I was part of a whole family, and my family was a large part of a little colored world, and for a while no one else existed.

Before evening was over, two white families stopped by to extend their greetings. The spell of color was broken, but not the spirit of Christmas, for the way Mack greeted them and their own warm response erased any feeling we may have had of intrusion.

Mother, Father, and I went home with Ted's family. We had a quiet night and an inhibited breakfast. There were wide spaces of white linen exposed between the Haviland dishes, real sterling silver and individual napkin rings adding a bit of Down

East to the hushed austerity that prevailed. Ted's Episcopalian blessing was brief, dignified. The food was good, beautifully served, but limited. Involuntarily we slowed down. Pop tried to get two bites out of the tiny biscuits—wanted a second cup of coffee.

I tagged along when Ted showed Father around the place, pointing with pride to the pure-bred Shropshires and the Jersey cows. He was filled with new farming ideas, advanced methods that Mack ridiculed but most of his neighbors respected. Ted, who had been trained at Tuskegee, read weekly farm journals and government bulletins, and his was the only library in the township.

With a feeling of relief we returned to Mack's.

"You all come on in here an' eat some food," Mack said. "That birdseed my brother give you won't last you down the hill."

Pop threw back his head and whooped. "True, Brother, true! We didn't have a Lord's thing but pretty dishes. Where's the turkey, Lady Williams—that delicious, delectable last part over the fence?"

It was high noon before we reluctantly started for home, stomachs full, hearts glad, and the rear end of the sled packed with food for our supper, with canned goods and lard and dried fruit and jelly and a quarter of a hog, its frozen white skin visible through its cheesecloth wrapping.

The worst part about going away was the coming home late at night to a cold house. Gus had fed and watered the stock and had milked the two cows, but he was afraid to leave a fire, so we stood around in our coats until Pop got the stove going, then opened the big box and ate some more of Mrs. Williams' Christmas dinner.

Far into the night we could hear Dick's voice and Tom and Harry's laughter. Dick was taking the Williamses apart, one by one. "That Mack, he's a bear. A bear, man!"

"A black bear," put in Harry.

"Unquestionably!" Dick continued. "He could whip Jack

75

Johnson and Jim Jeffries settin' down."

"An' never stop talkin'," said Tom.

"Stop talkin'? What you sayin', son? That man stop talkin' he'd die sure as you're born. Drop dead as that old nag Ted calls a racehorse."

At that sally the boys broke out into unrestrained laughter. "That mule? Lord today! That little yella Negro stand up there with his ugly face hangin' out in this Dakota breeze and say that bag of bones was a racehorse?"

Dick settled down to his lies. "Why, son, he's got papers, he's got papers that say Sir John . . ."

"Sir who?"

"That's right. Sir John. Honest to Gawd, that shine done christened that mule after some sweepstake nag. Well, this paper with the pedigree is 'bout two feet long. He's got it rolled up like a diploma, with ribbon and the gold seal stamped all around the edges."

The boys went off into another gale of laughter. "What'd it say, boy? What'd this here thing say?" coaxed Tom.

"How'd I know what it says? I ain't been to no Latin school. There's about two feet of fine writin' in Latin. So fine and so Latin can't no one read it, least of all that fool from Tuskegee."

"Tuskegee? What'd you mean, Tuskegee?" Harry had never heard of the school.

"Will you quit bein' ignorant? Tuskegee is a college some place below the Mason Dixie."

"What's it for?"

"What you think it's for? Didn't I say 'twas below the Mason Dixie? It's for Zigs, that's what it's for."

"Did Ted say he went to that school?" Tom asked interested.

"Yes, but what makes you think he stayed? Now tell me that?"

"What about the paper?"

76

"Didn't I tell you the print was too fine to read? Nobody know what it says but the Latin who wrote it, and he threw away his book and glasses, give himself up."

"If that's a racehorse," said Tom dryly, "I bane a blue-eyed Swede, aye iss."

"Oh, Gawd!" moaned Dick. "Nigger, you and them blue eyes. Them baby-blue eyes. Father, father! I caun't stand it!"

New Year's Day, Billy Swanson galloped out from town with a telegram. Pop took it with shaking hands. "Here, you open it, Mary."

"Maybe somebody's dead," said Billy, cheerfully, as he got off his horse.

"It's addressed to you, Tony. You read it."

Pop read in silence. He read it again. He began to holler. "Oh, my Lord! Just looka here. Mary, Mary, it's from the Governor." He grabbed Mother in his arms and danced her around in a circle.

"Stop your noise, Tony, and read it. What does it say?"

Pop read aloud: "Dear Sir: Report at Capitol at nine o'clock Tuesday to be sworn in as private messenger to the Governor. Stop."

"But Tuesday, Tony, that's tomorrow!"

"Great Scotts! That's the truth. Help me pack; where's my clothes?"

Tom picked up the telegram. "This was sent two days ago; hadn't you better answer it?"

"Yes, yes! Mary, get me a pencil. Here, take this down while I get my clothes. Tom, you get the team ready. I got to make the next train."

Tom looked at Billy and winked. "Train don't get in till four-thirty. 'Tain't one yet."

"Git the horses ready, anyhow. Ain't got time to argue with you, boy!"

Billy began to laugh softly. Pop had removed his pants and

77

put on his cap. He was walking around waving the telegram in the air. "Honorable Sir. No, scratch that out. Most Honorable Sir."

"His Majesty," said Harry.

"You git out of here! How can a man think with all this noise? Go on, git!"

Mother sent us to the kitchen and shut the door. "Will he get paid for it?" asked Billy.

"I guess so," said Tom. "Ought to pay pretty good."

"Say, that's all right." Billy sobered. "Must be something important, for them to send a telegram all the way out here for."

"The Old Man worked at the capitol in Des Moines, too, you know."

"He did? Say, he must be smart. But he did look funny walking around in his underwear like that." Billy began to laugh again.

"He's gonna butt his brains out gettin' packed," Harry predicted.

"Yeah," said Tom. "Sure be a relief when he gets on that train."

It was Pop, the city man, who brought a bit of country to the farm administration, for he was sworn in, still clad in his sheepskin suit and his sheep-lined boots.

"Shades of reconstruction!" exclaimed a Minneapolis reporter. "Now where in hell did he come from?"

My father spent the next sixty days telling them where he came from, what they did there, and how. There were many who could well listen. Most of the new officeholders, like Governor Frazier, had never held an office above township level, and some had never been inside a state capitol. Before long, farmer-politicians were seeking Pop out.

"Will you set with us, Tony?" they asked. "We never been to one of these here fancy things. All them dishes and things— Tony, you been around, we'll set by you an' watch, see how you do. All right, Tony?"

Pop put them at ease. "Jest take it easy," he said. "Let the other fellow lead. Eat slow, don't reach for nothin' like you do when you're out threshin'. You'll be all right; I'll give you the eye."

Nobody seemed to know just what the duties of the new messenger were, except, of course, the new messenger; so, when North Dakota's fifteenth legislative assembly opened, my Pop sat behind a big mahogany desk at one end of the long reception room in the executive offices and received the Governor's callers. He was happy. For sixty days, at least, he would escape the torturous winter on a lonely farm. Sheepskin had given way to blue serge, his shoes were shined to gleaming perfection, and the gold-rimmed glasses and the gold lodge chain added dignity. Once more he was shaking hands, rubbing elbows with the public, and it gave him back some of the confidence he had lost during his brief struggle with the soil.

Next to his office was that of the Governor's secretary, Nelson A. Mason, a pleasant young lawyer who became one of his lifelong friends. The Governor himself was something special, and Mason and Pop were two of his greatest admirers. Frazier was a big, jolly man, florid of face, and with no more hair on top of his head than Father. Everything Pop had observed in other capitals and among officials elsewhere he gladly passed on to the new party, and even the Governor was among those grateful.

Father roomed with the Smiths, one of the very few colored families living in Bismarck at the time. Ed Smith, who ran a clean-dye-and-pawn shop, was king of the colored folks. Negroes coming to Bismarck usually stayed only on his approval. He went their bail when they got into trouble (and most of them did), and he loaned them money when they were broke (and most of them were). His fees were high—Ed Smith prospered. He was a handsome, brown man, with a ready laugh and a funny story, with a shrewdness beneath his slow good humor that earned for him the name of "Black Jew."

"I'm a race man, myself," Ed confided to Pop from behind the coats and suits. "I like to see my people do things, be somebody. We need decent, respectable folks out here. Now take my wife; she hasn't got anybody to associate with but white folks. Oh, they're nice enough, treat us fine and all that, but they're not colored, see."

"How did you ever get 'way out here?" asked Pop.

Ed grinned. "Why'd you come?" He didn't wait for the answer. "When I was a young feller, I ran around all over the country. Bummed in here broke, got a job working right here in this very shop. Already knew a little about cleaning and dyeing, liked the business. Benny, the Jew who owned it, got sick, and I ran the place for him two years, then, he died, I bought it, went back to Memphis and married, then fooled my wife up here. Been here ever since."

"You do a nice business here."

"Yes, I'm doing all right. But since we got the little one, my wife wants to move. Don't want to bring the kid up ignorant about his own people. Junior, he's only seven, but he thinks he's white. Every year my wife takes him South to visit her folks. Nearly got her into trouble last time; ran over to the white folk's side of the depot and started to drink out of their fountain. You know how them peckerwoods took that!"

Smith shrugged his shoulders, spread his hands. It was Benny's gesture. He looked out over the rows of suits, the smile never leaving his face. A big cigar hung loose from his heavy lips. "Don't want him to learn how to run from white folks," he continued. "I was bred and born in the South, lived there most of my life, but I don't want my son to be brought up there either. A darky hung himself a few months ago, right there where you're sitting." Smith pointed to the wooden beam running along the ceiling.

Pop moved his chair.

"Yes, sir. I came down here to open up that morning, and there he was, hanging from that beam, dead as hell."

"You don't say! Must of been crazy."

"Yes, he was crazy—crazy with worry, crazy with fear. White folks down in Georgia was after him. He got away somehow and come North, kept coming farther and farther North. Arranged with some old white man he thought he could trust to give his wife and eight kids the money he sent them. Kept sending money, kept moving, couldn't hear from them, didn't know if they was dead or alive. He'd sit here at night for hours and just stare, not saying a word, not moving a muscle. I let him sleep in back of the store. That night he just give up. Better off, poor devil."

A week before the session closed Pop sent for Mother and me. After he fitted us out in new clothes, he took us to the Capitol and introduced us to the Governor and to all of his new friends. The closing night of the assembly was exciting. They set the clocks back so they could close at midnight, then proceeded to fight until dawn. Galleries were crowded, and people roamed the big halls as if they were going to a circus. I couldn't understand much of what was being said, but half the men down on the floor were angry and half were laughing—all were having the time of their lives. The farmers weren't much on oratory, but they made up for it in vehemence and noisy gestures. Behind every profane word, somebody yelled, "Strike that out!" Fist fights broke out in the corridors and on the floor. "He's got a gun!" somebody shouted into the milling crowd, and all bedlam broke loose. The police sergeants-at-arms had their hands full. It was wonderful.

The farm was quite a letdown after the exciting week at Bismarck, after running water and inside plumbing, but I was glad to be home again. Sport ran around in little circles and leaped upon me, his big, padded paws flailing my shoulders and his hot tongue flailing my face, reaching farther behind my ears than I was ever wont to go. It was good to be home.

Soon came the warm chinooks, melting the snow, and again the rocks of Hansmeyer came out of their hiding, but we were no longer afraid. The dreaded winter was over.

5) BIG CAMP MEETING

With spring came the excitement of the birth of living things, and with new life came new responsibilities, new roots in the soil of a country we now called home. Our firstborn was a calf, a damp, curly, red and white baby with big, rabbit ears and wobbly legs. Soon it was sharing honors with a velvety, mouse-colored colt. Harry loved the colt. Out of his strange conglomeration of Negrowegian horse talk evolved the recondite and inglorious name, "Speevadowsky." The colt never had a chance.

Multiple life in the form of eight squirming, squealing baby pigs and one runt turned the farm into a day nursery. The litter's mortality rate was high. After the sow had lain on two, Mother took over the tiny runt, greasing his scaly sides and feeding him warm milk until he, too, died. When I appropriated little Jerry for my doll buggy, Pop intervened. He got special pleasure out of caring for the pigs, especially in feeding them. Feeding was his business.

School was fun, now that the Koch cousins had admitted me into their exclusive circle. They hated Miss Breen, mostly because she was a teacher, so I hated her out of loyalty to them, and immediately my deportment suffered.

During noon hour we played "school," a game expressly for Miss Breen's benefit, each of us taking turns being "teacher." Tillie would push her glasses down over her pug nose and walk up and down the aisle, looking cross-eyed, and I would poke my pupils with a book and issue impossible commands in a horrid voice. Miss Breen pretended she didn't see, couldn't hear, so we drew large pictures of her on the blackboard, big, atrocious caricatures with an undeniably Breen profile.

Teacher didn't allow us to play with our rulers, and that irked, so I dipped one end of mine into an inkwell and began flaunting it around. When she came for it she got a handful of ink—as planned. That night at the supper table Ollie told about the ruler. Dick laughed loud and long with the rest of them, then went out to the barn, got a horse, and rode home to tell Mom. My mother measured out a bit of justice that would have done Miss Breen's soul good—if she had a soul.

Hating teacher had other drawbacks—namely, teacher. Her means of retribution were many and effective, so we devised a nasty little game called "Mad." We'd spend the morning making faces at one another, then split up at recess and approach the other pupils. "I hate Tillie," I'd tell Lena Jensen confidentially, "don't you?" If Lena didn't cooperate, I'd go a little further. "She thinks she's smart, and her clothes are Old Country." Taking careful note of Lena's comments, I'd go on to the next victim. At an appointed time the three of us would meet, compare notes, then hate each other's enemies. I didn't always enjoy my deceit, for I knew the cousins would eventually form other coalitions and frame me. When they did they called me "black" and "nigger," and I was alone in my exile, differentiated by the color of my skin, and I longed to be home with the comfort of my family; but even with them I would not share my hurt. I was ashamed that others should find me distasteful. I could not afford the luxury of hate. I soon discovered that the little game was not for me.

Early that spring I was given the most wonderful thing in the world—a pony. Pop and Mom refused to accept pay for boarding the Nordlands' pony all winter, so Skippy was prevailed upon to part with his Bessie. I couldn't sleep the first night I got her; I was up with Pop at five and out to the barn, petting and talking to my pony. Bessie was beautiful and spirited, with long black tail and silky mane, her rich brown coat glossy from constant care. Skippy didn't want to show it, but he missed his pony. He came to visit Harry a lot that summer, but he always went to the barn to see Bessie first.

"If you ever mistreat her," he told me fiercely, "I'll take her back home. Promise me, won't you?"

I kept my promise. I stole oats for her from the working horses when they hardly had enough strength to pull the plows, and for hours at a time I curried and brushed my pony and braided her mane and tail. With my dog and my pony I was happy beyond the realm of people, for I had found a friendship among animals that wavered not, that asked so little and gave so much of loyalty and trust, irrespective of color.

With the beginning of spring work in the fields, Pop's farming instincts began to diminish. Two months at the capital made him lust for another means of escape, so, when Oscar Olson told him of the Holiness Camp, a two-week religious festival held at Jamestown every June, Pop began to think. Where there were gathered together a number of people, he reasoned, there must be a cook—or the need of one. The messenger letter had worked out so well he again took pen in hand and wrote to the good Nazarenes.

"You know," he told Mother, "I bet those folks'll be willin' to pay ten dollars a day for a real chef. I know they ain't never had no real honest-to-goodness chef cook. If you all can get along without me. . . ."

84

Mother smiled. She was glad Tom did not hear.

The camp officials were delighted. Pop could hardly wait until June. He sharpened his French carvers in April and began assembling his cook's clothes in the month of May, and, while Tom plowed and disked, Pop tended his precious pigs and composed menus for five hundred righteous people.

"You know, Mary," he said, "I always did say the good Lord will provide. And He do, Mary, He sure do!"

Mother and I gave Pop a week's start, then we, too, set out for the big camp-meeting grounds.

A young minister met our train and took us to the camp bus. We rode along beautiful tree-lined streets, whose heavy foliage interlocked far overhead, and passed pretty homes with clipped hedges and flower beds. Surely this could not be North Dakota. Surely less than two hundred miles could not make such a difference. But it did.

At the north end of town the bus rattled through a gate marked "Jamestown Holiness Camp Grounds," went down a long row of small white tents, and stopped in front of the combination kitchen and dining room.

Pop rushed out to meet us. He had changed again. On the farm he was lost, confused, dependent upon the Lord; at the capital he was suave, genteel, dignified; but here in a hot kitchen, he was again Tony the cook, quick, sure, skillful. His staff of young men and women, mostly divinity students from the nearby college, were alive, clean-cut youngsters, happy in their task and happy in their Lord. Never had he been given help that cheerfully did so much yet received so little. When we arrived Pop was having trouble with the white folk's religion, again hard put with the "Praise Gods" and the "Hallelujahs." New to him was this taking God over by the fiery stoves or back behind the meat block with the French carvers. Cooking was mean, aggravating work, where a man wrestled with the demon heat, was plagued by incompetent seconds and temperamental bosses; but here it was different—all day long they sang and shouted the name of the Lord as they worked.

85

Even Dr. Kane, the great evangelist, invaded the kitchen, slapped Pop's sweating back and said, "Praise the Lord, Tony! Say 'Praise the Lord'!"

"I'm a busy man, Reverend—got to get these folks fed."

"You're not too busy for God, are you, Tony?"

"No. It's not that. Just cookin' and prayin' don't mix."

"You're a Christian, aren't you, Tony?"

"Course I'm a Christian!" Pop bridled.

"You've been born again, haven't you, Tony?"

"Course I've been born again." Sweat rolled down his face.

"Don't you believe," said Dr. Kane, "that you can serve food and serve God at the same time?"

Pop took his big ladle out of the soup and laid it carefully down on the table. "Now what must I do with a man like this?"

Dr. Kane put his arm around Pop's shoulder, put his lips close to Pop's ear. "Say, 'Praise the Lord,' Tony. Say, 'Amen'!"

By the end of the season my father could stop in the middle of baking a soufflé and say, "Amen."

Our tent was one of the larger ones in the first row by the dining hall. It had a double bed, a canvas cot for me, a folding chair, campstool, and washstand. Out of deference to his rheumatism, and for an additional fifty cents, Pop had had a wooden floor installed. I was a little disappointed. All those tents, and still no Indians. But life in a tent had its advantages; there was very little housework, and there were over five hundred neighbors with children. Because of the proximity of the tents, we kept our voices low, and, because a tent is a tent, we kept our shadows likewise.

Next to the playground was a small tabernacle for children. The p. k.'s (preachers' kids) were friendly to me, either out of a sense of Christian duty or because they really liked me, I never knew which. The only time I was reminded of my race was when a group of town toughies ganged us at the playground, and for my benefit hurled a few "nigger, niggers" along with the sticks and rocks. After that episode I was a little less aggressive, a little more reluctant to be a leader among my friends.

86

Thanks to the tabernacle classes, I was soon able to recite—for no particular reason—the names of the books of the Bible, both Old and New Testament, all in one breath; and I could rattle off a Psalm or a verse with ack-ack precision and just about as much feeling. Recently, at a friend's home, when it came my turn to give a Bible verse, there was a pause that wasn't refreshing. The only thing I could remember was "Jesus wept," and a nine-year-old prodigy beat me to that.

At night parents took their young to the evening services at the big tabernacle. The first part of the meeting was given over to singing, as the evangelists walked about the stage swinging their black-clothed arms to the rhythm of revival music, stopping now and then to clap their hands or shout, "Sing it, brothers and sisters!"

After the songs and long prayers and the reading of the Scriptures, one of the greats in evangelism brought the message. The popular ones prefaced their sermon by telling funny stories, then, gradually warming up to their subjects, preached and stormed and brought down upon the intent congregation the wrath, the love, and the power of God.

The climax was reached in the call for sinners. Each preacher made an eloquent plea: the slim ones, pointing gracefully towards heaven, tiptoed around, whispering sweetly, then stopped suddenly, stamped the floor, and shook their clenched fists at the very pits of hell; the fat ones jumped up and down in one spot, their voices going where their bodies could not.

There was a lot about hell at those meetings. I trembled beside my mother, doomed to eternal fire with the flames of purgatory lapping at my feet, for I was of an age now to be responsible for my own soul—and pay full fare on a streetcar. Leaping down from their pulpit, the preachers walked up and down the sawdust aisles, pleading to the congregation as they sang, "Almost persuaded now to believe. . . ." Men and women flocked down to the front of the tent, and knelt in prayer and repentance baring their souls to God. Some stood up and cried and shook hands with the elders, laughing, testifying through their tears; those in a trance were carried off to cots in the rear of the bookstore, where they lay between heaven and hell, fighting with the devil. It was more like Colored Baptist than Colored Baptist, and I came away feeling guilty and afraid.

The breaking up of camp was a sad, disillusioning thing. We stayed over an extra day, while Pop supervised the storing of the equipment and put the place in order. Mother and Father didn't say much coming home on the train. For Father it was the end of something dear to his heart; for Mother it was a pleasant interlude and rest from the arduous duties of caring for the family. I sat at the window watching the green grass turn to brown, breaking the magic spell. Again I was riding over my prairies, looking out towards the purple haze of my distant hills. There was no struggle in the changing. My happiness, my home has ever been the present, my hopes and dreams the future; the past dying suddenly, quietly, leaving no mourners in my heart.

The monotony of the dry, hot summer was broken by Claude and Pinky, two colored youths from St. Paul who had bummed their way to North Dakota to work in the fields during school vacation. Claude was a handsome boy, tall and bronze, with brooding black eyes and manners we had long since forgotten. I fell in love with Claude. He told me beautiful stories about his native Minnesota, about Lake Minnetonka and the Falls of Minnehaha. It was like reading *The Song of Hiawatha,* listening to Claude, for his voice rippled like the Indian waters he knew so well, and when he recited poetry he sang on a golden harp, played on an enchanted flute. And I was much charmed.

Pinky was light like Sue and wild like Dick, the son of a priest. During the week, they worked for neighboring farmers and made our home their headquarters. On Sundays Ben and Sue rode over, and sometimes the oldest Williams boy came late Saturday and spent the night. When Dick heard, he, too, came home. Pop sat back and listened to the boys talk, sat back on his seniority, feeling particularly patriarchal and a little old-fashioned. It was a new sensation for him. The boys brought with

them a breath of the cities he loved, a breath of youthfulness—
and Dick. It was good to have Dick home again.

Our crop was better that fall, and, with both Harry and
Tom manning bundle racks and Pop hauling grain, we realized
enough to make a down payment—at last—on a farm of our
own, two hundred and forty acres of land in Sterling Township on a beautiful hill near the Widow Weiss. We were pretty
excited about our new home. Every Sunday we drove over its
virgin soil, planning the house we would build, laying out the
barnyard, the lanes, the pastures. Pop took new heart, put a new
faith in the land, and Mother dreamed her dreams again.

After threshing season Dick pocketed his money and went
off to the cities. Harry bought a bicycle with his share of the
threshing money, and Tom got a new double-barreled Win-
chester. The bicycle fared badly in the rock-strewn wagon ruts,
but it was new and shiny, and for a while it became more desirable than Bessie, so Pop gave me a tan riding bridle, and
again there was peace.

Even with the new gun, Tom frightened more coyotes than
he killed. Two big ones who came to the pasture every night to
feed on the carcass of a dead horse studiously avoided the traps
he set for them, so early one morning Tom went to meet his
foes. The dead horse was in a little ravine, between two hills.
Tom dropped down on his stomach, gun in hand and began a
slow belly-crawl up the hill. Coyotes usually travel in pairs, one
feeding, while the other watches. Tom arrived atop the hill si-
multaneously with the big, bad wolf, close enough to rub noses.
The element of surprise being equal, both escaped unharmed.

My brother's interest suddenly turned to skunks, weasels,
and badgers. Tom collected enough hides to pay for his traps,
an ice cream freezer, and a smoke bellows that no one knew
how to manipulate.

Sue Evans eloped late that fall with the hired man and was
married in Moorehead, just across the state line. North Dakota
don't allow no mixed marriages going on around there! Uncle
John got the sheriff and trailed the couple to Minnesota, but they

were too late. And now there were three Irishmen in the Evans household, for Ann's brother had suddenly arrived for an indefinite visit and brought his wife, Zorine. We weren't at all agreed on Zorine. She seemed to be a pint-sized combination of Mexican chili beans and Negro TNT. Zorine could swear—and usually did for ten consecutive minutes without taking a breath or repeating herself, making my camp-meeting feats sound a little on the sissy side.

When winter closed in again we had a nickle-plated heater, with warming rails for our feet and a place on top for a simmering kettle. Before Christmas we butchered our first hog. Something went wrong with the scalding, so my brother Tom took Pop's good razor and shaved him. They had the body stretched out on a table in the yard before I ventured out of doors. Tom was waiting when I did.

"Well, Tovey," he said sadly, "it sure is too bad."

"What's too bad?" I asked gazing fearfully upon still death.

"Don't you recognize him? It's Jerry."

My eyes popped open, my heart sank.

"Yes," Tom went on, wiping his eyes—there was even a catch in his voice. "He jumped right under the knife. Tried to stop him, but it was too late."

"Mamma!" I had my breath now. I started for the house. "Mamma, they killed my pig! They killed Jerry!"

"No, they didn't," she said. "You know better than to believe Tom. You know he's always saying something to hear you holler. And you always do," she added despairingly.

Out in the yard Pop looked up from the hog, looked at Tom. "Boy, what you want to start all that noise for?"

"That's the cryingest little darky I've ever seen," Tom hedged. "When is she goin' to grow up—and shut up?"

There are a lot of parts to a dead hog, and we tried to eat them all. The good pieces were cut up and hung in the granary to freeze, and the odds and ends appeared upon the table in various forms. There was headcheese, soft brains, pig's feet, chitterlings, sweetbreads, liver, maws, heart, and a tail. Then there was the rendering of lard that brought on crackling bread. It was a long time before I came to eating terms with the recently departed. The frozen meat was brought into the house to thaw out a day or two before it was cooked. The day the hog's head joined the family circle on a chair behind the stove was an unhappy day for me. Those little blue eyes, staring recriminatingly out from the clean-shaven face, followed me about the room. Tom talked to the head, called it Deacon Death, offered it food, and put a towel around its jowls to alleviate an imaginary toothache.

There were times when I felt the family wasn't exactly bright.

That Christmas Tom cut down on the candy and ordered a phonograph. It was several days before we found the crank, sealed up inside the sound box. The ten "selected records" that accompanied the machine had a lot to do with molding our musical tastes and prejudices that winter. John Philip Sousa's band became Pop's favorite because he once heard Sousa back East. Mother and I played the Hawaiian "Aloha," and thrilled to its plaintive notes. For a while I dreamed of coral islands beyond the blue Pacific; then Harry sat on the record, and I joined Pop and Sousa. Bert Williams' "Preacher and the Bear," with the "Two Black Crows" on the reverse side, was the most used and abused record of all. The boys played it until its scratched surface was warped and cracked. When the words were no longer distinguishable, they gave their own version of who got the worm, with variations that would have delighted the recording company's heart.

Soon after Christmas Dick came home, wearing a white shirt and smoking cigarettes right in front of Mom and Pop— and nobody stopped him. Never once did he offer to help with the chores, just talked and bragged about the good times he had in the wonderful city; but he didn't seem in too much of a hurry to return. He said so many girls were after him he had to leave. He said it was awful. After two days at home he went back to

Driscoll, where he had a more appreciative audience.

When Dick was gone, Tom and Harry lay upstairs in their bed and laughed until they cried. "Did you hear that lying jig? Did you hear him doin' all that big talk?" asked Tom.

"If the city's so hot, then why didn't he stay there? Tell me that. Why did he come back here to the sticks?"

"You said it, son. But you see where he is?"

"He must of heard we bought a farm."

"What's that got to do with him? He ain't put none of his sweat and money in it."

"All his money's on his back, and Dick, he ain't never raised no sweat for nobody. Him and his white shirts and white handkerchiefs, in the middle of the week too!" Harry snorted his disgust.

"And did you see that hair? Slick as a onion. Look like a cow licked him."

"What hair, man? That wasn't hair, that was grease."

"If he'd fell down, he'd slide from here to "Minnie."

"Minnie who?"

"Minnehaha, you fool." They both went into gales of laughter. "Oh, that lying man!" said Tom. "That big-mouthed, lying darky!"

6) BROKEN DREAMS

In the middle of February a chinook swept over the icy
prairies, melting the heavy snow, bringing sudden, unseasonable
spring to the Dakotas. On the second day of the thaw Mother
complained slightly of feeling ill, and grew steadily worse as the
week drew on. Mom was hardly ever sick. Old Doc Reeves
came out from town, felt her pulse, took her temperature, and
left some pills. She'd be all right, he said; it was nothing.

The next day I stayed home from school—the first day I
had missed that term. I felt grown up, staying home to take
care of my mother. After lunch, when Pop left with the school
rig, and Tom was in the barn doing the chores, I got out the
ironing board and placed it across two chairs. Mother often let
me iron little things; she'd be surprised when she woke up.

The bright February sun flooded the room and sparkled on
the melting snow outside, causing small streams of water to run

from under the deep banks of snow. My mind was far away on the soft spring breeze, as I pushed the heavy flatiron over a faded blue shirt.

Mother stirred. Her breathing became louder, more difficult. I put down my iron and went to the bed. "Mom, Mom," I called softly, but she did not answer me. I held her head up so she could breathe, but her body was limp and heavy, her eyes open but unseeing, and the breathing was harsh, scraping now, deep within her throat.

Then it ceased.

"Mom!" I called again; still she did not answer. Gently I shook her. Her head rolled over on my shoulder, and suddenly I was afraid. I laid her back on the pillow. She did not move. Slowly I backed away towards the door, found the knob, and slipped quietly outside. Sport sat on the step whimpering, whining. I started for the barn, but he did not follow me.

"Tom! Tom!" I called. "Come in and see what's the matter with Mom." I faltered, unable to describe this nameless fear that had come over me. "She acts funny," I finished lamely.

Tom dropped his pitchfork and hurried to the house. I followed, the feeling of impending disaster growing in my heart, clutching at my throat. For a long time he sat there holding her hand, feeling for her pulse. I waited; still he did not speak. He rubbed her hands, listened to her heart, then carefully placed a chair behind her pillows and propped her up in the bed. Finally he spoke.

"Mom's awful sick," he said softly. "I'll have to go for the doctor." He saw the fear in my face. "Or I'll stay," he offered, "and you go. Which do you want to do?"

"I'll go," I said, "I'll go."

"You'll have to ride fast," he warned. "Better take Major. Gallop all the way. Tell Pop to turn back an' get the doctor, quick!"

Major, seeming to sense the urgency of his mission, pranced and fretted as Tom lifted me up on to his back. Tom released the bridle, hit him on the rump, and with a mighty leap we were out of the yard and headed down the road towards town. I rode as I had never ridden before, saying a kind of prayer as I clung hard to the mane of the flying horse, asking God to let me keep my mother. Major never slowed down for the big hill. As we dashed over the top, I could see the school rig turning the corner just outside of town. Pop was standing in the road beside the team when I rode up, his face gray and tight.

"What's the matter?" he cried, but he knew without asking. Nothing short of death would cause Tom to send me to town on Major.

"Get the doctor!" I said, trying to get my breath. "Tom says go back and get the doctor. Quick, Mom's worse!"

"Harry," Pop called as he lifted me from the horse. "Take Major and go for the doctor. Hurry, boy, hurry!"

I climbed into the school rig, glad to be relieved of my mount, feeling the importance of my message, some of the fear gone. Pop whipped up the horses, galloping them all the way home.

Dick came late that night, big-eyed and quiet. John and Ann came, offering to send for the Williams families, while Harry rode over to tell the Olsons. All night neighbors sat up drinking coffee and eating sandwiches. Afraid to go to sleep, I followed Tom and Pop around the kitchen, avoiding the living room, where Mother still lay on our bed.

In the morning, Old Lady Anderson came and laid her out on a sheet spread across some boards to await the coffin from Bismarck. With the stove down and the windows open, the living room was icy cold, filled with the smell of white carnations and death. I wanted to comb Mother's hair the way she always wore it, but I was afraid. "Touch her," Father urged, "and you won't be scared no more." But the fear of death gripped me, a fear so deep and horrible that I could not go near.

Ed Smith sent a colored circuit preacher down from Bismarck, and with the cheap black coffin and pine box came a large wreath of flowers from Governor and Mrs. Frazier. I didn't have a black dress, so I put on the white eyelet with the

95

blue-ribbon sash, and Tom helped me with my hair ribbons.

The ceremony was brief and simple. Dick took it harder than any of us. Father was beyond grief. After the funeral we got into the school rig and followed the spring wagon with the coffin, driving slowly through the ice and mud to the little cemetery on the hill.

They lowered my mother down into the frozen earth at the close of day, as the sun sank behind the snow-blotched hills. We stood on the brink of the grave, listening to the clods of dirt fall upon her coffin while the neighbors sang "Nearer My God to Thee." And, for the last time, there were six of us.

Ann took me home with her, but I would not stay. "Poor little thing," she'd say to all who stopped by their farm. "Got no mother; don't know what will become of her. I feel so sorry for the little tyke."

I stood it a week, then gathered up my things, got on my pony, and rode home. Sport was joyful, but my father didn't speak. Putting on his hat, he walked out into the yard, followed the fence down to the grove, and stood with his hands clasped behind his back, looking up towards the heavens. I was afraid to go into the house, for I could see Mother everywhere. With Sport close beside me, I went back to the barn, rebridled Bessie, and rode towards the new farm in search of my brothers. Tom and Harry, with pick and crowbar, were prying rocks from the soil of our new home, but there was little joy and enthusiasm in the task.

"Hello, Tovey," said Tom. "What you doing here?"

Harry stood by dumb and awkward.

"I came back home." I tried to sound casual. "Aunt Ann talks too much."

There was a long silence. I sat relaxed on my pony while she munched at the grass at her feet. Tom did not look at me. "All right," he finally said. "But you've got to work."

"What you think I've been doing?" I countered. "All day long Aunt Ann calls: 'Sister, run get me this; Sister, run get me that. Your legs are younger than mine,' she says."

"Want some lunch?" Harry handed me the basket with a sandwich and some potato salad left in it. I slid off Bessie and sat down on a rock to eat.

That night Pop wrote to a wealthy cousin of Mother's who lived in the East, asking her to take me, but, to my relief, nothing ever came of it.

For weeks Pop hardly spoke a word to us. He cooked the meals and cleaned the house, walking around in a halo of grief, whistling or humming the old hymns, the troubled hymns of Zion. Harry and I turned to Tom for everything. He directed my bath as he sat on a barricade chair, his back to me and the stove. Even an ambidextrous octopus would have had difficulty following his instructions, but I did a lot of splashing and puffing to consume the fifteen minutes allotted me. Mrs. Nordland and Mrs. Olson came over to look after my clothes, and Jewel came half an hour earlier in the mornings to help comb my hair. My first thought, after the shock of death was one of freedom: now I could wear what I wished and tie the ribbons on the ends of my braids like the other kids—but I was soon disillusioned. Tom made me change my clothes after school and learn to fold the legs of my long underwear, so that my stockings fitted smoothly over them. Jewel and I worked hard at the end-of-the-braid project, but it was no use—my hair was too short. The bow slid off as fast as we tied it on.

I made one attempt to capitalize upon my semiorphanhood, but it was short-lived. Tom caught me selling subscriptions to a little magazine and made me return the money—a prize of a gold chain and locket, notwithstanding. "It's begging," he said. "We don't want nobody's sympathy, and you don't need no tin locket anyhow."

Then Tom made me a life-size rag doll, a bit gruesome as I remember it, for his skill with a sewing machine was only somewhat less spectacular than his idea of a doll's physique. The monstrosity became a household pet, used by the boys as a cross between a ventriloquist's dummy and a football, and arousing the coyote in Sport. When Pop found it sitting cross-legged in

97

the coal scuttle, he smiled for the first time since Mother's death.

At school for a few days all was sympathy and understanding—that is, for a few days. Miss Breen wasn't given to sentimentality. When she suppressed a sixth-grade revolt with the open palm of her hand, there were no repercussions at home, nor was there consolation. I don't know how hard she slapped the cousins, but she caught me squarely on the nose, and the blood clotted and I thought I was going to faint, but I didn't cry. For once I didn't cry.

When school resumed after Easter vacation, we had a new teacher.

The burden of the house fell upon me when Pop and the boys began work in the fields. Tom washed the underwear and the overalls, and Pop cooked the meals, but the cleaning was all mine, and I hated it. Left alone at the house all day long, I sought the companionship of my dog and pony, and always there were the drifting clouds that carried my dreams and the purple hills that beckoned to me from the rim of another world. And the clouds mingled with my tears, and the distant hills comforted me.

That summer Sue's baby was born, a beautiful boy with a million blonde curls and big brown eyes, fairer even than his Irish father. Sue, now living in Bismarck, wrote to Pop asking him to let me spend a week with her and the child. Gladly he hustled me off on the train, but two days later I was back home with my battered suitcase—and smallpox.

Tom swore I had leprosy. Old Doc Reeves came eventually and put up the sign—just in case—then vaccinated the boys and gave Pop permission to come into town for supplies. Pop was immune. Tom was afraid of me, refusing to touch anything I touched, running if I came towards him. Even my dishes were segregated, and I found my towel on a new nail on the other side of the house. Two days after Doc left, dear brother Tom went into voluntary exile in the hot room upstairs, where he sat by the hour, his yellow face covered with salve, his hands held rigidly before him—finger tips barely touching—for all the world like a bumpy Buddha, for he was completely and painfully pocked. When he emerged from his attic throne, his face and body were healed, but I resembled a rusty sieve.

"From now on," pronounced Father, "you stays home."

That summer the Koch cousins herded their cattle near our farm, and I had company. They left the cows grazing on the broad slope near the Bend while I taught them how to shoot gophers and tin cans with a .22, and they taught me how to swear in German. Then we found Tom's yeasty malt in the vent hole and became more ill than drunk—and that ended my herding.

New clouds appeared in the sky that spring. The war clouds of Europe hung heavy over America; then we, too, were at war. It affected us little at first. Pop had difficulty making wheatless bread—black bread—and we ate brown sugar instead of white, but we had known days before when there was no sugar, no flour. And no war.

I was alone that August morning when Dick came walking across the prairie. It was the first time he had been home since Mom died, and I knew it was hard for him to come now. I met him at the gate.

"Hello," I said.

"Hello, Tovey. Anyone at home?" Dick stopped outside the door to greet Sport, who jumped and barked about him, frantic with joy.

"No, they're up to the new place," I said.

Slowly, reluctantly, he went into the house. "I'm going to join the army, Tovey," Dick said, not looking at me. I felt a sinking in my heart, felt my whole family slipping away, but I couldn't spoil this wonderful moment when Dick was confiding in me, trusting me with his big news. He looked at my woeful face. "Yep, Tovey, I'm goin' to fight the Huns. I'm goin' over there and git the Kaiser." He turned to the stairs. "Come help me find my things."

He stuffed a few things in his pockets—a shaving outfit, a pocketknife, a picture of a girl. "You go downstairs while I change my shirt," he said. When he came down he was his old self again, brisk, curt, impatient. It was easier that way. "Well, good-bye," he said. "Tell Pop and the boys I'm on my way. Take care of my dog."

Dick walked out of the house and into the warm morning sunshine. Tears swam in my eyes as I watched him go swiftly down the road, without a parting wave or a backward glance. I sank down on the wooden step, my arms around Sport's neck. I cried then, shed tears that my mother would have shed had she been there when her firstborn went marching off to war. Then came the avalanche of tears, all the pent-up tears since Mother's death, tears I would not shed before. As the sobs wracked my body, Sport freed himself from my grasp and ran back and forth in front of me, barking in alarm. Slowly the tears subsided. I looked over the prairie, and Dick was gone.

The price of grain soared as the war continued. Flax went up to $3.50, $3.75, $4.00 a bushel. At $4.08 Father sold a thousand bushels while the little blue flowers were still in bloom. The next day the price fell below the four dollar mark and stayed. It had been a big gamble, and Pop wasn't a gambling man, but he knew he was near the end of his farming, that he could not keep the boys at home much longer. All he wanted now was enough to get out of debt and get away, so he had gambled on the flax and won. That year we had a bumper crop, the new land yielding more than the thousand bushels. Our new granary was filled to overflowing, and even I was put to work hauling the precious grain to the elevator.

I loved the long, solitary ride through the golden autumn sunshine during the brief North Dakota fall, when the days stood still and the warm silence was unbearable in its poignant beauty. I sat on the seat high on top of the green wagon, loosely holding the reins as the horses labored slowly along with their burden. Sometimes I tied the reins to the seat and ate the shiny coffee-colored seeds or scooped them up in my palms and let them run through my fingers like millions of tiny sequins. When I came to the elevator, I carefully drove the load up the steep ramp on to the scales to be weighed and dumped. The horses needed no urging going home. I talked to them through the twilight above the rumble of the empty wagon; I sang my German songs or recited "Little Gottlieb"; and sometimes I sat silently on the high seat or stood down in the bottom of the deep wagon, drinking in the full glory of white sage against purple shadows, watching gold-streaked heavens turn blue with approaching night. At home I unhitched and tended my own horses before joining the threshers at the table. I was a big girl now.

News of our flax crop spread among the farmers. There was a touch of mystery, a touch of the occult about this black man from the city who came a poor man but now was rich. When Pop went into town, a stranger approached him in Anderson's store.

"How you do it?" he asked.

"Do what?"

"How you know when to sell you flax? How you tell when price is biggest?"

Pop was still bewildered by his good fortune, more sure than ever it was the work of the Lord. "I trust in a Higher Power," he answered reverently.

The man stared. "A higher power?" he repeated. "A higher power?" He turned and walked away, more sure than ever that this higher power was black magic.

First cards, then letters began to dribble in from Dick, all addressed to me, inquiring about the others. He wasn't out of quarantine before he was threatening to do away with the Kaiser. "I was excited the first days," he wrote from Camp Lewis, "but I'm all right now. Tell the boys I say hello and to hell with the Kaiser as I am going to get him." The next letter was from Private First Class Thompson, Camp Grant. The flu was raging, but he was well and cocky. "I am the running guard now. I am an expert rifleman. My score was 98%. I can shoot 250 yards and hit a bull's eye. My lieutenant says he is going to make me a leader of a bombarding squad. That is a very dangerous place, but I must do my best. I am going to France pretty soon and see Bill Kaiser and end up the war."

Pop was proud of his soldier son, but my brothers read Dick's letters and howled. "I can understand that 'bout him a runnin' guard," observed Tom, "but which way is he gonna run?"

"Same way he been runnin'. Him and that rifle gonna run amuck, sure as you're born. Run amuck with everything else he had. Remember when he run into that streetcar in Des Moines?"

Pop's eyes were on his Bible, but every once in a while his stomach shook, and he put his hand over his mouth, and I knew he was finding his heathens much more interesting than his Hebrews.

"Read that thing again, boy." Harry handed Tom the letter.

"This is the prize lie. 'I can hit a bull's eye at 250 yards.' I know that boy can shoot the bull much farther than that."

"Umm umph! Him shootin' a bull's eye and can't even milk a cow!"

"Oh, my soul!" Pop closed his Bible and laughed with Tom.

" 'I am going to France pretty soon,' " Tom read, " 'and see Bill Kaiser and end up the war.' " He put the letter down.

"Him," said Harry, "and the United States Army."

Our flax fame outlived the forty-eight hundred dollars we realized from it, for there were many debts accumulated from the years before, and the new home, if we kept it, would need much to make it livable. Well drillers came before the ground froze and sunk a well. It took them three days to strike good water on the hill, drilling through the rock and gumbo. While the drillers worked, the boys fenced in the big pasture with heavy barbed wire.

Pop and I drove twenty miles in a cold October wind to a cattle sale to buy another cow, but Pop got so interested in a secondhand fur coat he forgot about the cow. When we pulled into the yard that night, Harry, coming out to take the horses, looked at the huge black coat and asked, "Where's Pop?"

"Boy, who do you think this is in this here coat?"

"Oh," said Harry. "Then where's the cow?"

"We didn't get a cow," I said, sensing Pop's ire, "and shut up!"

The coat was a touchy subject. The boys began to grumble; said they, too, wanted something out of the crop besides glory and callouses. They wanted a car, but Pop compromised on a motorcycle and put them off until spring. This was no time to go into debt.

On the fourth of November Dick was passing through Ohio; on the fifth he marched up the streets of Scranton, still on his way to the port of embarkation. On the eleventh the war ended with him still in New Jersey, one foot on the boat. He spent the holidays back in Camp Grant with the measles—the German measles.

After Christmas Pop left for the legislature, leaving Tom in charge. Immediately he had trouble with me. I was afraid to sleep alone. He reasoned and rebuked, but it was no use; so he slept downstairs with me at the foot of the bed, my head covered with quilts and blankets, pillowed against his feet.

When the Nordland children came over on Sunday, we had a glorious time. If it was nice outside, we skated on the slough and skied down the pasture hill, and when it wasn't, the boys wrestled all over the house, while Sport barked and Jewel and I took refuge behind the couch. During the week, Tom stressed work more than play, so Harry and I went on a strike. It didn't last long—Tom stopped cooking. "No workee, no eatee," he said, and organized labor received a setback. Washing the sticky separator with its innumerable tin parts was the bane of my existence. Every night when I came home from school it stood waiting for me. When Tom criticized me for not getting it clean, I threw down the dishcloth and issued an ultimatum.

"I'm going away," I said. "You can wash your old separator to suit yourself. I'm through."

Nobody paid any attention to me. I got as far as the clothesline when I sank into snow up to my knees. I stood there waiting for someone to come for me, to call me back, but I heard

103

only the cold north wind and saw only my dog sitting at the corner of the house, patiently waiting for me to return. Slowly I retraced my steps, slipped silently into the house, and again nobody paid any attention to me.

That night, when the boys went out to do the chores, they found Dixie lying helpless in the snow, her feet entangled in the barbed wire of the corral gate. For half an hour they worked with her, trying to get her up on her feet, but she was too weak to make the effort, so they hitched Major to a singletree, fastened it to a rope around her body, and Tom pushed from the rear while Harry urged Major ahead. It was dark now and bitterly cold. I went to the house for the lantern, and when I returned the boys were quarreling. There were words, angry and bitter. They tried again, and the singletree broke.

"You dumb nigger!" Tom came from behind the mare, his fists clenched.

Harry struck out blindly. Surprised, Tom stumbled and fell backward. I began to cry. Harry ran to the barn and in the darkness bridled Buck and rode out and into the night.

Tom wasn't hurt, the blow only grazed his chin. "Let him go, Tovey." There was no anger in his voice. Tom got another singletree and tied it to the rope. "Here, you drive for me. When I say 'Ready,' make him go as hard as you can."

Rested—and probably inspired by the lively intermission— Dixie lunged to her feet on the first try. We got her into the barn and made comfortable for the night, then went to the house. Tom was sitting by the stove reading when I dropped off to sleep.

I awoke the next morning asking for Harry. "He's all right; he's at somebody's house." Tom tried to appear casual, but his forehead was lined and his eyes were bloodshot, as if he hadn't slept all night. The dog came over to the bed and jumped up on me. "It's blizzarding outside," Tom said, "so I brought Sport in."

"How long has it been blizzarding?" I was thinking about Harry, wondering if he was somewhere out there in the storm.

Tom read my thoughts. "Not long," he said. "Git dressed

and wash up. I'll fix you something to eat."

At noon Tom fought his way to the barn. He was gone a long time, and when he returned he said Dixie was down again and the door to the cow barn was sealed by a huge drift. We ate a little, tried a game or two of checkers, then gave up. Tom stopped trying to make conversation. We sat by the stove and waited for the storm to die down, hoping Harry was safe.

By nightfall the storm was over. As soon as I was asleep, Tom bundled himself in sheepskins, turned down the lamp, and slipped out the door, leaving Sport to watch over me. All that night he and Major lunged through the drifted snow, across the white-capped prairies, inquiring for Harry at farmhouses, searching in the moonlight for his body in the snow. He returned at dawn, his toes and fingers frosted, his cheek frozen. Dixie was dead.

After lunch we both set to work with snow shovels, digging a tunnel to the door of the cow barn, and when we pried it open the two young calves and a colt were dead, their little bodies stiff, their starved stomachs swelled tight in death. Sport sniffed gingerly at the colt, then dashed out through the tunnel. I don't know how long he had been barking before we heard him, but when we came out of the barn Harry was riding in through the gate.

He grinned sheepishly through half-frozen lips as Tom helped him dismount. "Some storm," he said.

"Better go in the house and get those things off." Tom tried to hide his excitement. "Tovey, you go with him and put on the coffeepot. Don't let him go near the stove," he warned.

"Where you been, Harry? Where you been?" I begged, pulling him towards the house. "Was you in the blizzard, was you?"

"Naw," he said beating his hands against his sides. "I was over to Olson's. Been ridin' through them snowbanks since morning."

"But ain't you hungry?"

"Of course, I'm hungry. Stopped at Gus's about noon and had some coffee, but I couldn't stomach that food of his. Bachelor

105

cooking!" Harry made a wry face.

Tom came in with an armful of wood and a bucket of coal. Harry jumped to help him. "What you want for supper, boy?" Tom beamed. "You name it, and I'll cook it."

"Well, George," Harry's voice became patronizing, "you can just bring me some bird's tongues—a la carte—and a portion of roast hog on the half shell, well turned, George, the way you Southern Negroes cook it, and some hot biscuits and fried corn. If you don't mind." Harry stretched his long legs on a second chair. "In other words, darky, just open up all them cans and heat well." He signaled me with his finger. "Oh, Tovey, I'll have my demitasse in the drawing room."

I poked him in the stomach and dashed for the kitchen. Sport jumped between us before he could trip me.

We were halfway through the meal when Harry noticed Tom's frozen cheek. "Where'd you git the rose?" he asked.

"We had a blizzard, remember?" Tom said nothing about his night ride. "Dixie is dead," he added bluntly. Harry picked up his fork, put it down again. For a minute no one spoke. "She died last night—in the barn. Couldn't be helped," Tom added kindly.

"Dixie dead," said Harry slowly. "What'll Pop say? He's gonna have a fit; he was crazy about that mare."

"Yeah, I know." There was a touch of resentment in Tom's voice now. "But he wasn't here to look after her. We was, and we did the best we could."

"Poor Dixie. You got her in the barn?"

"Tovey and I got her in, then she got down again in the night. She's dead," he said with finality. "And that's all there is to it."

Dixie wasn't the only thing that died that winter. Tom wrung the neck of a chicken he found floundering around outside the coop, its feet frozen—and I died a thousand deaths. When he entered the house bearing the body and the bloody head, I fled, without hat or coat, to stand outside the house with my hands buried in Sport's warm hair, waiting for my brother to finish with his gruesome business.

106

Tom came to the door. "You crazy? Come on in here before you freeze to death!"

"Not until yy-you get that chchch-chicken picked." My teeth chattered, my ears stung, my bare head felt tight and swollen.

"Come on in here. That thing's been picked long ago."

"Let mmm-me see it," I insisted.

Tom shut the door. He didn't return right away, but when he did he had the naked fowl in his hand. Timidly, gratefully, I followed him inside.

"Shut the door, Tovey," called Harry. "Gowan, slam it."

With my eyes on Tom and the chicken, I pushed hard on the heavy door. Something wet and soft touched my hand. I turned. The bloody head of the chicken, with its beady eyes and frozen comb, hung suspended from a string before my eyes. For a long minute I could not move, could not speak. The bones in my legs turned to rubber, my head swam. A hot wave of nausea swept over me.

"Not in here." Tom grabbed me by the arm and pulled me back outdoors. "Boy," he called to Harry, "take that thing down, clean down, and out of here. Give it to the pigs."

Tom was worried. I didn't cry, wouldn't eat. "Get that cookbook," he told Harry; "we're gonna make Tovey some broth. Some good old chicken broth."

The first of March Pop came home laden down with fruit and clothing and some new sixteen-inch records for the phonograph.

At the depot Tom told him about Dixie and the storm. "No use writing you," he said. "We did all we could."

"Yes, I know, I know," Pop said softly. Tom looked at him curiously. "Ain't your fault, Son. She'd a-died if I'd a-been there, too. I read all about the storm. Thank God you all all right. Why couldn't it of been that fool colt, Speeve?"

"I saved her hide for you, but it's kind of holey. She froze fast."

"Thank you, Son. Lots of stock and people died in that

107

storm. Was fifty below some places—papers was full of it. Wonder you all ain't dead. You say Harry and Sister all right?" he asked for the third time.

"Yeah. They're O.K."

"Didn't give you no trouble, did they?"

"Naw. We got along fine."

"You didn't scare your sister none, did you?"

"Me scare her? She's all right. But I'm sure glad you're back. We're kinda tired of my cooking."

"I know it's the truth!" agreed Pop. "I know it's the truth!"

Tom could tell I wanted to ask him something by the way I followed him around the barn and hung around the separator while he finished with the milk, but he waited until the whine of the machine died down and the thin stream of cream tapered off to slow, measured drops. "How's school?" he finally asked, taking the disks apart.

"We're going to have a play."

"You in it?"

"Yes," I admitted. "Say, Tom"—it was now or never—"would it be all right if Teacher blackened my face?"

"Blackened your face?" he shouted. "You crazy? Ain't you black enough now?"

"But the rest—Ollie and Tillie—she's gonna blacken them up, too."

"They're white; they're not like you. What'd she want to blacken your face for, anyhow? What kinda play is that you gotta be black?" Tom scowled at me. "Blacker," he amended.

I wasn't too sure; Teacher hadn't told me much about it. She gave out the parts, then called me aside at recess asking me if I'd mind if she blackened me up. I had a vague feeling it wasn't necessary. When I hesitated, she said the others would be black, too, so I said all right, I'd ask my brother.

"It's a play about Lincoln," I explained, near tears. "All the sixth grade's in it. Four of us are slaves, Jewel . . ." I remembered Jewel's long blonde hair and blue eyes and wondered how she'd look in blackface. "Jewel's gonna be one."

"Well, you ain't!" Tom said flatly.

The next day I told Teacher I couldn't be in the play; I didn't have to tell her why.

"You can have any part you want," she promised, hastily, and handed me the script.

The list of characters consisted of four slaves, an overseer, and the master. The master was Rudolph. I didn't like Rudolph —he was pink and chubby and Teacher's pet. In Norwegian he called me what sounded like "stika naggie." I knew what it meant, but I couldn't prove it, so I took the part of the master. Teacher excused the master and freed the slave. "If Lincoln could do it," she said wearily, "then so can I."

As soon as the snow melted the boys got their motorcycle, a Harley-Davidson, beautiful, graceful, and noisy. Bessie and the bicycle faded into oblivion in the face of the new gasoline monster. Pop wouldn't let me ride with Harry, but I clung to Tom and buried my head in his back as we whizzed over the open prairie like a streak out of hell.

Just once did we get Pop to take a ride. There were still six payments left, and the boys felt their vehicle would be more secure if they could win his wholehearted approval. Pop mounted cautiously and with misgivings. Tom started off slowly, carefully picking his way over the rocky road. Pop began to relax —it wasn't half bad. They rode as far as the new farm, turned, and headed towards home. A horn tooted behind them.

"Stop this thing and let that car pass," shouted Pop.

Tom carefully turned off the road on to the prairie. The car slowed down. The men inside could not believe their eyes. Negroes out here in the middle of Dakota—on a motorcycle! The man at the wheel waved good-naturedly as they passed.

"That's a Ioway license. They're from Ioway, Pop. Wonder if we know 'em?"

He didn't wait for an answer. He stepped hard on the accelerator, and the motorcycle leaped over the deep rut into the center of the road and roared out in hot pursuit of the departing car. Pop got his mouth open, but he couldn't get his breath, and if words came he could not hear them above the infernal din of

109

the motor. They gained on the car, but the driver, thinking they wanted to race, speeded ahead. Pop hung on to Tom with both arms as his feet bounced off the treads and flapped helplessly in the wind. Pop prayed a little, asking God to take care of his motherless daughter when he was gone. He knew he'd soon be gone now, so he shut his eyes and waited. He didn't feel the motorcycle swerve when Tom turned in at our gate, he didn't hear the engine stop in front of the house, and he didn't hear Harry laugh, because Harry was doubled up on the ground trying to get his breath. Tom started to dismount, but feeling Pop's arms still around him, looked back. His father sat still and rigid.

"We're home, Pop. Wake up."

"Is—is I all right?" Pop slowly opened his eyes. Tom helped him off. "Boy," he said solemnly, "don't you ever ask me to get on that thing again as long as you live." Pop started for the door, staggering a little, still dizzy from the ride. "Lord, Lord!" he said, half to himself, "What have I done? First death, then war—now this thing. My whole family be wiped out 'fore we get it paid for."

"Now I've done it," said Tom. "He won't be a bit of good for weeks."

"Not next week, anyhow," offered Harry. "Not 'till we're all done movin'."

Tom set the motorcycle up on its stand. His face was sober. "Two years ago I'd a-been tickled to death leaving Hansmeyer's place for a farm of our own, but now . . ."

"When you figure on leavin'?" asked Harry.

"Not till after the crop's in, 'long about fall."

"You gonna tell him?"

"Tell him what?" I asked, coming up behind them.

"Where'd you come from," said Tom, "and why ain't you in the house doin' your work?"

"Tell him what?" I repeated.

"Tell him you're out here meddlin', that's what," said Harry. "Now git!"

7) OUR LAND

During the moving I was sent to Charley Koch's place, where I remained to finish the school year at Driscoll. It was fun living at Ollie's house with her jolly mother and father and the ten boisterous brothers and sisters; but at the end of each week I eagerly listened for the explosive putt-putt of the motorcycle that heralded Tom's coming, anxious to crest the last long hill, to see the little granary gleaming like a mystic castle in the blood-red glow of a surrendering sun, for of all the family, I alone was happy on our land, content to call it home.

The two small bins of the granary had been turned into bedrooms, lighted only by one high window. In the big room we cooked and ate and lived. It was crude, with its bare rafters and wide barn door, but new and clean, the pungent smell of lumber blending with the earthy smell of recent grain, and to me it was good. The horse barn, with sloping roof and roomy stalls, the

111

big corral, and the long lane leading to the pasture were as we had first planned them. And in place of a windmill, a gasoline engine pumped the water, for there were those days when the winds were stilled—long, hot days when the stock lined up along the dry trough with panting tongues and pleading eyes.

I was glad when school was out, and I could again be with my family and my pets, but home was different now. Over it hung the apparition of Mother's dreams, the shadow of Mother's death. Gone from my brothers were the old fun and frivolity, replaced by a cold soberness that drew them farther and farther away from Father, and I lived between two camps: the one guarded by self-pity and silence, the other by bitter restlessness.

Things went badly on the new farm. First the horses got the mange. Ignoring the lush green pastures, they stood around in the corral, lean and listless, rubbing off large patches of hair on barbed wire and the corners of buildings, the great bare spots on their bodies covered with a dandrufflike scale, the bony ribs plainly visible.

No sooner had the horses recovered from their scourge than the grasshoppers descended upon us. Vague rumors preceded their coming. The state agricultural college issued bulletins, telling the farmers how to treat the grain, while unbelievable stories of the devastation of horses and cows as well as crops circulated like wildfire. The farmers became alarmed, called meetings, but even as they met and talked, the pests appeared.

Hordes of them came—big, strong-legged fellows with yellow enameled bodies and powerful, lacquerlike wings, darting and zinging through the dry, hot air, leaping upon the growing grain, stripping each stock, leaving it naked. Hurriedly the syrupy poison was scattered over the crops, but calves and poultry ate of it and died, while the grasshoppers lived on. They were everywhere, flying against windshields and clogging radiators of cars, getting into houses, in the food, in the drinking water, zooming into our faces and down our necks. Wagon ruts were caked with their mashed brown bodies. Then suddenly they were gone.

112

The sun beat down upon the prairies, hot and devastating, drying up the little water that was in the big ravine down in the pasture, leaving it a spongy mire, crusted with alkaline. Seeking relief from the intense heat, the cows waded into the mud, and not all of them waded out again. We lost the best milch cow and two of the young calves.

Even the two weeks at camp meeting failed to shake Father out of his stolid taciturnity, and the boys became more cynical, more bitter, hating now the land and the loneliness and the futility of fighting against the elements. In 1919 unrest was everywhere. Race riots broke out in many cities that summer. Dick, writing from Chicago, said it caught him at the home of his North Side employer, where he stayed until it was over. He had a fine job chauffeuring, he said, making good money, living a bright, colorful life. "How," he asked, "can you folks stay out there in that Godforsaken country away from civilization and our people?" The boys read his letters and laughed no more, for their scorn had turned to envy.

A few days later Dick sent a copy of the *Chicago Defender*, the first Negro newspaper I had ever seen. It was full of the riots. On the front page was a large picture of a Negro hanging from a tree. Followed an account of a Southern lynching in all its diabolical horror, of a man being dragged behind a speeding car through the streets of the Negro section, past his own home, of the mutilating of his body, of final death from a rope, to the jeers of the mob, of flames licking his nude body, and white men and women cutting off burned black fingers, burned black ears to carry home in gory triumph, souvenirs for their young.

For a long time, I could see the lifeless body dangling from the tree. To me it became a symbol of the South, a place to hate and fear. And Dick's civilization was a riot, where black and white Americans fought each other and died. I wanted never to leave my prairies, with white clouds of peace and clean, blue heavens, for now I knew that beyond the purple hills prejudice rode hard on the heels of promise, and death was its overtaking. And I wondered where was God.

113

I made my debut into rural society that summer clad in blue crepe de chine, riding a brown pony. I was twelve, and it was my first basket social. Harry was antisocial, and it was his prerogative to stay home, so I persuaded Pop to let me ride in alone and go with the Koch cousins.

With Pop a cook, food wasn't much of a problem, but Tom's conception of the basket beautiful was. With bits of green tissue from the crown of a new cap and hand-painted flowers, the likes of which grow nowhere, in or out of this world, we made my basket.

"You're gonna have to carry this thing under your arm," Tom warned. "Them paste handles are only for looks."

The basket completed, I began to worry about my own adornments. The shoes I had ordered to go with the silk dress never arrived, so Tom and I dug around in Mother's trunk until we found a pair of old-fashioned gray kids that had hardly been worn. My stubby toes didn't come near the sharp-pointed tips, but they were better than my black school shoes—much better. The dress itself was somewhat of a problem. Its long crepe de chine overskirt had an uneven hem line bordered with silver braid which didn't lend itself easily to sewing machine altera- tions. That night only the bright cloth rose on the shoulder was reminiscent of the beautiful formal I had worshipped so long from the pages of the catalog.

"You'd better ride sideways," Tom suggested, as he led Bessie up to the door, "or else pull that dress up from under you."

I couldn't sit sideways for six miles, so I put the blanket across the pony's back and, with my gaudy basket under one arm, rode off to my first grown-up party in my first silk dress.

It was dark when I galloped into the Koch's yard. Tillie was already there. As the hired man led Bessie to the barn, Ollie pulled me into the house to show her mother my dress, my real silk dress. By the time all of them had touched and patted it, from the sticky-fingered babies to the grown sons and daughters, the crepe was wan and drooping.

When we arrived at the schoolhouse, the sixth-grade room

114

was decorated with paper chains and flowers, and the seats had been pushed against the wall, leaving the center of the floor free for dancing. Teacher's desk, stacked high with baskets, awaited the auctioneer. The little string orchestra was playing "Pop Goes the Weasel" when someone pushed us into the circle. We were shoved and swung around by shy farm youths and big, awkward men, all dressed in their Sunday clothes, hair slicked back with water, torturous bow ties stiff beneath their chins. They were a rough but good-natured lot, talking and laughing and calling to each other in broken English or in their native tongue.

My poor dress fared badly. The rose, first to go, was recovered by one of the Qualle boys, mashed and crumpled. As I stopped to pin it back, someone caught me by the arm, and the rose was gone forever. When they rang Teacher's bell at nine o'clock, the crepe was hanging from my waist in limp, jagged bunches. I found the cousins in the crowd, and together we climbed up on top of the desks to watch the auction. One box sold for eleven dollars, but for the most part they averaged about four and five dollars. As the lively bidding proceeded, boys and men paid for their possession, found the blushing owner, and retired to a desk to eat.

Knudt Nelson bought mine. Both handles had broken, and there was a large, damp spot on the bottom where the dessert lay, but it cost only a dollar and a half. Few went cheaper. Knudt, a big, nineteen-year-old Swede, was as loud as he was tall.

"Where's my partner?" he bellowed, holding the basket high above his head.

"Here she is." Tillie gave me a vicious shove. Her basket was still on the table.

"Well, what are we waitin' for?" Grabbing my arm, Knudt steered me across the room amid giggles and shouts. I burned with embarrassment from the blue hair ribbons down to the tops of those awful shoes, but my partner was enjoying it.

"Who's your new girl?" and "Look who's robbin' the cradle!" they yelled, and Knudt called them flat-headed Polacks

115

or square-headed Bohunks and mildly suggested they were jealous.

I had never eaten alone with a fellow before. I played with my food and kept my eyes on the desk, but Knudt was wholly uninhibited. Cleaning up his share of the meal, he began throwing my half-eaten sandwiches about the room, and in no time at all we were bombarded with food. After the grand march he escorted me to the door, where the cousins were waiting.

Outside the schoolhouse we began to run.

"Ma said I had to be home by ten," panted Ollie, "and it's nearly ten-thirty. Let's cut through the alley, back of the hotel."

Mrs. Koch was waiting for us, but she wasn't angry. "Why don't you stay all night?" she urged. "Tillie's stayin'."

"Yah, why don't you?" chimed in Ollie. "Ain't you scared to go home alone?"

"I can't stay; Pop's looking for me home. He'd worry."

"Did you kids have a good time?" asked Mrs. Koch, eyeing my dress.

Tillie pointed to me and giggled. "Her and Knudt. She got that big slob Knudt!"

"He's just as good as Otto," I flared. "You had to eat with Otto!"

"Oh, God!" groaned Ollie. "And what did I get? A hired man, Ma Jensen's old hired man!"

"Ain't none of 'em no bargains," said the woman, "but you kids would go."

Bessie was led up, big-eyed and nervous. Bessie didn't take much to night life. Saying my good-byes, I rode bravely off over the prairies, bright moonlight in my hair, bits of German potato salad in my hair ribbon, pretending Prince Charming was riding beside me, and he wasn't Knudt Nelson.

In September I began school in Sterling on Berg's route. Mr. Berg was section boss, but one never knew who would come for us or how. Most of the fall we were taken in the Ford by Mrs. Berg, but there were mornings when we rode into town

116

on a handcar, and there were other mornings when we walked in; but ride or walk, we were nearly always late. The Bergs were full of profanity and fun, and we didn't really care if we never got to school, especially when Tootsie drove. Tootsie Berg had dancing eyes and curly black hair, and every girl in Sterling imagined herself in love with him. Me too.

The Sterling school was a modern little two-room building with a furnace instead of stoves. The children stared the first day or two, some of the boys called me "nigger," but I didn't chase them, didn't cry, so they gave it up, because it wasn't any fun that way. And when they found that I could run faster, push the swings higher than most of them, I had many friends.

Riding home from the Nordlands' one Sunday afternoon, soon after the beginning of school, I met Harry walking down the road, a bundle under his arm. He was going to Driscoll, he said; the bundle was nothing. He went on. That night Harry did not come home. We ate supper in silence. The next night when I returned from school, Tom, too, was gone. Pop said they were going to live in St. Paul for a while, then he closed up like a clam and began the soft humming and whistling as he did after Mother's death.

Together we stacked the forty acres of winter wheat, and alone I milked the six cows before and after school. At night I got out the arithmetic book and did my homework, while Pop sat nearby, reading his worn Bible. Sometimes I tried to get him to help me, but his mind wasn't on A and B and their bolts of cloth. The farm was lonely without the boys. I dreaded to come home at night to its empty silence, to my father's brooding gloom, but there was still my dog and pony. The boys wrote often. Somehow they had found each other in St. Paul and were working in a packinghouse. With their first check they sent me a folding camera, and I sent them pictures of all the animals so they would not forget.

The unplastered granary was cold and drafty that winter, the wind whistling around our feet and over our heads far more than it had at Hansmeyer's. The gasoline engine became my

117

special problem, for Father knew nothing about machinery. Having watched Tom, I knew that a new gasket, that clean spark plugs—even a kick—would sometimes help, but there were days when none of these expedients moved the little motor, and those were the days we pumped, the bitterly cold days when the twenty-eight head of cattle and horses stood passively at the ice-caked trough, drinking as long as the water flowed.

Volunteering one bright Saturday morning to take the cream into Driscoll, I placed a wagon seat on the two front runners of the light sled, hooked it to a team of horses, then wrapped a blanket around my legs, and, with the five-gallon can hung on the side, started down the road. My sled was tiny and low to the snow, but so light that when I turned in at the Gunderson farm, half a mile away, the can swung out to the side, and my team bolted. The hired man caught the horses and held them until the Gundersons' cream was tied on the opposite side to balance the weight, and I again sped off down the road.

After depositing the cream at the Driscoll depot I drove over to the Evanses'. There were goings-on that day at the Evanses'. Ben was home with his new wife—a frail, sad-eyed only daughter of a West Coast dress shop proprietor. Helen Evans' reluctance to help with the house and farm work infuriated Ann. When I arrived things were so interesting I stayed longer than I had intended.

The gray haze of an impending blizzard was already settling down. Before I had gone two miles, the snow began to swirl and blow about me. I wanted to turn back, but all I could see now were the two horses before me. Quickly the road drifted over. I slacked the reins, wrapping them round the end of the seat, and let the horses have their heads, for I knew they would take me home. Suddenly it was dark. A coyote howled off to the right, and a new fear gripped me. The team slowed down as the snow deepened. I stopped them so I could get up on the back of the tallest horse, away from the snow and the coyotes, but as I stepped out of the sled I sank in over my knees, and still there was no bottom. Quickly I scrambled back on the low seat, and the horses plunged on. I knew where I was now; the snow had drifted in the deep ravine, leveling it, but somehow the horses had kept faithfully to the narrow road. It was still a good mile and a half home. The coyote howled again, farther away now. I was too afraid to notice the cold, afraid of the coyotes and the storm and what Father would say. I felt the sled turn left, and I could tell by the eagerness of the horses that this, at last, was home. Sport bounded out to greet me. Pop was there in the yard, waiting.

"Thank God!" he said. "You're safe, you're safe!"

He helped me into the house, for my feet were like clubs, my eyelashes coated with ice. Father set a bowl of hot soup before me.

"The team. I'll put the team away first."

"I'll do that; you eat."

"All right," I sat down again. Then I remembered the cows. Pop couldn't milk, and the cows would be waiting. "I'll milk soon's I eat."

Pop had his hand on the door. He stopped then, but didn't look around. "The cows is milked," he said simply.

My mouth fell open.

"I had to do something. I couldn't set here waitin' and waitin' with you out there in that storm." He paused. "Got right smart milk, too." There was pride in his voice. "Almost two buckets full."

That night my father began to plan again, and his plans did not include things agricultural. "As soon as it gits spring," he said, "we're gonna have a auction sale, a great big auction sale, and git rid of all this stuff—farm and all—and I'm gonna take you away from here. You lost yourself in your last blizzard. This ain't no kinda life for you. Or me."

We were eating our supper a few nights later when Ole Gunderson drove up to our door. "Hey, Thompson!" he shouted. "Got company for you."

Pop opened the door, and there stood Ben and his wife. "Hello, Uncle Tony. Got room for a couple of guests?"

"Where in the name of common sense did you come from?" Pop asked, eyeing the bags in his hand.

"Go on in, Helen," Ben pushed the girl inside. "Be right back. Gotta help Ole with the trunk."

Helen stood huddled in the middle of the floor while Pop stared. The two men placed the trunk inside the door. Ole was the first to speak. "I was comin' back from Steele," he said. "Run into Ben, here, walkin' towards town. Said he had some trouble with his dad, so I drove back and got her and these things." Ole was openly appraising "her." Word had got around about Ben's pretty wife. That she was white was taken for granted, Ben being what he was. But why, people asked, did he have to go all the way to the Coast for a wife?

"Won't you stay and have supper?" Pop wasn't enthusiastic.

"Naw. Naw, thanks," said Ole. "Old lady's waitin' supper fer me to home."

When the door closed behind him, Pop turned to Ben. "That's right what he say? Did John put you and this girl out?"

"Put us out? Man, he threw us out! Hello there, Sissy." Ben gave me a playful shove and danced around the stove. He was already enjoying his troubles. He turned to the girl. "Take off your things, honey. Uncle Tony, this is my wife, Helen." Ben began to laugh. "It was some battle, Uncle Tony. You shoulda seen it. Ma'd been gripin' ever since I brought Helen home, sore because she didn't get out in the barn and pitch manure. Helen don't know nothin' about no farm work; she's use to servants and maids, ain't you, baby?" Ben tweaked her ear, and she smiled back weakly.

"Well, whatever happened, you got to stay somewhere." Pop put two more plates on the table. "Come on, you all, pull up to the table. Sister, you get some more bread."

Ben stretched his long legs out under the table. "Then Monday night," he continued, "Sue come home with her baby and that bum of a husband of hers. She was jealous of Helen's looks, so she sided in with Mom. They kept naggin' the poor kid till she was in tears half the time. Dad didn't say anythin' until the letter come."

120

"Letter? What letter?" Pop looked up.

"Well, you see, Helen wrote to tell her folks about the place and happened to mention Dad was colored, and man, oh man!" Ben whistled. "What'd she do that for? He wrote to Dad and, among other things, called him a nigger. Made Ma madder than it did Dad—you know how she is about anybody calling us names—so they said we couldn't stay in their house another night and to get our so-and-so's out of there. We didn't move fast enough for 'em, and Ma threw a skillet at me when I sassed her; so the kid here began whooping it up, and I was glad to get out of there."

Ben stayed with us for a few days, then hooked a freight for the Twin Cities, promising to send for Helen in a couple of weeks. I liked the girl. It was nice having a woman in the house, but as the days went by with little word and no money from Ben, she gradually drew into herself. A dull listlessness crept over her until she hardly spoke, hardly ate. Pop and Helen must have had a wonderful time those dreary winter days while I was at school. Each sat on his side of the stove, saying nothing. Pop spent as much time in the barns as possible, but Helen had nothing to occupy her time. Once she took the beautiful dresses from her trunk and washed them, ruining them, then she returned to her chair beside the stove and sat staring into space.

When Pop saw Ben wasn't going to send for her, he said she had to go. He said he couldn't allow her to stay with him day after day. He said people would say things. He said whether they said things or not, the girl was driving him crazy, so he went down to the Gundersons' and had a long talk with Ole's wife.

The next day Helen went to the Gundersons' and sat beside their stove until her father relented and sent for her.

Early in the new year Pop was called to Bismarck for a special session, so I stayed with the Gundersons, Ole helping me with our chores. When the Bergs moved away in midwinter, Ole Gunderson took over the school route, his hired man, Arlee Davis, driving. I didn't like Arlee—he was from the South. He

121

never said anything directly to me, but he had a snide way of saying things that made me uncomfortable, like talking about coons as though they were animals, yet instinctively I knew he meant Negroes, and I was always glad when I got out of the rig. After Arlee came, I stopped going with the Gundersons to community parties in Sterling and after a while stopped going to the Gundersons'.

For a time I, too, had a boyfriend. But only for a time. Rags Bohm was one of the dirtiest of the dirty little boys we three seventh grade girls taught when the lower grade teacher had the flu. I'm afraid I displayed more brute strength than mental superiority, and Rags was impressed. On Valentine's Day I received a little piece of flowered wallpaper inscribed laboriously with the immortal words: "I love you—Rags." Any feeling of reciprocity that I may have felt died suddenly and ruthlessly following a rumor that head lice were running rampant in the school. The Board, at Mr. Bohm's suggestion, voted to investigate. They began with his son, Rags, and went no further.

It may have been that taste of teaching, or the admiration I had for the current teacher, or maybe I was just showing off, I don't know, but when we were asked how many planned to attend college, I alone raised my hand. The teacher called me to her desk and praised me for my ambition, and all of a sudden I really did want to go on with my schooling. I was sure it would make Mother happy, wherever she was, and make my father very proud.

In the spring Pop sold the farm back to the elevator man he had bought it from—and for nearly twice as much as he had paid for it. In April we had the auction sale, selling everything but our personal belongings. When the Nordlands took Bessie back home, and when Uncle John promised to keep Sport for us, I was partly mollified. We spent the last night with the Gundersons, and in the morning Ole drove us past the empty granary, over the snow-crusted road, and into town to take the train for Bismarck, our next home.

8) GENTLEMAN JANITOR

Bismarck was a beautiful prairie town along the banks of the muddy Missouri. Less than twenty of its ten thousand people were Negroes, all living south of the tracks where the streets were unpaved and the sidewalks were broken and crumbling. Ed Smith's young son and I were the only colored children in town.

We moved into a small three-room house on Maple Street, whose living room led directly into the middle room, and from there it was only a step down to the tiny, low-roofed kitchen and the makeshift shed, but to me it was a mansion with ivory halls. Pop furnished the living room in Spanish leather and bird's-eye maple, buying colorful peacock drapes for the narrow windows. When I learned the drapes cost eight dollars a yard, I split them in two, and there were peacock bodies on one side and tails on the other, but enough now for the other room and Pop was pleased at the sign of thrift in a time of plenty. A huge, hard-coal heater completely filled the middle room, the red glow from its isinglassed windows casting a mellow warmth over the house, and for the first time in a long while we were warm on both sides.

Our immediate neighbors were white. Except for a few old timers—very old people who came up the river on boats when the town was young—and one or two couples who were legally married and visibly employed, the colored were mostly down-under-the-hill folks, and folks who lived under the big hill that led to the river bottoms were mostly bad, both black and white.

But even on top of the hill we were not above suspicion. On our second night in town I was washing clothes by lamplight in the little shed when a husky voice yelled, "Open up in the name of the law!" While I went for Father, a policeman broke down the door. He looked rather sheepishly at the washing machine and apologized, he said he saw the dim light and thought we were moonshiners. He said he was Jergeson, the chief of police. Pop told him who he was, and Jergeson said yes, he remembered him now, and welcome to Bismarck. So Jergeson stayed for coffee, and Pop told me I'd better finish the washing in the morning.

Word soon got around that Pop was a rich, retired farmer. Money and the city made him a new man—again dapper, handsome Tony. For three hours each evening he worked as custodian at the Bank of North Dakota, a Nonpartisan venture across the tracks, and the rest of the day he walked around in his gold-rimmed specs, the gold watch chain swinging across his vest, a purple handkerchief—silk and perfumed—peeking out of his blue-serge pocket. Pop never referred to himself as a porter or janitor. If pushed, he spoke fleetingly of certain janitorial aspects of the position, and few suspected, as he strolled up the street, immaculate and smiling, that he had a date with a mop.

Pop lavished money on me while it lasted, trying to make up for some of the things I had missed—for some of the things he had promised Mother. He sent our clothes to a laundress,

124

engaged an expensive dressmaker, and brought me a silk parasol I didn't really want and twelve-dollar shoes I soon outgrew. I went through two gold wrist watches in a year's time, and was the only kid on our side of the tracks with an allowance.

Our house soon became a rendezvous for the children of the neighborhood. Pop liked having them around, liked the noise, so he entertained them with his stories and fed them with his good cooking.

Jessie McRafferty, who lived across the street, took me to school my first day. Jessie was a pretty girl, almost a grown lady, but she didn't let the lady part stand in the way of her principles and her Irish temper. She and her friend, Alma, were the only girls on the South Side who attended North Ward Junior High way up on the hill. Jessie and I waited for Alma, but when the girl saw me, she stayed on the other side of the street.

"Alma!" Jessie called. Alma tossed her head and kept walking. "That dirty snob! That lousy, white-headed Swede!" Jessie stamped her foot and whirled around, her hair falling about her face like a smoky cloud. "Who in hell does she think she is?" she asked defiantly.

We crossed the tracks and started up the long hill together.

"Tomorrow," I said apologetically, "you go with her. I can go alone; I'll know the way by then."

"The hell you will! If you're not good enough to walk with that son of a bitch, then neither am I." Jessie took me by the hand and began to run. "Come on, kid, let's beat her there."

I liked to run; it helped me to forget the humiliation, overcome the threatening tears. There was something clean and free about running against the crisp morning air with the clear sky above and the pavement smooth and challenging. I ran easily, effortlessly, beside the larger girl, doubling her stride, matching her speed.

Jessie looked at me admiringly. "Say," she said, "you *can* run."

The school yard was full of laughing, shouting children, grouped near the door waiting for the last bell. As we came panting up the long walk, a sudden wide-eyed hush fell over them, and Jessie pulled me inside before they recovered. We went directly to the principal, a cool, impersonal woman, not too pleased having me, half hoping I was in the wrong school. I was small for my age, and those agriculture certificates from Sterling didn't add anything to my mental prestige. The lady had been at North Ward for a long time, teaching now the children of her first pupils, and in all that time there had been only two colored children enrolled. One was very light, nearly white and the other very bad.

I was placed in Seven B, which was composed of delinquents and prodigies—those who had surged half a year ahead or dropped half a year behind. I made no bosom friends among the kids north of the tracks, but most of them were friendly. No one molested me while Jessie was around, but in the spring she eloped, and I was left to fight my own battles, so there weren't any. Every Friday afternoon for half an hour we played games, either silly girl-boy games or something quiet and subdued with a bean bag. The girl-boy games were most popular, and I learned to dread Friday afternoons. For a while the nice little girls sat by me out of politeness, then gradually one or two of the bolder boys plumped themselves down beside me. When I was "it" I sat by the same boys, but it wasn't always a safe gamble. Sometimes they reacted violently and the class tittered while I squirmed, but usually I could depend upon Keith Adams, the dentist's son. Ray Jones was the harum-scarum son of a prominent lawyer, and everyone expected the unusual of him, so when he began sitting by me at every game, the kids laughed, and the teacher raised her eyebrows. And I gave Keith a rest.

Alex Barnes didn't like me. He jumped in mock alarm when I passed his desk, and made horrid faces when I looked at him; when I stopped passing his desk and looking at him, he began shooting paper wads. I retaliated in kind, and young Barnes became less active with rubber bands but more vocal in his invectives. When I wore my new dress and new hair ribbons on the last day of school, Alex looked at me for a long time, then nudged Keith.

126

"She's a cute little coon, isn't she?" he said, without emotion and without malice.

Uncle John, on his first trip to the city, brought Sport, bound fast to the back seat of his model T. When the dog saw me, he jumped through the side curtains, and it cost Pop five dollars. It was good having my dog again. He was mystified by the noise and the people, but the kids loved him. Sport's coyote blood was the cause of his death. One night a drove of dogs set upon him, and he crawled home with his beautiful yellow coat mud-stained and bloody, his back broken. The next morning we found him lying in the shed whimpering, his big brown eyes filled with pain. The veterinarian said he could not live, so Pop had Jergeson shoot him while I was at school, and for a long time I was afraid to go to the shed.

That summer a wealthy Jewish family and their maid moved into the big brick house below us and opened a new grocery store on the corner. The Cohn home was an amazing place. Each one of them slept in a separate bedroom on a massive feather mattress with pillows half as large as the bed. Deep, rich rugs covered the polished floors, heavy satin draped the windows, and everywhere was Old World red plush and purple velvet. On Fridays candles burned when the sun went down, and new and mysterious dishes appeared on their table, dishes the jolly little Mrs. Cohn prepared with her own stubby, bejewelled hands.

Sarah, youngest of the two Cohn daughters, was a chubby, lively girl, her head a tangled mass of brown curls. Sarah and I became inseparable. When she got her bicycle, I got one, and when she got a uke, so did I. Together we rode our bikes out to the river and played our ukes for the ferry pilot in exchange for rides; we invaded the library, the capitol, the penitentiary; we climbed the little ladder to the railroad tower house, where we read the guard's funnies, and we talked the streetcar conductor out of our fares. People gave us money, took our pictures, bought us pop and ice cream.

When Bismarck began its children's band and built its swimming pool, Sarah and I were right there, only Sarah got a

127

saxophone and learned to play and Sarah learned to swim. Pop sent me to the Nuns to take piano lessons and made arrangements for me to practice at the home of the blind lady on the brink of the hill, but it was short-lived. I was up to the "First Waltz" again when the blind lady's baby was born. Everybody, including Uncle John, said the baby looked more like Pop than it did like the blind lady's husband, so I didn't go over for practice any more. I knew what people said wasn't true, but the baby was very dark to be a white baby—but, then, some colored babies could be very white, so I went back to my ukelele and the swimming pool.

I never got very far as a swimmer, but I liked going to the pool with Sarah, because when we came out her hair looked just like mine—the matron said. Soon after the pool opened, Joe Green, one of the Negro toughies from below the hill, arrived in a bright red bathing suit on his muscular brown body, but they wouldn't let him swim. Joe wanted to get his gang and tear up the pool, water and all, but Pop and Ed Smith talked him out of it. I asked Pop if I would have to give up the pool when I got big like Joe Green, and he said he didn't know, prejudice was a funny thing. It ran every way but out.

Occasionally Sarah and I wandered into enemy territory, neighborhoods where the kids called us names; but if they called me a coon, they called her a kike, and when I was with her there was none of the embarrassment I felt when I was with my other friends, even the loyal ones who fought my battles.

It was inevitable that I should finally find my Indians. In between the bluffs along the river was the Indian school for girls. There were no wigwams, no squaws, no warriors, only big wooden buildings with little girls in pale blue dresses, their faces stolid and sallow, not red; their bobbed hair straight and black. Some of them ran to blue eyes and blonde tresses, and I was glad they couldn't blame my father for that.

I liked the Indian girls, but if I found in them a kindred spirit my Cherokee blood wasn't to blame. Sarah and I baffled them. At first they followed us around the yard watching as we

128

played on their swings and iron bars, circling around us when we stood still, closing in on us, never saying a word, then touching us lightly with their fingers and giggling. One Sunday we put on a show in their gym. We did handsprings and sang and danced and played our ukes. The school faculty stayed discreetly in the background until the show was over, then thanked us for the entertainment and invited us to stay for lemonade and cookies. The whole school followed us to the main road to say good-bye.

"You come back," said one girl shyly, "come back, come back soon."

Pop and his friend Mason had organized Grace Baptist Church before we moved to Bismarck. Meetings were held in private homes until a church could be bought with the generous contributions of their Capitol friends. At first a visiting minister came once a month, but as the membership increased Reverend Daily and his wife came down from St. Paul, and Grace Baptist became the center of social activity on the South Side.

Reverend Daily's congregation was colorful, and at times quite volatile. Owing to a paucity of Christians, the preacher brought in the down-under-the-hill folks, converting and putting them to work on rallies and money-raising dinners. Some of them were excellent cooks, most of them could pray the devil himself out of purgatory, but their religion was a fleeting thing. As fast as the Reverend pulled them up the hill, they backslid right down again, so he made arrangements to use the First Baptist pool to baptize the sinners. But he hadn't taken into consideration Biddy and Baby. They were sisters from the red-light districts of Montana and the Dakotas, and were very fat. Biddy, getting old now and evil, could still do battle. Every Saturday night Baby got quietly and completely drunk, her hangovers lasting through collection time Sunday, when she suddenly got shouting happy.

Pop wouldn't tell me exactly what happened during the ceremony at First Baptist, but somewhere along the way Reverend Daily had "Sister" trouble. In the battle that ensued, a battle of right against might, Jergeson and his pulmotor were on right's side a long time after might was dry. Biddy didn't take Communion the next Sunday. Ed Smith sat in the amen corner and laughed softly to himself most of the service. When Pop accosted him for the collection, Ed whispered something, then laughed right out loud. Biddy turned around very slowly and looked at him with those evil, red eyes, and Ed got very quiet.

Soon after the baptizing, Reverend Daily and his wife returned to St. Paul. Because Pop was already a deacon, some local preachers came down one night and ordained him so he could carry on until we got a replacement. It wasn't very easy, "laying the hands" on Pop. Every time they put their hands on his bald head, they slid off again, and Ed Smith got back in his amen corner and snickered some more, and this time Biddy and Baby joined him.

Soon other hands, female hands, were about to be laid on Pop. Miss Willie Mae O'Toole caused quite a stir when she arrived in town with her fox furs and six pieces of luggage. Depositing her belongings in the hotel where she was to be housekeeper, she went out to find the colored people, and came straight to our house. She was a stout woman, neat but overdressed—not very bad-looking, not very good-looking. After services Pop took to walking her back to the hotel, via the ice cream parlor. I tagged along for the ice cream, but I don't know why Bart Groves followed. Bart was a simple-minded young man who portered at one of the barber shops. Pop tried everything short of insult—then he tried that—but Bart just hung his head and fell in step with me and ate Pop's ice cream. I wouldn't have thought much about it—Pop and Miss O'Toole, I mean—if Bart hadn't asked me how I'd like her for a mother. Then when Sarah looked up from skipping rope one evening and said, "Here comes your new Ma." I saw red.

"She's not my mother!" I said hotly.

"Oh, no! You just wait and see. Everybody knows she's plotting to marry your father."

I couldn't play any more. I felt sick all over. Her marrying

Pop was bad enough, but she couldn't ever be my mother. So I followed them home that night, and sat down on the davenport and just looked at her.

"What's the matter, Sister?" Pop asked. "Don't you hear them kids callin' you?"

"Yes," I said.

"Then go on out there an' play or tell 'em to keep still."

I went to the back door and told them I couldn't come out because I had to watch my father. He was being trapped. The kids said they'd hang around the window so they could see, too. Miss O'Toole didn't stay long.

"What did you set there lookin' at that lady like that for?" Pop asked.

I came to the point. "Are you going to marry her?"

Pop exploded. "Oh, my soul! Me marry all that woman! What kind a taste you think I got? No, child." He was serious now. "If I ever marry again, it'll be somebody you like, somebody nice an' refined like that widder in St. Paul."

So I stopped worrying about Miss Willie Mae O'Toole and started worrying about a widow in St. Paul, that friend of Daily's who wrote all those letters. Suddenly Pop left for the Twin Cities to attend to some business, he said, and when he returned Miss O'Toole was gone.

The Widow Brown was a fine-looking woman, according to her pictures, and her two grown sons were fine-looking, too; but Pop didn't put their pictures on the library table with the Widow's. I found them in the bureau drawer with his stiff collars and a stack of the Widow's letters. I had a letter from her, too. "You must be a very dear little girl," she wrote in a beautiful Spencerian hand on lavender paper, "and I hope I shall love you as much as your dear father does, but we both believe you are yet a little young to have a fur coat." She said other things, too, but I didn't read them. It was enough that she had scotched my chance of ever owning a fur coat.

"If you marry her—or any other woman," I told Pop, "I'll run away!"

That February I entered high school, and a whole new world was opened up to me. High school was fun. Because the building was crowded, we midyear subfreshmen were assigned temporary seats in the assembly hall among the seniors—and that was my undoing. The boys drew pictures for me and engaged me in sham battles with paper wads; the girls took me out to the cloakroom and combed my hair and smoothed my clothes, then coaxed me to write poems about their current loves. Having long since despaired of ever memorizing the poetry assigned us, I had begun to compose my own verse. The teachers encouraged me, and I lost my shyness and became bold and, I'm afraid, a bit of a problem. They gave me a corner in the school paper for my humor and poetry, and my own penciled newspaper, *Snap,* was passed surreptitiously around the school and into the homes of my admirers.

Pop served his last session at the Capitol that winter, for it was the beginning of the end of Nonpartisan League control. I don't know whether he saw the handwriting on the wall, or whether it sprang from the goodness of his heart, but Pop decided to give a stag for his Capitol friends. It had to be a stag— our house being what it was—so we cleared the front and middle rooms and ran borrowed tables straight through to the hard-coal heater. The whole neighborhood contributed to the dinner in either household loans or donated labor. Pop cooked for two days, mixing the ingredients in our kitchen and cooking them across the street in Flynn's big oven.

The guests began to arrive early. For some it was their maiden trip across the tracks; for some, the first home-cooked meal since they left home; for nearly all of them, the first time in a Negro home. There were hearty greetings at the door, loud, he-man exclamations of delight as the pungent odor of roast pork and oyster dressing permeated the room. The house filled rapidly. Word of the stag got around, and more came than Pop had invited. "We knew you wouldn't mind, Tony," they explained. "You can't turn a starving man away." They laughed and crowded in, and Pop beamed with true Virginia hospitality, then sent me out to borrow more plates and silver.

Pop was lining them up when there was a belated knock at the door. It was Mr. Mason.

"You're late, Brother Mason," Pop chided good-naturedly. "Come on in and fall in line."

Mason hesitated. "Tony," he began, "I'm sorry I'm late, but I ran across a friend of yours on my way over. Said he didn't have any place to go, so I brought him along. Do you mind?"

"Course not, man! Bring him on in."

Mason stepped aside, and in the doorway stood Governor Frazier, his bald head shining, his face wreathed in smiles. Pop was speechless.

"What do you mean, snubbing me, Tony? Why, I always thought you and I were friends?" said Frazier.

"The Governor! The Governor hisself, come to my humble home," whispered Pop softly.

"For he's a jolly good fellow," sang the men.

Pop climbed upon a chair and led them in another round. The singing and word of the Governor's presence brought the neighborhood crowding around the house to get a glimpse of His Honor. After grace, Pop disappeared into the kitchen and returned bearing a whole roast pig standing upright on a huge tray, a red apple in its mouth, a sprig of parsley around its tail. A roar went up from the table.

Governor Frazier was one of the last to leave. There was enough food left for the neighbors and their kids, so we had a second party at midnight, and everyone helped with the dishes. Mrs. Flynn kept repeating, "He ate on my table. The Governor of North Dakota ate his dinner on my table. I'll keep it as long as I live."

Shortly after that memorable dinner Governor Frazier was recalled. This unprecedented event was closely followed by one equally amazing. The same people who thought him unfit to complete his term as Governor elected him to the Senate of the United States. Mason remained his secretary and went to Washington. When the job at the bank folded, Frazier wrote for Pop to join him, but he declined; said he was too old to start out in a new place, too old to keep up with the fast pace of the nation's capital, so he opened a secondhand store in a barn.

Pop knew nothing about furniture, but our money was getting low, the legislature was no longer a source of income—and the barn was empty. It was also dank and gloomy, sitting partly on top and partly below the hill. By renting the bottom half to a couple of Missouri mule dealers, we managed to make the rent. Bismarck housewives were a little startled when they answered the front door bell and found my father in a light gray suit, straw hat, and cane, inquiring politely about their old furniture; but it wasn't long before he found out it would be better to be less immaculate and more observing. You can't test stovegrates and fireboxes in a Palm Beach suit, any more than you can buy a mattress with the bed made up, so Pop learned. As our money dwindled, there was something symbolic about the braying of the mules below.

When Ed Smith moved his family into the new house on the other side of the tracks, I got my second job—that of mother's helper to Mrs. Smith. Pop said I was old enough—and our finances low enough—for me to start making my own spending money. Housework was hard and I missed my playmates, but it was the Ford that brought me home. Smith, who had opened up a dance pavilion on the river, had talked Pop and another man into operating a taxi line between his place and town; but after two trips the partner resigned, and Pop found himself with a car he was afraid of. The mule-man taught me how to drive, and Chief Jergeson pretended he didn't know my age. I depended upon the public to crank the car until I caught on to the short, quick twist that did the trick. After that I could turn off the engine when I stopped and have a sporting chance of getting home again.

After twenty-five years of wrestling with the soil, Uncle John went advantageously bankrupt and moved to Bismarck. He and Pop formed a partnership in the furniture business, which, of course, did not work. My uncle was clever at repairing and

134

upholstering, but this asset didn't quite offset his family. Sue and Ann raided the store every morning, appropriating the best furniture for themselves, leaving nothing much to sell. Pop grumbled to John, and John yelled at Ann, and Ann swore and said it was as much theirs as it was Tony's; she'd done without all her life and she'd be derned if she wasn't going to have something decent now. So Uncle John took the store, and Pop opened a lunch counter in a poolhall.

It wasn't a clean break, however, for we still spent our holidays together, and I played with Sue's little Benny when people didn't bother me too much. People never seemed to get used to the idea of the child and me being related, like the time when the carnival came to town. Sue gave me half a dollar to take the boy on the merry-go-round. Benny was such a strikingly handsome child, with his blonde curls, that he attracted everyone's attention, especially the lady who operated the merry-go-round. She began asking questions when she came for the fares, more questions than Miss Breen had asked back in Driscoll. She never did take our money, for every time the music stopped she returned with a new set of questions, and we rode all afternoon.

Uncle John had some explaining to do, too. After Pop pulled out, Ann would go to the store in the afternoon to help out, she said, but she usually just sat and waited for somebody to look at her funny or say something. Occasionally she was rewarded, like the time the man came in and asked for the proprietor. Ann said, "I'm the proprietor. What do you want?"

"I thought that nigger back there ran the store," said the man.

Ann began to redden and swell. "Well, that there 'nigger,' as you call him, happens to be my husband. An' you'd better git to hell out of here before I pick up somethin' an' let you have it!"

"You know Ann runs away more trade with her big mouth," John confided later to Pop.

Pop looked surprised. "Is that so?" he said. "Can you imagine that!"

Under John's gifted hands the store began to prosper in

135

spite of Ann and Sue. He could fix anything and make what he couldn't fix. People soon got used to the family, were careful of what they said, and saved all the bad things until later when they fell out with Ann—and they usually did.

That summer I won three races and got religion. I could always run faster than the other kids in the neighborhood or in school, but now it paid dividends. By Labor Day I had won nearly ten dollars at various picnics in and about Bismarck.

For a long time now I had been hanging my head at camp meetings and local revivals when Christians raised their hands and sinners went to the mourners' bench, so I had a talk with Mable Flynn just before we left for the annual camp meeting at Jamestown. Mable, too, was disturbed about her soul, so we decided that if there was anything to "getting religion," I should get it and bring it home. Pop must have had the same idea, because the preachers closed in on me one night at the tabernacle as though it had been prearranged. I knelt in the sawdust a long time, and nothing happened. Dr. Kane knelt beside me with the other preachers and tried to hurry it up.

"Won't you believe, little sister, won't you believe?"

"Believe what?"

"Believe Jesus saves."

"I'm not saved. I don't feel any different."

They prayed some more, then tried again. "Do you believe now?"

My handkerchief was wet from crying, my knees hurt, people were leaving the tent.

"Raise your hand and say you believe. The change," they promised, when I hesitated, "will come later. First you must have faith."

So I stood up on my paralysed legs and held up my hand and said, "All right, I believe."

Explaining it later to Mable was difficult. She wanted concrete evidence of the change. "When the ticket seller at the Orpheum asked if you were twelve, you said no."

"But I'm not twelve; I'm fourteen," I defended.

136

"And you told that policeman Biddy was your mother." Mable was getting technical. The open-air pavilion across the street from our house gave a dance every Saturday night, and we kids danced, too, when no one was watching. Biddy and Baby were sitting in a car watching the sights when a policeman started after us. Sarah and I dived into the car and under the wide skirts of the two sisters. Mable tried, too, but she was too fat. That's when I said Biddy was my mother. Under the circumstances, I was the only one who could get away with it.

"And it would have worked," I pointed out, "if you kids hadn't claimed her also!"

"We're sinners," Mable reminded me. And I knew in my heart that I was, too.

It was funny, the way we got on the other side of the tracks. The South Side had a certain stigma, of course, but we would have gone right on living there if it hadn't been for Watkins Products. Mrs. Kuntz, their agent, not only sold Pop a bill of goods, but also rented him their house on her first call, so we moved to the West Side into the little white cottage with the lilac bush and the green picket fence, to sidewalks and paved streets, to a house with a bathroom. Eventually the bathroom got a bathtub, and finally a two-burner oilstove was installed, but in the windowless room oil fumes mingled with steam from the heated water, and bathing became a blind race against unconsciousness.

Our house sat on a corner across from a vacant lot, so the only close neighbors were Mr. and Mrs. Kuntz, who lived in a made-over garage in the rear of our yard, and the Harmons to our left. As a result of earlier difficulties between the two families, a high fence separated the house. The Harmons' kitchen window looked directly into ours, and there Mrs. Harmon sat all day long, watching from behind her starched curtains. We hardly ever saw Mr. Harmon, but the four little boys fretted behind their fence and tried to make friends through the cracks. Mrs. Harmon didn't approve of Negroes for neighbors. She was sure if she watched long enough she would see something im-

137

moral or improper or unclean, so she kept her lonely vigil, and was eventually rewarded. The washings I put out didn't bear the *Good Housekeeping* Seal Of Approval, especially on days when the pool was open, so Mrs. Harmon remarked, loudly enough for the whole block to hear, that my wash looked a sight. It did.

Pop was irked by the constant watching, and he felt sorry for the little boys jailed in behind the fence, so gradually he began to break the lady down. Every morning he'd come outside by the kitchen window and bow politely to the starched curtains and say good morning to the kids. His whistling about the yard and garden drew them to the fence like a magnet. He talked to them as he worked, apparently unmindful of the woman's watching eyes. Little by little the curtains began to part, slowly Mrs. Harmon began to nod, then smile. It wasn't long before she came out on her back porch to sit and listen to what Pop said to her boys, before the little boys were slipping over the fence and into our yard.

By midsummer Mrs. Harmon was a good neighbor. She never came over to visit, like the other neighbors were now doing, but she and her husband often hung over the fence in the cool of evening, talking about the garden—and the Kuntzes. And when Pop took me fishing, all four little Harmons went along.

We were nicely settled in our new house when Harry, tall and handsome now, came home with a broken leg and a wrecked motorcycle. He never knew who hit him, but he assumed it was the man who took him to a St. Paul hospital and paid the bills. As soon as his leg mended, he got a job at a garage and began paying room and board. I don't know what Harry did for social life, but he took the car nearly every night, and I don't think he rode alone.

When I graduated from a foot racer to a sprinter Pop took me to every picnic in the community and some that weren't, running me against young ladies, old ladies, boys, and even men, when the crowd demanded it—and the purse was large. Strangers would walk slowly past me at large public gatherings

138

and say, "You wanna win, kid. I've got five bucks on you!" Of course, I never saw them again or got any of the money, but it was nice to know they won, too.

My first real competition came when our school participated in the spring high school festival at the state agricultural college at Fargo. Miss Wallace, our gym teacher, raised enough money from candy and rummage sales to hire a bus to take sixteen of us to the meet.

All along the way people came out to see what in the world. The grown-ups stared, but little children looked at me and sometimes asked questions. I still cannot understand how those kids who had never seen a Negro before, who were too young even to read, always arrived at the same conclusion.

We were two days getting to Fargo. It rained, bogging down the dirt road and the bus with it, so we pushed most of the last seventy miles. Darkness caught us the first night at a little town which boasted of one hotel and one cook. When the manager saw eighteen muddy, hungry people descending upon him he followed the resigning cook and turned the place over to us—for $18. We cooked our own dinner and slept three to five in a room, except, of course, the driver. I had asked Gwyn Doyle, the third baseman, to sleep with me, but when Miss Wallace asked her, too, of course she chose Miss Wallace. As a compromise, Miss Wallace had a cot put in their room for me, and, while Red McGee and the others raised Cain down the hall, I had to go to sleep.

We made Valley City about two the next afternoon, stopping only long enough to eat. After the beating our finances had taken the night before, we went to a little restaurant on a side street, one the driver recommended. When we walked in, the men at the counter stopped eating, and the one waitress looked at me and blinked. The track team wasn't allowed to eat sweets, so we had planned to sit with the other girls and bribe them for their dessert. I selected the pianist, one of the Frazier twins. Softening her up wasn't very hard, with her feeling partly responsible for me because of our fathers. Already she had mended my torn stocking and taken a sliver out of my hand, so she would have been a pushover for dessert, only Miss Wallace said she was sure I'd like to sit beside her. And she had me by the arm when she said it.

The waitress took all the orders at our table but mine and started away. Miss Wallace called her back. "I believe you forgot her order."

"Oh," said the girl innocently, "does *she* want something, too?"

I didn't get an opportunity to answer that or to select my food either. Miss Wallace was very efficient.

It was still raining when we pulled into Fargo late at night, a weary, woebegone, mud-smeared group, not a school yell left in us.

The rain continued all the next day, but Saturday morning broke clear and chilly. At six we were up greeting the sun, running down the fire escape, trying the cinder path. After breakfast we registered and drew numbers. While we sat around the dorm waiting for two o'clock, Red and I got into a fight over the window seat. I said the longer I stood, the slower I'd run, and Red said I couldn't run anyway, so I went over to the "enemy's side." The enemy was three little Fargo girls who had made previous overtures of friendliness. All afternoon I stayed with the enemy, rooting for Fargo while they rooted for me, much to the confusion of onlookers. Miss Wallace came for me after I won the fifty-yard dash.

The night the awards were made the auditorium was crowded, but a large motherly woman sitting on the bleachers made room on the bottom board and pulled me down between her knees. When I went up to get my gold knife, she led the applause.

We left right after breakfast the next morning, but not before the three little enemies came tearing down the walk to say good-bye.

At home we were all heroines; the whole town was proud of us. A man in the post office told me he was glad I won because he won, too—twenty dollars, he said. I didn't touch a textbook for a week.

Grace Baptist petered out soon after we left the South Side, for Chief Jergeson raided above and below the hill, and the congregation vanished. I turned Lutheran, like the new neighborhood, until confirmation time, then followed a girl friend from the next block to the Evangelical church.

I came in handy. Once a year the church put on an all-nations pageant to raise funds to support the missionaries. My role was Mother Africa. They didn't ask me to blacken my face —all I had to do was put on a long white robe and follow Mother India and say: "Help me, too. My people need you!" I don't think Pop even knew I was in the play, the first one, I mean; but after her Evangelical debut, Mother Africa was much in demand. Missionaries of other denominations also needed financing. No telling where it would have ended had it not been for Priscilla Running Horse and her real Indian headgear. Priscilla was to follow me, but with feathers she followed too closely. The Presbyterian church was hushed, expectant, I raised my arms, fixed my eyes on the rafters. "I, Mother Africa. . ." Priscilla moved. I came down past the pulpit and out over the little curtained rail in much better time than I made at Fargo.

I was left pretty much on my own when Harry returned to the Twin Cities. Pop was at the restaurant when I got up, and I was in bed when he came home. Sarah and I started around the world on our bikes, and got nearly ten miles, when a storm and a traveling salesman brought us home before we were even missed. We spent a lot of time at the river while the new bridge was being built, and when the ice broke up in the spring we played Robinson Crusoe on big, loose cakes, flirting with death. In summer we roamed along the river where the treacherous current undermined the banks, watching trees and great chunks of land tumble into the water about us.

In school I was learning many things in spite of my love for the gymnasium, even things about myself, like the statement in our textbook that said Negroes were black folks with kinky hair and a thick skull that education could not penetrate. I made a prevaricator out of the author by getting 97 on the exam, then cut class the day of the "black analysis." The pupils wanted to know which was wrong, the book or I, and the teacher was in a spot until some bright kid remembered there was an Aryan in my family closet; so the white intelligence that hovered around on my dark shoulders was accounted for and excused.

Assembly speakers were often as embarrassing as textbooks and songs like "Polly Wolly Doodle" and "Old Folks at Home." I learned to hate those songs as much as I did the speakers who couldn't sit down until they had told a "darky" story, for invariably the student body turned to see how I was taking it. Sometimes I'd turn and look, too, just for the hell of it.

Early in my senior year Pop gave up the restaurant business and opened another secondhand store across the river in Mandan, which meant giving up our little house when the lilacs were in bloom, meant being short of money when I needed it most, and meant going back on the other side of the tracks to stay with Aunt Ann and Uncle John. Peggy and Jerry Stein roomed with the Evanses. They said they were married, but Peggy packed a little suitcase and stayed out lots of nights, and Jerry never said a word. Ann said that, as long as they behaved themselves in her home, it was none of her business what they did outside. Pop didn't like my being around Peggy, but it couldn't be helped. I liked Peggy. The first blues music I ever heard was on her phonograph. The sad, slow, pulsing rhythms fascinated me, and I begged Peggy for stories about the big cities, about colored people, because she had lived many places.

I did a little better when the new gym teacher took us to Fargo that May, winning two gold medals and a bronze one, but I came up against a new opponent called prejudice, and lost, hands down. I had begged Clara Heldt to go downtown to a show with us, against Clara's religious judgment. Clara had never been to a show, but she was my pal. I had no roommate this time. The others went in the theater ahead of us, because I was still having trouble with Clara and her conscience. When

142

we got inside the lady usher said, "Upstairs, please."

"You," she said, stepping over to me, "have to sit upstairs."

"But our friends are down here," I protested.

She took a step closer. "I know, dear," she lowered her voice, "but it's a rule of the house."

I stood there a moment, puzzled, then a red flame of humiliation and anger spread over me, blinding my eyes, burning my throat. Leaving Clara on the steps, more confused than ever, I rushed out of the theater into the bright afternoon sunshine. For a long time I walked up and down the broad streets until the flame burned itself out, then walked until I found the depot, where I knew I could get my bearings and make my way back to the college.

A matron approached me. "Hello," she said. "Ain't you the one that come in here the other day with those high school girls?"

"Yes," I admitted.

"You ain't lost, are you, honey?"

I could feel her gray eyes on me; kind eyes they were, but I couldn't stand kindness now. "No," I said, "I can find my way."

She walked with me to the door. "Be sure you get the car that says 'College,' now. Don't take no other car but the one what says 'College,' and then when everybody else gets off, you get off, too."

I didn't go down to dinner that night, and I was grateful the teacher did not come to me, but I waited for Clara. I knew she would come. "I'm sorry," I told her. "I shouldn't have coaxed you to go to the show. I wish I hadn't gone myself."

"But why," she asked, wrinkling her broad forehead, "did they want you to sit upstairs? Up there were white people, too. I know; I looked."

"They were afraid someone wouldn't want to sit beside me, I guess—the downstairs people, I mean."

"The girls said you could of sit between us, they said you could of sit in the middle." I didn't answer. "Don't you worry," she consoled. "It was a no-good show, anyway. I didn't like it."

143

Back home, in the rush and excitement of graduation, I soon forgot about Fargo and segregation, for as class poet I was forty-six stanzas deep in eulogies for eighty-one seniors—the last thirty-five got gypped.

Our commencement speaker talked about the ship of life, the commencement, the beginning of things to come. We were men and women, he said, and the world was ours. The next morning I set out for the local newspaper office to find my niche in the world. Keith was there finishing up the school annuals. I didn't want him to know why I had come. Quietly I asked to see the editor. He came out of the inner office, spoke to Keith, and looked quizzically at me.

"Did you want to see me?" he said loudly.

"Yes." I hesitated. "I'd like to speak to you."

"What about?"

I lowered my voice. "I-I want a job."

"A job?" he yelled. "Sorry, haven't a thing right now. Sorry."

Keith pretended he did not hear. I hurried out of the office and back down below the tracks. Maybe I was grown-up—I wasn't sure. It was like that time at camp meeting when I was down on my knees at the mourners' bench. The time had come, I believed, but I really didn't feel any different.

9) WHERE THE WEST BEGINS

Mandan marks the beginning of the real West. It is here Mountain Time begins, here the Indians come from the reservation to greet the tourist trains and dance at the big rodeo; here, on this side of the river, live the rattlers; and farther to the west, in the Bad Lands, is the town of Medora, once the ranch home of Teddy Roosevelt and his fabulous friend, the French nobleman, the Marquis de Mores.

The town was proud of its historical significance, worked hard to maintain it. Few Negroes had ever lived in Mandan— never more than two or three at a time. Most of its seven thousand people were Russian-German, living in Dutch and Russian hollows, bits of the Old Country, complete in their quaintness, transplanted deep between the sharp hills at the north end of town. Scrubbed wooden benches leaned against light blue and pale green houses, earthenware jugs stood by the doors. English was seldom spoken.

Here Pop opened his secondhand store in a little four-room house on Main Street between Wagner's Hotel and the Morton Construction Company. For a long time the store smelled. Its former tenant made and sold moonshine, and the tenants before him had babies—so many babies they were said to have slept sideways in the bed. Pop scrubbed the store, drenched it with creosote, and burned sulphur, but it retained the sour odor of bad liquor and something else—customers. All night long men tapped on the back doors and windows calling softly for a bootlegger named Joe. They thought Deacon Thompson was running a speakeasy.

When I joined Pop in Mandan, our neighbors were already our friends. I was a godsend to Elsie Wagner, living in the rear of the hotel with her parents and brothers—and the old men who sat around in the lobby like gray vultures, their eyes following every female figure, their mouths drooling tobacco. Elsie and I became inseparable. Pop said that every time he looked up there was Elsie, and that when he looked again we were both gone. The elder Wagners said it was the same with me. "She's a gute girl, that Era Bell," Mrs. Wagner would say, and Pop would tell her, "I'm glad she's with your girl. Let 'em have fun while they're young, laugh while they can. What you s'pose they always laughin' at?"

"Oh, God, I don't know!" Mrs. Wagner would smile her tired smile. "They laugh alla the time, always laughing. They don't need not'ings to make them laugh."

We didn't know, either. Sometimes we would just stand before a mirror and giggle, and when we'd catch Pop watching us we'd giggle all the harder. He'd laugh, too. He'd shake his head and say to himself, "Lord, Lord! I wonder is they crazy sure 'nuff?"

In all Mandan there was not one Baptist church, so with many apologies to his past faith, Pop succumbed and went to Mass. "They all right," he commented dryly when we got home, "but I'm too old for that religion." He rubbed his knees. "Them prayer-benches and all that gettin' up and gettin' down—and

146

with my rheumatism, too—Lord today, I wouldn't last out the week!" He looked at me. "You join if you want to, one religion just as good as another with you 'cause you ain't goin' to do no different no way."

"They wear hats to church," I replied. "I hate hats."

So Pop and I went over to the pretty Methodist church, where they stayed put in their pews and sang doleful hymns and took Deacon Thompson on probation and accepted me and my sins in full.

As rodeo time drew near, Pop's excitement grew with that of the town, and the call of the kitchen was strong upon him. "Lots of money to be made out there at that thing," he reasoned. "Now, I could sell some chicken sandwiches an' make a killin'." So, when the rodeo opened, Pop, like the Indians, pitched his tent at the fairgrounds and began to hawk his wares. Afternoons and evenings I sold sandwiches over the oilcloth counter, while Pop mysteriously converted each wizened, over-aged hen into sixteen golden-brown, highly inflated morsels at a quarter a sandwich. Business got so good I went to Bismarck and got Gwyn to help us. Carnival people, fed up on the traditional American hot dog and hamburger, flocked to our stand, and even the Indians deserted their tents and tepees—after I found Priscilla. She was living with the other Indians at the far end of the racetrack, where spotted ponies grazed on wild grass, dried meat hung in long strips on ropes between the trees, and dogs snapped at the flies and scratched their mangy sides. When Priscilla came to visit me, she asked for a hot dog.

"Try chicken," I urged. "You've got dogs at home."

"How much?" she asked.

"Ten cents to you." I looked at the old woman beside her. "Is that your mother?"

"Yes." She said something in Sioux. The woman pulled her shawl around her thin shoulders and smiled at me. She said nothing. "My mother don't speak American," said the girl.

Old Country, I thought. Only it wasn't Old Country: it was this country. Nearly all my friends were second generation;

147

their parents spoke the mother tongue, wore the native clothes, had the ways of the fatherland, even the Indians. In a sense I was second generation, too, only Pop had no other language, but in the ways of the world he was far ahead of me. My Latin and geometry didn't make any more sense to my father than they did to my friends' fathers. They didn't make too much sense to me.

"Both of you try chicken," I offered, giving them the biggest pieces I could find.

The next morning the old lady returned. Gwyn and Pop tried to wait on her, but she stood at the counter, silent and unmoved. When I came at noon, she was still there. "Chick-on," she said, holding out a dime.

"So that's why she waited for you. Tell her chicken's a quarter, and we don't pick out no more big pieces," Pop said peevishly.

"More," I said, picking up a quarter from the cash box. "Like this."

She shook her head and smiled. "Chick-on."

"Pop," I pleaded. "You know I can't talk Indian. This is Priscilla's mother. Priscilla is my friend from the School. Can't we let her have it this time? She likes your cooking; she'll tell her friends, and you'll get lots of trade."

Pop had visions of the whole tribe descending upon him with dimes. "Give her somethin' an' git her away from here. She been takin' up cash-customer room all day. Then you go find that friend of yours an' stop them folks, hear? I got no time to interrupt my cookin' to go fightin' Indians."

I slipped off to the stables every chance I got and rode the white trick horse that belonged to the boss of the rodeo.

"You like horses, don't you, girlie?" he asked one afternoon when I brought the mare back.

"Crazy about them."

"Ever do much ridin'—hard ridin'?"

"Are you kidding? I come from a bronco busting family, wild Montana broncs, real horses." I neglected to mention Bessie.

148

"Yeah? How'd you like to ride for me, travel along with my outfit? I'd teach you some tricks—you've got a way with horses— and you'd be a good drawin' card."

Some of the bravado went out of me. "I don't know," I backed down, "you'll have to ask my father." And that ended that career.

I loved the Indian war dances. Every evening they gathered in front of the grandstand in the twilight, dressed in all their fine feathers and elk's teeth and beaded moccasins, the chiefs and warriors wearing long headdresses and carrying hatchets in their fringed buffalo pants. Beneath the war paint were gentleness and quiet joy in their make-believe. The dance was a picturesque thing, weird and exotic. A tall brave would step out into the center of the chanting circle, head bent low, knees pumping high, dancing to the throb of the tom-tom; a strenuous dance it was, punctuated by bloodcurdling yells, a dance that raised beads of sweat on his naked, brown back, made his makeup run down his high cheeks. While the bucks danced, I often joined the squaws in a smooth little sidestep around the edge of the circle until some brash individual asked what tribe I belonged to: the Crows or the Blackfeet.

I hated to see the roundup close, see the carnival people and the Indians move on. The money Gwyn earned was to help pay her tuition at the state university in September. I wondered which would be nicer, going with the rodeo as a trick rider or with Gwyn as a freshman, so I went home to Thompson's Secondhand Store with Pop.

Hardly a morning passed that some hobo or tramp didn't cross over the tracks and come to our store. They were like Slim, the I.W.W. who helped us thresh: happy-go-lucky, philosophical, radical, religious; all ages, all nationalities, come to buy or barter for clothing, shaving equipment, pocketknives, pans—yes, even Bibles. One old man came and went with the birds. He had a gold chain—a beautiful chain, with a large cross at the end. The first time we saw him, he talked with Pop about God, about brotherly love. Pop asked him where he was going.

"Nowhere," he said. "Can't stay long in one place. I like to feel free, to not be beholdin' to any man, so I follow the birds and talk with God, and I am happy."

"You hungry, too?" Pop looked at him closely.

"No, no," he said pleasantly. "God feeds me."

"He feeds me, too," Pop countered. "We'll have a bite together. I was just goin' to make some coffee anyhow."

After they had eaten, the old man pulled out his chain and broke off a few links. "I have no money." He held the links out to my father.

"No, no. I don't want your chain. You don't owe me nothin'."

"Take them, brother, they are for you."

"I'm a Christian, too. I can't do that," Pop protested.

"Then keep them, brother, till I need them."

Pop kept the chain in the Bible where it said, "Inasmuch as ye have done it unto one of the least of these." Each time the old man came, his chain was shorter and shorter. He would take no money, so Pop fed him, gave him shoes and coats, and they talked about God, took up where they left off as if it were only yesterday. The last time we saw him, only the big cross remained. Pop took his links from the Bible and slipped them into his bundle.

"I got a feelin'," Pop said when he was gone, "that he won't come back no more. He's come to the cross, and his journey's most nigh over." But every spring when the birds flew North and every fall when the tumbling tumbleweeds began to roll, Pop stood at the door and watched the tracks. He did not come again.

When Elsie and her brothers started to school in the fall, I wanted to attend the local business college, but there was no money except the thousand-dollar note the elevator man still owed us for the farm. Crops failed miserably after we left Sterling, and land values decreased until the note was worthless.

"Maybe I could get something out of it," I told Father.

"How you goin' to collect when the lawyers couldn't?"

150

"If I get anything, can I have it?"

"Yes, Lord, if you get it."

I sat down and wrote the elevator man a letter about the business college, and he sent me a check for seventy-five dollars. Pop never quite got over it, but he let me keep the money. In October I went up to the high school and talked to the principal. It was a little irregular, he said, but if I thought I could make up the work, why, yes, I could take a postgraduate commercial course; so I went back to school and kept the seventy-five dollars.

My first day wasn't too happy. As the principal and I started down the hall for the commercial room, classes began to pass down the long, dark corridor, and the students were upon us before they noticed me. Some stopped stock-still and stared the way people did on Main Street, some shied away, and one big, husky boy even screamed. I hurried along, trying to keep up with the long strides of the principal, ignoring the confusion that followed in my wake.

The blonde shorthand teacher was wholly unprepared for my coming. As she talked her big, gray eyes never moved from my face. She was seeing her first colored girl.

"She'll work hard and catch up," the principal was saying; "I'm sure she will."

"Catch up! Why, we're a month ahead of her now. A whole month, and I already have one backward class."

"I know, I know," he soothed. "She'll take her work home, she'll practice hard. Won't you?" He stopped short with sudden apprehension; but I was so busy returning the stare I nearly missed my cue.

"Well," she said peevishly, "I'll try it. But if she can't keep up, she can't stay."

I stayed, and had a wonderful time. The first few days the little class was divided between those bent upon being nice to me and the others. By the end of the second week they were all bent on being nice to me, vying to walk home with me. Teacher changed, too. With nothing else to do except shorthand, I caught up so rapidly she urged me to join her bookkeeping class and

151

she let me practice typing when there was an extra machine. And when there wasn't I used the principal's portable. Soon I was writing for the school paper, taking part in all their activities, and creating a few of my own. Teacher made little effort to discipline, for I was good for the Polish boy. The Old Country solemnity was disappearing from his face, his spirits went up and his marks went down, but he was smiling like the rest of us, and Teacher was glad.

I couldn't resist the gymnasium long. I played basketball with all four class teams and stayed after school to practice acrobatics, because right then my desire was to become a lady contortionist. There being only one shower in the girls' dressing room, several of us went in together. At first my new friends watched me undress, watched to see if the color went all the way up and if any washed off in the water, and I think they were glad when it didn't because they knew then I wasn't a phony.

That winter I found another interest—the *Chicago Defender*. By enlarging upon and fictionalizing the commonplace events of the Evans and Thompson households, I created enough news to become a correspondent. My first feature, an attack upon Marcus Garvey's "Back to Africa" movement for Negroes, brought my first fan mail, a letter from one of his followers who even scorched the outside of the letter; so I gave up social reform, assumed the pseudonym of "Dakota Dick," and became a contributor to the "Lights and Shadows" column as a bad, bad cowboy from the wild and wooly West. The Mandan Chamber of Commerce could not have done better. Came friendly letters from colored pen pals beyond the hills. When an article to *Physical Culture* magazine netted me three dollars, I traded contortionism for journalism and hooked my wagon to a literary star.

The secondhand business was especially good in the fall, when farmers came from miles around to buy trucks and carloads of furniture. Most of them could speak little English. Pop knew five or six words in German, and from there on he made motions. He got pretty good with his motions, usually selling at one of his three prices and making money. Customers liked to haggle over the price, liked to feel they had talked him out of a dollar or two, so Pop went up above the price and let them talk him down, and everybody was happy. Sometimes he got a man that did not argue, and Pop felt bad because he had overcharged him, so he made it up to God in the church collection. The women were hard on him. They talked their language, used his motions, and paid him what they liked. When two came in together, Pop threw up his hands and hollered for the Wagners, but he didn't holler very loud, because Pop loved his customers and they loved him. He went to their homes and fussed with them over their goods, then sat down and drank their coffee. He came home with vegetables and fresh strudel and German coffee cake as well as furniture, but he was bothered.

"Why don't you put that shorthand business down and learn to talk these folks' language so you can be some help to me?" he asked.

So when Mrs. Wertz put a sign in the hotel window which read: "EXCHANGE GERMAN FOR ENGLISH," I went right over. Mr. and Mrs. Wertz and their little boy, Kurt, were straight from Berlin, where Mrs. had taught in the University and Mr. had been an accountant. They didn't know a word of English.

Mrs. Wagner was delighted. "That is fine," she said. "Both learn."

Pop was amused. "I'd certainly like to see that, I would. You sure this woman can't talk no English?"

She couldn't and my repertoire consisted of the German equivalent of such words as "bedbug" and "crazy" and the songs "Du bist" and "Zu Lauderbach habe." Frau Wertz was a patient woman. We sat at a table in her room, an English-German book between us. She'd say something and smile and nod her head, and I'd say, "Ya, ya," and wait. Then she'd point out the English and make me repeat in German, and she'd repeat in English, and we'd both nod and smile. At the end of the hour I ran down the stairs and into the store like an escaped refugee.

"Well?" Pop looked expectantly. "What you learn?"

153

"Es gefällt mir."

"What that mean?"

"I don't know."

"Oh, my soul! You already don't know what you sayin' now; why didn't you ask her what you learnt?"

"I did ask her."

"What'd she say?"

"Es gefällt mir."

"Umph!" Pop turned away. "I'm sure glad she don't charge nothin'."

My first colored boy friend was Bobby, an inmate at the Training School—a boys' reformatory. Bobby's story was a sad one. His unmarried white mother deserted him when he was a baby, and he never knew his father. He lived with different families, some colored, some white, until he was ten; then, because there was no other place for a little colored boy, they sent him to the School. Pop was disturbed about that, but it wasn't Bobby's fault; he couldn't help being born. He stopped by for a few minutes when he came in town on errands; he never said much, just sat looking at me with his big, solemn eyes, happy in those stolen moments of freedom.

When I began to correspond with Wilbur, Pop was more than disturbed. Wilbur was a prisoner who got my address from the *Defender* and asked me to write to him. He had run over a little white girl in Richmond, Virginia—an accident, he said—so they gave him five years. He didn't want his mother to know; it would break her heart, so would I write and cheer him up? For Christmas Wilbur sent me a poem about a fragrant flower in a crystal bowl, and Elsie, sharing it with me, said it was beautiful. I could marry that one, she said.

When the saxophone player came over, Pop began to read *True Story*. He found a copy in the drawer of an old dresser and started to throw it away when the cover caught his eye. "Is Your Daughter Safe from Temptation?" it asked in big, bold letters, and Pop began to read. When I came home from basketball I found the magazine on my table. The next day it was still there.

"Did you see that magazine?" he asked.

"It's an old one," I said.

"I don't care how old it is; I want you to read it, read every word of it. It—it tells you things I can't tell you; things you ought to know." Pop was having a hard time saying what he meant. "Now you read it, you hear?" Poor Pop. I'd been reading them for years.

The saxophone player didn't last long. He lost his instrument in some kind of game and moved on. Pop felt sorry for the next one, a porter in a Bismarck hotel. He was an old man of thirty-five or forty, with atrocious clothes and heinous grammar. When he came over, I called Pop and got out the checkerboard. While they played, I read.

Coping with my near-romances must have aroused something in Pop, because he made one last effort, unearthed one more widow. The first indication I had of the dear lady was the arrival of a large picture in a silver frame. Pop hung it over the rolltop desk, and every time I made an entry in the ledger or went into the cash drawer, I looked at a woman in a rocking chair on a front porch in Kansas City. Then one day Pop asked me if I could run the store alone for a week; he was going to Kansas City.

Staying alone in the store all day long got terribly dull, so I began to paint. I painted everything in our room, including the broom handle and rolling pin. Before the paint gave out there were three blue chairs, a red dresser, and a pink table. Then, out of an old packing box and a bucket of water, I made a shower that had the velocity of Boulder Dam—and that should have discouraged me, but I got to thinking about the seven-day mantel clock. If an electric bulb replaced the insides, I reasoned, it should make an artistic lamp. I was busy disemboweling the clock when the bell jingled and a well-dressed man walked briskly in the door. He paused by the clothes rack, his nose in the air, walking stick poised at his side.

"Where is the proprietor?" he demanded in an Eastern accent.

"He isn't in. May I help you?" I had given up telling the

155

people I was the proprietor. They never believed me.

"No," he said coldly. "I'll wait for the proprietor."

He perched himself on the end of a chipped Chippendale settee, his back rigid, his eyes aloft. A large diamond sparkled on his finger; a rancid, black cigar burned slowly in his hand. I worked silently on my clock. I released a screw, and a spring shot skyward. The man jumped.

Half an hour later I was still removing springs and cogs. The black cigar had burned out, and the man began to fidget. "Are you sure"—his voice was level, hard—"that the proprietor is coming back?"

"Yes, sir."

"Has he been gone long?"

"No, sir."

"Well, where did he go?"

I laid the screwdriver down on the desk and lifted out the mechanism. I shook it, but it wouldn't tick, hadn't ticked much since that spring departed. I looked at the man. He was about to burst, his knuckles were white over the handle of his cane, his eyes black and angry.

"Who?" I asked.

"The proprietor!" he roared. "Where is he?"

"Oh, him," I smiled. "He went to Kansas City."

Whatever it was that the man wanted, I didn't sell it to him.

The lamp-clock was a temporary success. I left the $10 tag on and kept it burning in the window all night.

Pop had sold the Ford when we moved to Mandan, so feeling the need of locomotion, I proceeded to make a car. Taking a kerosene tank from an oilstove, I fastened it behind the seat of my bicycle, used a rolling pin for a bumper, an umbrella for a top, and a strip of canvas to form the body. When the monstrosity was completed, I hung an "Out for Lunch" sign on the door and rolled into the street. Progress to the end of the block was slow and precarious. Cars slowed down, followed; people gaped and grinned. I made a right turn. It didn't crash or snap;

156

it just collapsed slowly, settling down about me in a heap at the corner of First and Main. The creative instinct was bruised, but not crushed. Work on a tea cart was interrupted by a card from Pop. He'd be home a day early. There was little time to wonder about the widow; the store had to be put back together again, and the clock would be difficult. I had three springs, a coil, and five cogs left over.

Pop came alone. He seemed awfully glad to get back; he acted as if he had just escaped something. I hastened to show him the ledger, how much money I had taken in. "I got five dollars out of Old Lady Gross," I boasted.

"You got money out of her?"

"Sure. It was easy. I just told her you said she was bad pay, and she blew up, said she'd show you."

"Oh, my Lord! Now I've heard everything. Hereafter all the . . ." Pop saw the dresser. "Great day in the mornin', where'd you get that ugly red thing from—and them blue chairs." Pop walked into our room, picked up the broom. "If I'd been gone just one more day, I wouldn't a-had no store."

"I sold that old chiffonier," I said hastily.

Pop was staring at the word "Gas" painted in white on the tank of a kerosene stove.

"What'd you get for it? Five dollars?"

"Guess again."

"Ten dollars?"

"Again."

"You didn't get more'n twelve dollars for it, I know."

"Fourteen ninety-eight!"

Pop sat down. "You mean that old yella chiffonier with the glass knobs?"

"Yes. That Caesarean one."

"That what?"

"Well, Caucasian, then."

Pop began to laugh just as had the man and woman that bought it. "Caesarean, Caucasian" he repeated. "Child, don't you know ain't no wood called that? You talkin about Circassian

157

—and we ain't had one of them for a year." Pop went back to the front and looked at the mantel clock. "You forget to wind this clock?"

"What clock?"

Pop wound it. Shook it. "Humph! That's funny. Thing don't run; must be dirty." He took the tag off and marked it down to $7.50. "Let's eat," he said. "I'm hungry."

While we were eating, the bell jingled.

"I'll get it," Pop said. He took the customer in the back room; then they went to the front again. "Sister, where's that canvas cot I had here? Did you sell it?"

"What canvas cot?" Suddenly I remembered. "Wait," I said. "I know where it is." I led them to the back yard.

Pop got between the man and the shower and kept talking. "I don't see no cot."

"Follow me," I said, and started climbing up the side of the shed.

"Where in the name of common sense you goin'?"

"Penthouse. Come on."

Pop looked at the man. "Mister, are you sure you want a cot?"

The man grinned. "This penthouse; that I got to see." He scrambled up the low coal shed and over on to the roof.

"You got any more of my furniture up there? If you have, don't you come down till you git it." Grabbing an end of the bed, Pop turned to the man. "Mighty decent of you to help us get this down. I'm no good on top of things—makes my head swim."

"Oh, I buy it," said the man. "Me have what you call penthouse, too."

The dry hotness of summer closed in upon us, dull and listless. I hadn't even high school to look forward to now, and college was financially out of the question. Beyond the bluffs of the river the white clouds were beckoning again, not to the happy hunting ground of the red men, but to the happy-happy

158

land of my people; so I wrote to Harry in Pittsburgh and Tom in Minneapolis. But they wanted no part of me. Remembering that the Ed Smiths now had a store in St. Paul, I wrote to them for a job and got it.

With what was left of the seventy-five dollars and Mrs. Smith's promise to look after me, I said good-bye to Pop and Elsie and boarded the train for the Twin Cities, my mind full of the future, of the big, busy world ahead of me, the world of colored girls and boys as well as white, of colored stores and churches, of big city lights, a job.

Mrs. Smith met me at the station, and when we got to the store Tom was there waiting. I could tell by the scowl on his face that he disapproved of my coming.

"Have you got any money?" he began as soon as we were alone.

"Yes," I said. "Some."

"How long you going to stay here?" he demanded.

"Oh, I don't know." Feeling that I should express some future ambition beyond clerking in a grocery store, I floundered around in my mind for something to say, something impressive. "Unless I go back to school," I added.

"Did you and Pop have a fight?"

"No!" I was angry. I didn't have to fight to get away from home; I had as much right to leave as the rest of them. I wanted to go out into the world, too.

"Sorry I couldn't get over in time to meet you," Tom said, relenting a little. "Had to come all the way from Minneapolis. How'd you happen to come here?" He motioned towards the Smiths at the other end of the store.

"They hired me."

Tom wasn't impressed. "About school. What school did you have in mind?"

"The university." Only rich kids went there, rich kids and girls like Gwyn who could make their way any place. I felt safe.

"The one in North Dakota?" he continued doggedly.

"Why, yes. I guess so." I was suddenly inspired. "But the

159

University of Minnesota is right here. It's bigger and better. I could work for my board and room and I'd be close . . ."

"How much does it cost to go to the other one—the one back home?"

"I don't know. It's in Grand Forks. I've never been there."

"Well, you find out. I'll pay your tuition. Maybe you can get yourself a job to help out. I don't want you staying here in this big city; I ain't got time to look after you; I can't be responsible."

Tom was like a stranger; the city had made him dour, cynical. His voice was sharp, he didn't smile or joke like he used to, and didn't even call me "Tovey." I thought of Pop back there in the store all alone, and I began to feel homesick in spite of myself.

Between waiting on customers on the grocery side of the store and washing dishes on the restaurant side, I was kept fairly busy. A few colored girls came in, but only one talked to me. She was Lee, a nice-looking, brown girl with happy eyes, who lived with her mother and sisters down the street from the store.

"What time you get off tonight?" she asked.

"I don't know. When they close, I guess."

"My God," she said softly, half-smiling. "That'll be midnight! I'll wait for you if my mother don't make me go in. I'll be just outside the door."

Lee was right. Every time I untied my apron, Mrs. Smith found something else for me to do. By a quarter to eleven I was free and tired. Selling chairs and tables was much easier than selling a peck of potatoes, and Mrs. Smith used a cash register, not a simple ledger book.

"I thought you'd never come," said Lee. "My mother's sitting on our step; let's walk the other way."

We walked a block or two in silence, but it was a friendly silence. I could feel Lee's warmness, her easy zest for life. The tree-lined street was dark, here and there shot through with moonlight, and there was the smell of summer roses on the night air. We passed by little houses, big houses, close-clipped lawns,

160

well-tended hedges, bare yards, rusty gates: homes of colored people, rows and rows of houses owned by or rented to colored people. Occasionally we passed young colored couples, quiet, respectable people, strolling along in the darkness, and I stared as Miss Breen and the white kids had once stared at me. This, then, was the life I had dreamed about, the people I belonged to. Soon I, too, would be one of them, welcome within their gates.

"Where you from?" Lee was asking.

"Mandan. Mandan, North Dakota."

"Ain't it awful cold up there in the winter?"

"Not so very."

"Not many colored folks up there, are there?"

"No."

"You'll like it here after you get acquainted." We turned and started walking back. "But these Negroes ain't going to be very friendly to you at first. Unless you're dressed to death or got money to burn, they can't see you for dust."

"Do you work?" I asked, changing the subject. I didn't want to think about their not liking me.

"Yes, it's just a little old piece of a job, working for a white lady, doing housework. It's hard work, but she pays pretty good, and Ma always needs the money."

We stopped in front of a white-looking woman sitting in the shadows of the trees on the steps of a wooden porch; two little brown girls were curled up beside her.

"Leona?" asked the woman irritably. "Where in God's name have you been?"

"Ma, this is Era Bell, the new girl that's working for Old Lady Smith."

"Umph. God help her!" The woman frowned.

"She just got through a little while ago. I waited for her."

"Well, this is no time of night for decent girls to be walking the streets. I don't allow my girls to do it," she said pointedly.

Lee was right about a lot of things, especially the girls and boys in the neighborhood. There were few enough white-collar jobs for colored in St. Paul, and they resented my coming from

161

out of town and taking a job that should have been theirs.

Mrs. Smith paid me only five dollars a week, then cut it to four when I got a typing job one day a week for the Twin Cities' representative of the *Defender*. The job terminated abruptly when Tom came over to see me one night, the first night I was late, and my employer let me out of his car at 9:30. Tom's fears were realized.

One day a handsome young man came into the store and asked for me. "Miss Thompson?" he said. "I'm Claude Neal. Don't you remember me? I spent a summer at your farm." He turned to Mrs. Smith. "She was just a little girl last time I saw her. Used to hold her on my lap." He smiled at my embarrassment. "My mother wants to meet you. I've told her so much about your folks, she wants you to come over to dinner Sunday. Sort of pay back some of the good meals I used to eat at your house out in Dakota. You'll come, won't you?"

I looked at Mrs. Smith. "Why, of course she will." Mrs. Smith was flattered for me. The Neals were *something* in St. Paul.

"All right, then, I'll be by at two."

Claude smiled his slow smile, and I was in love all over again.

Sneaking out of the store, I ran over to Lee's house. She couldn't believe it. Why, I didn't know you knew him! Everybody in town's crazy about that man. I'm going to tell Myrtle; I want to see her fat face when I tell her!" Lee sobered. "What you going to wear? His ritzy sister will be there; she's a singer in St. Louis, girl, you're really in society now!"

I wasn't thinking so much of society as I was about what to wear. It meant spending part of my college savings to buy a dress; and this sister and the rest of his family—they sounded awful.

By the time Claude arrived Sunday I was a nervous wreck. I fidgeted with my gloves—Lee had insisted on the gloves—and I squirmed in my new girdle. Mrs. Neal met us at the door and kissed me. In the living room I met the young Neals, the father, and the beauteous Ruth, tall, poised, and gay. Ruth crossed her legs and lit a cigarette. I couldn't smoke. I couldn't even get my legs crossed, for they kept slipping off my pudgy knees, and when I sat back on the davenport they stuck straight out in front of me. When I sat on the edge, my back tired. I wished I hadn't come.

Dinner was a nightmare.

The table was full of gleaming silver and sparkling glasses with tall, delicate stems. I sat paralysed between Claude and Ruth. While the plates were being served, I studied the intricate salad and the top-heavy glass of tea and decided against them. The family began to eat. I put my fork into the mashed potatoes—one could always count on mashed potatoes—and was halfway to my mouth with it when Claude spoke to me. I jumped, and the fork clattered noisily against the plate. Ruth came to my rescue.

"Dad," she called to her father, "who waved your hair?" All eyes turned to the end of the table. "That's a two-dollar marcel if I ever saw one; and at your age, too. Ma, you'd better watch him. These old men in their second childhood are a riot!" She launched into a long story about an old man she had met in St. Louis. All through the meal she kept the floor, kept them off of me. I shall never forget Ruth Neal as long as I live.

That night over on Lee's steps, minus the gloves and girdle, I gave a glowing account of the day. "After dinner," I said dreamily, "Claude and I were at last alone."

"Where didja go?" asked Lee breathlessly.

"Oh, in the back yard under a tree."

Her eyes popped. "What did he say?" She jumped up. "You gotta tell me!" She pulled me into the house, into her mother's bedroom and locked the door. "Did—he kiss you?" she whispered. "Come on, you can tell me."

"You won't tell anyone?"

"Cross my heart, hope to die."

"Well, we were out under that tree for two hours, Lee, but all I did was hand him tools while he worked on his car."

163

"The rat!" said Lee slowly, softly. "That damned, low-down, dirty rat!"

When September came I was glad to leave St. Paul, glad to get away from grocery stores and restaurants and rows of colored houses and colored people's gates—gates where I was still a stranger—and colored boys and girls who did not want me; to get away from greasy food and the acrid smoke of barbecue stands, from strange seafoods and slimy okra dishes. I felt hemmed in, apart from the rest of the world. I was willing to give all the beautiful flowers in St. Paul for one ragged tumbleweed, all the beautiful lakes in Minnesota for one alkaline slough. In all the Twin Cities I would miss only Lee.

After I bought my ticket and a few clothes from the money I had saved and that Tom had given me, I had only sixty dollars left, thirty for tuition and thirty for books and living expenses until I could find a place to work. And that was another thing. I had gotten the name of a Grand Forks family, the Walkers, out of the colored paper, and had written them about temporary quarters; but they had not answered.

So on Friday the thirteenth, a rainy Friday in mid-September, I set out for a strange town in North Dakota to work my way through college with nothing to offer but my hands.

10)   WORKING MY WAY

It was raining hard when the train stopped at Grand Forks. For a while I was lost in the mob of hilarious students who jammed the platform of the tiny depot. Frat brothers and sorority sisters loudly acclaimed old students, and Big Sister representatives came to the rescue of bewildered freshmen, but nothing happened to me.

Cold rain pelted against my Sears Roebuck coat, and the rabbit-fur hem hung its hairs and wept. The platform was deserted now. Across the street hung the dripping blue sign of the Young Women's Christian Association. Picking up my bag, I walked over to the building and stepped inside. The woman at the desk looked startled.

"Could I get . . ."

"We're all filled up. I'm sorry!" she said.

They probably were filled up, but I don't think she was

165

sorry. By now the cheap, rust-colored coat was giving off muddy orange rivulets that drained into the unhappy border, paused, then streaked madly down my beige stockings. The once perky hat was slowly taking on the shape of a welder's helmet. I, too, was sorry—a sorry sight to behold.

I hadn't the heart to try the hotels, so there was but one thing left to do: find the Walkers. It was growing late now, and the chill dampness was pressing against my skin. Finding my way back to the depot, I asked the ticket agent if he knew of a colored family by that name.

"Jim Walker, the brakeman? Great big fella?"

I didn't know about that, but there couldn't be two in a town that size. "Yes, Jim Walker. Could you tell me where he lives?"

The man came out of the cage and walked over to the door. "You go right down thata way, beyond the tracks, and turn left a bit. It's a nice yella house with a fence around it."

My eyes followed the stubby pointing finger "down thata way" to a narrow, muddy path that led straight into a large junkyard. I looked despairingly at my stained stockings. A yellow house was all I needed. "Thank you," I said, and went back out into the rain.

Past the junkyard, a block farther down the unpaved street, was a yellow house—a house so much nicer than the surrounding homes I began to wonder if maybe there weren't two Jim Walkers, after all. I opened the iron gate and walked up to the front door. From within came the sound of music—a high soprano voice rising above the automatic rhythm of a player piano. Not the husky, forced voice of the colored blues singers in the restaurants and honky-tonks of St. Paul, but a voice that rose above the rain and soared out upon the muggy afternoon air like the voice of an angel. But angels sing Handel—this was Handy and "The St. Louis Blues." It was the right house, all right.

Suddenly the music stopped. I knocked. I could not see them, but I could feel their eyes through the curtains. I knocked again. Slowly the door opened a little, and a middle-aged, brown

166

woman peered through the crack.

"Do the Walkers live here? Are you Mrs. Walker?" I asked.

"Yes," she said reluctantly. "What do you want?"

"I'd like to get a room for the night," I began. Three small heads appeared below the woman's face.

"Git!" The voice of the singer came from somewhere within the house, unmusical now, ringing out sharp as steel, piercing the rain, shooting through the three little brown bodies, and snatching them away as if by an unseen hand.

The woman's unwelcoming eyes were still upon me. "Do you take in—could you let me stay here tonight?" I asked.

"No."

The upper part of my coat was light tan now, and the fur had shrunk into a hard, dark line. Mrs. Walker looked at my coat. "I'm expecting my sister soon. We have no extra room."

"Do you know of any place where I might stay? I just got into town."

"I'm sorry, no!" She shut the door.

I turned and walked slowly away. Well, I'd take the first train back—back anywhere, it didn't matter—but secretly I hoped it wouldn't be St. Paul. I was ashamed to go home to Pop defeated, not even able to find a room in a strange town.

"Oh, miss, miss!" Mrs. Walker stood at the gate waving me back. "Are you Miss Thompson, are you the lady that wrote about going to the university?"

"Y-y-yes," I stammered.

"Come back," she said, holding open the gate. "I thought you were a street woman." Too happy to be offended, I followed her into the house. "We have to be careful," she was saying as she opened the door to her bedroom, "so many stray women stop in here asking for a place to stay." A small brown pool of water began to form at my feet. "You poor child, you must be nearly drowned." The voice was kind and motherly now. It made me want to cry.

"I wrote to you," I said, my teeth chattering from the rain and cold.

"Yes, I got your letter," she said, helping me out of my wet

167

things and into some of her dry ones. "I told Gertrude, that's my daughter." The woman peered over her glasses towards the closed door and lowered her voice. "All them kids is hers."

Gertrude was a small, coffee-colored girl with big black eyes and a pretty little heart-shaped face. It was hard to believe the three children were hers. It was also hard to believe, as I sat at the family table, that the woman who was heaping my plate so generously was the same woman who had turned me away less than an hour before.

It was a good meal, with lots of food and little adult conversation, but there was commotion at the younger end of the table, where Gertrude presided over her brood with a deft destructiveness that would have struck terror into the hearts of the more mature. Twice, when the situation became too vocal, Jim Walker laid down his knife and fork and pushed his chair back ever so little. The results were magic.

"So you're from Bismarck," said the big man, addressing me directly for the first time. It was more a comment than a question. Evidently he didn't think too highly of the Bismarck Negroes.

While Gertrude refereed the children through the dishes, Jim Walker brought a small bottle of dandelion wine from the cellar. I took mine doubtfully. I didn't like wine, but I never knew how much until I tasted the bitter brew of the little wild flowers.

"Jim likes you," said Mrs. Walker. "When he opens his dandelion wine, he likes you."

Early Monday morning I was across the tracks and over to University Avenue waiting for the streetcar. A funny little humpty-dumpty thing rocked down the tracks. As I stood at the rear, the front opened, closed, and the car was gone. Both sides of the broad street were filled with students hurrying towards the university. Another trolley approached, and I ran to the front. The back opened, and again I was left in the street.

A flivver full of hatless college youths slowed down. "Well, shut mah mouth, honeychile!" one mimicked. "Does you-all

168

want a ride?" They laughed and drove on.

I began walking up the long street, the crisp, clean breeze in my face, above me the blue skies of my North Dakota. I wanted to run, to escape the impending ordeal of entering a strange school, facing a new student body. This time there was no Jessie to take my hand, no principal to follow. Awe filled me as I neared fraternity row with its beautiful brick mansions, its long English manor houses, its big white Colonial houses, each with its odd Greek symbol, each pouring out its contribution to the school. I followed the students inside the campus, past the Law Building, the Science Hall, the Commons, and on to the Woman's Gymnasium. Students stared at me, nudged each other. Some smiled, nobody spoke.

In the gym, I fell in line under the "Freshman" sign and waited my turn. When I reached the first desk, the man looked up and smiled. He did not seem surprised. "So you want to enroll, too, do you?"

"Yes," I said.

"Take these over there to the table," he said, handing me the forms. "Fill them out, then bring them back to me."

When I returned, he was busy. They motioned me on to the next registrar, but I waited for the man who had smiled. "From Bismarck," he commented pleasantly, taking my papers.

"And Mandan," I added out of loyalty.

"Wait a minute, what have we here?" He began to read aloud the subjects I had selected. "Physical Education, Sports, Music Appreciation, Advanced Sports, Reporting." He began to laugh, and the man beside him looked up and laughed, too, as if they were glad to have something to break the monotony of registration. "You've got to take something besides athletics, Miss Thompson. Both Journalism and Music Appreciation are advanced courses. How much music have you had?"

"None," I said, ignoring those two encounters with the "First Waltz."

"Then why do you want to take Music Appreciation?"

I was embarrassed. "Athletics are pretty strenuous. I thought maybe appreciation would be kind of restful. I'm working my way," I added hastily.

He fumbled with the catalog, and the man next to him coughed. "Here," he said kindly, picking up a new blank. "There are certain subjects all freshmen are required to take. Let's get them down first, then we'll see what we can do about these others." The first thing he wrote was Physical Education.

After I paid my fees I was sent to the Dean of Women for placement. All the college jobs were filled, she said, as were most of the desirable places in private homes, but she gave me a list of names of job possibilities. She wasn't very encouraging.

Classes didn't begin until the following week, so the next morning I set out bright and early to find a home, trying the ones closest to the campus first. All had someone or they expected someone or they were sorry, they didn't think I'd do. I worked down the list and down University Avenue with the same results. One lady who kept roomers and owned a grocery store gave me half a promise. There was washing and ironing and scrubbing and cooking—hard work, she said quite frankly, and she wasn't at all sure I could do it; but if I didn't find anything else, I should come back and she'd give me a try. I returned to the Walkers' tired and discouraged.

"You won't find many places in this town that will take you," said Mrs. Walker. "They're awfully prejudiced here."

"But why?" I asked.

"I don't know. Used to be lots of colored folks here, nice people with families, but they all moved away. We and Jordans are the only ones left, except a few stray men. Wasn't for Jim's job on the railroad we wouldn't be here either."

"Aren't there any colored students at the university?"

"Lord, no! I think there was one boy a long time ago. He was studying to be a doctor or lawyer or something, I don't remember which, it's been so long."

Gertrude came in from the kitchen. "Find anything, hon?"

"Not much. Got half a promise, but I don't think she means it."

170

"What about Opal, Ma? She's looking for somebody."

Jim Walker looked up from his paper. "Her live at Blocks?"

"Beats nothing," said Gertrude. "Would be all right until she could get something else."

"Who is Opal?" I asked.

"She's a Jewish neighbor. She's got a little girl—a red-headed little girl." Mrs. Walker looked at me significantly, but I had white-headed cousins, so the inference was lost.

"Opal's all right. She's good-hearted, she'd do anything for us, divide her last crust of bread. Course she's a little wild," said Mrs. Walker.

"Lord God!" breathed Gertrude softly. "A *little* wild!"

After supper Opal Block was sent for. She was tall, with dark, luminous eyes; a mass of curly blue-black hair almost hid her sallow face, and a nervous inner drive made her sharp and jumpy, witty and profane—very profane. When Opal went home that night, I was with her.

The Blocks lived in a small house on that part of Grove Street that was known as "Little Jerusalem." My trunk and clothes were placed in the tiny entrance hall against the front door that was seldom used, and I slept on the davenport.

"I'm going to call you Thompson," said Opal. "Era Bell is too goddamn hard to remember." I winced, and she giggled. "What's the matter, Thompson? Didn't you ever hear anybody swear before?"

"Well, not very much."

"Then hold on to your pants, kid, you're going to hear plenty around here!" Opal liked to swear. She swore gleefully, naturally, without malice; swore at first to shock me, then tried to make me swear, too. She'd say, "Say, 'goddamn,' Thompson. Come on and say it!"

I wouldn't swear, so she swore to tease me.

Lucy and Sol swore, too. Lucy was four, and tougher than any little boy twice her age. Sol Block, who sold fish to farmers, was away most of the time. So was Opal. She was out of the house and across the vacant lot to her mother's as soon as she

171

got dressed, sometimes before. She never told me what to do. "Do what you got time for, do what you want to," she'd say. "Hell, Thompson, you know as much about this damn house as I do!" So she cooked the meals, and I did the cleaning, and we sent the laundry out. Lucy ran wild.

It was a long time before I could eat at the Blocks'. The kitchen table stood in front of a window which looked directly out on the chicken coop, where ugly, gray chickens hopped around on one foot, heads down, feathers moldy. I sat facing them except when Sol was away; then I sat at the end of the table and kept my eyes away from the window, but I had to look at Lucy. They carried her to breakfast right from bed, crusty and warm with sleep, her little girl body nude from the waist down. I could ignore the chickens, but I couldn't ignore the child without jeopardizing my happy home. Before the meal was over, many times before it began, we had company. We never ate without company. Opal's brothers, the two Bloom boys, Pa Bloom, Sol's friends, the Shohet, with his bleary eyes, long white beard, and black skull cap, came one by one, surrounding us at the table, sitting on the sink, on the floor, on the door of the oven, waving their hands, all talking in Yiddish at once. Now and then I caught a word. Moid meant me, but I couldn't tell if it was good or bad. I spent my carfare for cookies and jelly-centered bismarcks and walked to school up the back road along the railroad tracks where no one could see me eating.

I was crossing the campus to Freshman English when I ran into my old friend Gwyn. She wasn't in any of my classes, but I'd be seeing her in gym, she said, and told me to be sure to sign up for hockey. I'd make a good halfback. I caught a glimpse of Red and some of the others from Bismarck now and then. A few seemed embarrassed when they met me—when they were with their new friends—but most of them were the same.

A college classroom was much different from high school. Professors assigned long lessons, twenty—thirty pages at a time, called us "Miss" or "Mister," and were nonchalant, sometimes bored; but there were some, thank goodness, who didn't mind

172

teaching for a living. Like Mr. Lewis, the rhetoric teacher. He was young and good-looking and human—so human he stopped right in the middle of class one day to see if he could hear a pin drop. He asked the kind of questions that brought on that kind of silence. Professor Hart, the sociology teacher, was another one who made learning pleasant. When I found out he was from Tennessee, it was too late. I already liked him.

Hockey was a strange game. We played in the field behind the gym with clumsy shin guards and big curved sticks, charging at each other in wild pursuit of a little white thing called a puck. It was a kind of ground tennis with a golf-stick-patty-cake takeoff. When we practiced with the sophs, Gwyn and I raced and yelled like in the old days in high school. It was beautiful out there in the golden autumn sunshine, in the warm stillness of a Dakota afternoon. There was an equality of living and playing in which rich girls, poor girls, city girls, farm girls, freshmen, and seniors, were measured by the strength of their arms, the speed of their feet, the accuracy of their aim. So I ran fast and aimed high—so high I knocked a girl's legs out from under her, breaking my stick, but I made the freshman and varsity teams, getting 125 points towards my cup.

Dora Gordon was my best friend at school. Dora was essentially a nonconformist, and it was her admiration for the athletic, her love for the underdog, that brought us together. Sororities to her were snobbish and undemocratic, so we organized the Barb Club, an anti-sorority organization with two members. There were a lot of students who weren't rushed or pledged who found solace in the Y, in literary or musical clubs, but not Dora. She had been asked to join a sorority, but had refused. I hadn't been asked. Opal's brother said they didn't take Jews or Negroes or dogs. He said it was written in their charters. I didn't know whether to believe him or not, but I wasn't too disturbed, because I couldn't have afforded it anyway. So for a time, a very brief time, Dora and I wore one canvas glove and one overshoe and set out to reform the college world. The first cold spell ended our campaign.

173

Walking down University Avenue after hockey practice one evening, I told Dora about Opal's swearing.

"Why don't you tell the Dean?" she asked. "Off-campus homes are supposed to be approved; they're supposed to be investigated."

After classes the next day, I told my story to the Dean.

"Do you work hard?" she asked.

"Not very. They send the washing out, and I don't cook, but I do all the rest of the work."

"Do you have to be home at certain hours?"

"No. She doesn't care as long as I do my work."

"Then forget the swearing," she said. "I haven't any place to offer you, and if this woman is good to you . . ."

"Oh, yes, she is," I said quickly. "I'm just not used to that kind of language."

"Then make the best of it." She smiled. "Remember, nobody can make you bad unless you really want to be."

"She thinks it's all right," I complained to Dora. "She's condoning it."

"Maybe," grinned my pal, "the old goat swears herself. I'll bet she swears a blue streak."

Dora was a bit remiss herself. She had a habit of saying "Oh, God" to everything. I said "ain't" and a lot more things unbecoming a college student, so we began to reform each other. Every time Dora said "Oh, God," I hit her—not very hard—just enough to make her remember, and vice versa, but I got so many slaps, she increased her sinning to even it up. Dora's father was a retired teacher, and she probably used good English all her life; but my father's self-education, mixed with a "Yah, yah" and an "Ach, ach," and my more recently acquired "I yi yi," gave me a strange vocabulary indeed.

I was enjoying the "I yi yi" now and all that went with it, including the food. I didn't have to eat the food, because the Blocks had instructed the store on the corner to let me have anything I wanted on their account, but I was developing a taste for lokshen and kosher fleish cooked with garlic and Mrs. Bloom's

174

cabbage borscht. When Opal called me a kike, it was like Harry calling me a darky, for I was now one of them, running over to Ma Bloom's every other minute, jumping their fence like the boys, sharing Ma's scoldings as well as her food. I liked to watch her roll out the squares of flour-egg dough and fill them with chopped meat for the kreplach, to watch her make strudel and cookies, and to fight with the boys over the icing pans. I played football in the streets with the Grove Street Roughnecks, and at night helped them with their homework and told them about the university. Ma Bloom liked that. "See," she'd say, boxing them on the ears and pointing to me. "You should listen to that one. Some day you should be smart like her, too."

I hadn't been in Grand Forks long when I attended my first shindig. Early that evening neighbors began gathering in the Walkers' big living room. The guitarist came with his toothless second wife; Hal, the only Jordan who wasn't feuding with the Walkers, brought his drums and his Norwegian bride; and an ex-boxer with cauliflower ears brought his banjo. Joe Green, the same Joe Green from Bismarck, played the piano when he was in town—and out of jail. When he wasn't, they put a roll on the player, and the party ran to polkas and Hawaiian waltzes. Negroes, Jews, Irish, and Scandinavians came. There was an old lady with a goiter and one blue, one green, eye; an old man who was stone deaf; Mable, the fresh waitress; Duke, the fence—all dancing, eating, having fun.

I didn't know then the Duke was a fence. He was a tall, slippery-looking black man, with tight lips and shifty eyes. The first time I danced with him, he offered to buy me a new coat. I told Gertrude.

"If he asks to take you home, don't go with him," she warned. "Tell him you're with Opal. He's no good."

I told him, and he took both of us home.

Several strange colored men with strange names came to the Forks that winter, and, in one unpleasant way or another, I met most of them. When String Beans and Canned Heat, the Duke's cohorts, wanted to start a show with me as leading lady, I knew there was something wrong, because I wasn't show material.

"He ain't no more got a show than I have," said Opal. "That goddamned liar's just trying to get you over there. Don't you go, Thompson!"

So I never got to be a leading lady.

Jim Walker conducted the services at the little colored church on Second Avenue when the woman from the uptown mission wasn't there, and on those nights the Jordans didn't come. Each family had its side of the church, and even the kids dared not cross the aisle. Having been befriended by the dark-skinned Walkers, I owed them my allegiance, but, on the other hand, I had nothing against the fair-skinned Jordans, so I sat with the Walkers and smiled at the Jordans and hoped the Jordans understood, because they had a daughter about my age and a very cute son.

It was during a Sunday evening service that I ran amuck with Boston, a drifter like the others, only better looking, better dressed, and much smoother. No one seemed to know what he did for a living until that night just before the collection— he lifted my ten dollars. No one saw him do it, but he was sitting in front of me, his arm over the back of the seat and the coin purse was on my lap. Then it wasn't. We looked and looked, but no purse. When Boston went over by the door to whisper to the Duke, Mr. Walker got suspicious.

"Nobody leaves this church until we find the money," he said. "And if we don't find it, I'm going to search everybody in here!"

The Jordans bristled. No Walker was going to search them. In the confusion that followed, Boston disappeared, and I was given the evening's collection, nearly fifteen dollars.

My interest in writing met with unexpected encouragement and a few setbacks. Mr. Lewis read my first theme, a short autobiography, to the class. When he finished, he said, "Well, Miss Thompson, there isn't much of yourself; there are many misspelled words; but the general impression is so good that I can't help it. 'A!'" My next theme was a little more daring, less conventional, for here in college they took the broad view, they let you out on your own. For a while my papers returned with the neat praise for the writing and subtle hints about spelling and construction, but I paid small heed. It was during the height of the Darwin controversy, and I put everything I had into an article entitled "Evolution." The gist of it was that women were fine people, but all men were monkeys—and I misspelled "monkeys."

I followed the theme into Mr. Lewis' office.

He was magnificent. His phrasing, his tonal quality, his word shading, and his gestures were beautiful, dramatic. The little blond moustache didn't move, the gray eyes didn't twinkle. "You write well, I guess you know; you spell abominably, and I guess you know that, too." He was cold, cutting, precise. "It's about time, Miss Thompson, that you remember to forget that you're clever and get down to the brass tacks of learning to put your cleverness into civilized art."

Still unabashed, I wrote a poem for the *Student* and dropped it in the wall box in Old Main. It was printed, and all Grove Street read it. I wrote jokes and more poems, and the editor said, "Come again, we like you." I came so often they made me humor editor, mistaking my misspelling and poor rhetoric for humor.

To get things started in my new advice to the lovelorn column, I wrote imaginary letters and signed them with random initials. With seventeen hundred names, I couldn't go far without getting a right combination. I soon found out "B. J." was a well-known coed, and she wasn't about to elope with "L. W.," president of the Student Council, and there was double trouble, so I went back to conducting the hard way. I wrote poetry in bed by flashlight and made up jokes instead of taking notes in sociology, and Mr. Hart, not knowing what to make of the sudden rapt attention, gave me 90 on conscientious endeavor. The South wasn't half bad.

My schedule was heavy that winter with basketball practice two nights a week, three pages of humor four days a week, housework, homework, classes—and Lucy. I had to watch Lucy for self-protection. Sol didn't always bother calling in the Shohet to slit the chickens' throat kosher fashion, it being much easier —and cheaper—to wring their necks and throw them on the pantry floor. I had to watch the pantry to see when Sol threw them in and watch Lucy to see when she dragged them out. Lucy loved dead chickens, and you know how I feel. Lucy loved tools and weapons, too. She was happy when she was hammering nails in the table or sawing the legs off the furniture with butcher knives, so I'd put a big piece of stove wood on a chair, sit on one end of it and study political science, while she sawed on the other end. It was dangerous, but somehow that saw brought me closer to understanding the ways of the government than anything else.

I never put Lucy to bed—just waited until she fell asleep over her strange playthings, then carried her to the bedroom and coaxed off her clothes. When Sol was away and Opal was running around at night, I had to do a lot of bluffing if Lucy awoke. I'd go in the darkened room and play Sol with an "Oiy yoi yoi, mine babla, mine pootsala, mine krapala," and shake the bed hard. If she continued to howl, I'd play Opal and tell her to go to hell. If she yelled loud enough, Ma Bloom would hear and come running. I didn't like for this to happen, because right away she'd start asking for her daughter, and I never had a good answer. Then she'd call me a liar, cuss out her daughter's soul, and put the kid to sleep all in one triad. I never did learn her routine.

With the approach of Christmas I was the only one in Little Jerusalem with the Christmas spirit, so I asked Opal if I couldn't tell Lucy about Santa Claus and give her a gift. "She doesn't have to believe it," I explained. "I'll tell her it's just a story."

"She'll believe it, all right. She believes every damn thing you tell her. What about that line about your two little sons in jail and your husband in the Old Country?"

When Lucy got out of hand, I found it expedient to

threaten to leave and go to jail to see those two sons. "But it can't hurt her. When she gets in school, she'll hear about it anyway."

"Sure, go on, goddamn you, I don't care. But if you tell Ma, I'll kill you sure as hell!"

The night before I went home for Christmas vacation Lucy and I hung our stockings behind the hard-coal heater. When she went to sleep Opal called me to the kitchen. "You and your damned Santa Claus! I spent the whole radio payment." She began taking packages out of the pantry. The radio payment was ten dollars, but she had spent as much as eighteen dollars for silk underwear and told Sol she put it on the furniture bill. I don't think she fooled him any, because he could count better than he could read, but he never said anything about the bills until he got very drunk, then he sang and cursed and itemized each one at the top of his voice.

"Here, take this junk and go stick it in your stockings. Pull down all the shades, too; I've got a tree, and if Ma finds out, she'll have a set of dishes, and if the Shohet comes in, I'll have another redheaded baby, and I'll name it after you, Thompson!"

So in the wee hours of the night, Santa Claus sneaked into Little Jerusalem, and he did quite well, thank you, for both Lucy and me.

Tom paid my tuition for the second semester, and with an occasional cash donation from Harry and the ten dollars a month from Pop, wrapped in letters he had picked out laboriously on my old Oliver—for at seventy Pop was learning to type—I managed to take care of expenses. Clothes weren't much of a problem because we wore coats in all classes except gym, but carfare counted up. When Sol was home, he took me to school in the car, and sometimes the Bloom brothers ran me out in their truck. On practice days I walked the two miles at least one way, and that helped.

Soon deep in the activities of the campus, I made the basketball and volleyball teams and played on the non-sorority team in intramural tournaments. The Dean of Women was scanning my poems in her literature classes, and the coach was telling his frat brothers unbelievable tales of my feats on the basketball floor. Rumors of what went on in Mr. Lewis' class caused a number of students to request transfers to Rhetoric I. I didn't walk down the back road so much any more, only when I wanted to think or when I got lonesome for the prairie grass and the floating clouds, for on University Avenue there was Alpha, boasting of our friendship in Bismarck, and Louise Banks, the journalism student, who put me on the *Stadium* staff during the fund drive and got the sports editor of the *Grand Forks Herald* to take my articles on women's athletics. Louise was always in the midst of a love problem, and that spring it was a toss-up between a Swedish reporter and a Hindu chemist, and I wasn't a bit of help.

I had kept none of the Jewish holy days, Yom Kippur, Rosh Hashana, or Purim, but having given Lucy a Christian Christmas, I was willing to accept Pesach in all its fullness: matzot, the latkes, and lokshen soup, and the special delicacies. All went well for a day or two, and then Opal and I got hungry for bread and butter.

"Thompson," she said, "they won't suspect you. Go over to the store and get a loaf of bread and a half-pound of butter. I'm damned near starved. Come back by Second Avenue, and for God's sake don't let Ma see you."

We sent Lucy out to play with Rebecca's little girl, and after pulling down all the shades, feasted on pumpernickel bread and butter and boiled chicken. In the midst of our eating, Pa Bloom came around the house. We dived into the bedroom, bread, butter, and all. Pa came into the kitchen, stood there a few minutes, then went out again.

"Oh, God!" said Opal. "I swallowed the tail bone, the whole damned tail bone!"

We ate until we couldn't hold any more, then we hid what was left out in the hall behind my trunk. The chicken had been sitting on the back of the warm range for a long time, but we didn't realize how long until late that night.

We met at the bathroom door. "Merry Christmas," said Opal.

"Happy Easter," I replied. "You look worse than I do; you go first."

As soon as the ground dried and track practice began I got up half an hour earlier every morning and ran around the block, arms bent, knees high, breathing from the chest. We were entering a telegraphic meet with DePauw, and competition was keen. Those stories about Fargo were catching up with me, so I had to make good. Working out in the department's only pair of spike shoes, eating a special diet, and being rubbed down daily with alcohol helped, of course, but most of my success on the day of the meet was due to the Second Avenue Church and what happened there the Sunday before.

The woman from the mission had preached the sermon, collection had been taken, and we waited expectantly for the orchestra to do what it could with a hymn. They filed up to the front of the room, the guitar player with his guitar, the drummer, for obvious reasons, switching to the organ, and the ex-boxer, resplendent in tux and banjo. Joe Green was in the congregation. He was in jail when the orchestra practiced, and they didn't need him now. He began to protest. He said it was against the rules of the union, whether he belonged to the union or not—and he did not—so if he didn't play, they wouldn't either. The lady preacher beckoned the men to begin. I kept my eyes on Joe. His hands were twitching and his eyes were red like fire, but he didn't seem to have a gun. They said he once shot up a deacon's davenport in Devil's Lake. I was thinking about Devil's Lake and the way it got its name, when Joe suddenly stood up and approached the front of the church. The orchestra was playing "Crown Him Lord of All."

Joe Green did. Taking a quick step forward, he wrenched the banjo from the startled hands of the ex-boxer and raised it above his head. I was five rows down the Walker side when Joe

181

let him have it. I was up by the corner of the junkyard when the first part of the congregation emerged from the church. First came the kids, then Joe with the lady preacher hanging desperately to his coattail; then Mr. Walker and the mild Mr. Jordan, pleading; then the ex-boxer, bleeding, bits of banjo around his neck.

We won the track meet. I broke five North Dakota records, tied two national intercollegiate, and ran anchor in the relays— and again Grove Street rejoiced while I scrubbed and cleaned because, records or no records, it was Saturday afternoon. When I sent Pop the clippings and pictures from the Sunday paper, even Uncle John admitted that maybe a little education wasn't too dangerous a thing.

Before the year was over, I made peace with Mr. Lewis by turning in a flawless book review of a book I never read, and, in return for the "A" he gave me, I presented him with Little Thunder, a garter snake I found dying on the campus. With all his pink-ribboned finery and fruit-jar caging, Thunder wasn't received with enthusiasm.

"Thank you," Mr. Lewis said. "You don't know how deeply this touches me. I shall never forget you, Miss Thompson." I looked back when I got to the door, and he was half out of his seat like he was going somewhere—to open the window, for instance, because Little Thunder was dead, a long time dead.

When I was summoned to the office of the Dean of Women a day later, the case of Little Thunder lay heavily upon me. The Dean held out her hand. "Congratulations. I hear you've been elected one of the seven most athletic coeds on the campus."

"Thanks," I said, wondering when she'd get around to the snake.

"I'm proud of you," she said. "You've done all right in the past nine months; creating quite a stir in literary circles, too, Mr. Lewis tells me." So she knew, and she was smiling. "How about next year?" she continued. "I think I can fix you up with a nice place, one near the campus. I know of two or three people who would like to have you."

"But I have a place. I've already told her I'd be back."

"The swearing lady?"

I nodded. "She still swears, and she's still very good to me. Thanks, but I'd rather stay where I am."

That night I took the back road home, and home was Grove Street.

11) DISASTER

Vacation in Mandan was dull after the excitement of college. I spent the summer preparing to return and conquer the world. From Father I wrung money for new clothes, but he said I'd have to find some way to earn carfare, so bicycle joined trunk in the baggage car, and transportation difficulties were partially solved.

Muriel, oldest of the three Jordan girls, entered the university that fall. Muriel was pretty and dainty and allergic to athletics, but we found a common lack of interest in European history and joined the Cosmopolitan Club along with other minorities—and found Africa represented by an Englishman.

Beginning the year with an all-out for dear old alma mater, I got as far as women's sports editor on *The Student* and all-varsity in soccer when things began to happen. First I caught scarlet fever, and for three weeks Lucy and I rashed and burned, while Sol peddled his fish in the country, and Opal fretted under the quarantine.

"Let's get drunk, Thompson," she said one day, appraising Sol's barrel of grape wine brewing on the porch. "Let's see how it feels."

I didn't think wine would do it, but it did. Pa Bloom, who was immune to signs, came over and sat with Lucy while we slept it off. When I was again free to return to classes, hockey was over, but not my troubles. Coal gas escaping from the heater one night put me in a fair way of missing a lot more things than hockey. Opal, herself partially overcome, stumbled to the phone and called the folks. Pa Bloom, again coming to our rescue, found her slumped over a chair and me on all fours circling the dining room table. Lucy was sound asleep. Newspaper accounts of our asphyxiation were good for three class cuts and a movie.

Next I caught a train. Muriel, Izzy Krueger, and I usually crossed the track by the junkyard, taking the short cut to University Avenue, thus saving ten to fifteen precious minutes. On this particular morning, following a heavy snowfall, we were already late when we reached the tracks, so when a long freight blocked our path—headed towards the university—Izzy said, "Let's hop it." Muriel was hesitant, her father being a railroad man, but we were two against one. Izzy put our books and purses in his briefcase so our hands would be free, and when a flatcar glided by we jumped on. It was fun. We waved to trainmen as we passed, and they waved back, cheerfully at first, then excitedly, pointing to the ground and yelling, but we couldn't understand what they were saying. The train gradually picked up speed. We neared the athletic field, and still there was no sign of slowing down. Izzy looked at us and shrugged. Trains usually stopped at the siding behind the powerhouse, but not this one. Izzy yelled to us to jump, and led the way just to show how easy it was; then I took off. It felt just like flying, only my wings were under me like feet. Muriel made a perfect one-point landing, head first in a snowbank, and two long, skinny legs waved in the morning air.

185

Mr. Jordan got a letter from the safety-first department of the railroad company, and Muriel said I'd better meet her on the avenue for a while, until her dad cooled off.

After my experience with Grand Forks men, I was a little skeptical of Otto, a dining-car cook. When he offered to take me to a show, I said yes, Gertrude and I could both go. After the show we went to a restaurant. I noticed a man take a coat from the rack, but I didn't think anything about it until a few minutes later, when a policeman came over and tapped Otto on the shoulder and asked him if the blue coat was his. Otto wasn't at all disturbed. He excused himself, paid our bill (bless him), and went with the policeman. We didn't know until we read the paper the next morning that a gun was in the coat pocket, and by that time all Grand Forks knew it, too. I read the article and breathed a prayer of thanks. It said ". . . two lady companions." Praise Allah, no names.

Chemistry and German got more and more in the way of my athletic schedule; then suddenly chemistry closed in upon me. Johnny Kelly, our lab teacher, was an easygoing senior, long on patience and short on words, but even Johnny had his limits, and they were reached the morning I took the instructions too far. Our experiment called for ice, which the storeroom didn't have, so I borrowed the janitor's long-handled shovel, got it full of snow, and brought it up four flights of stairs. Johnny took the shovel and the snow out, then returned and asked me to follow him. Halfway around an empty lecture hall on the way to his office, I stopped. He didn't miss me until he reached the door, but the pause had given me time to prepare a defense. Inside the office Johnny hesitated.

"Mr. Kelly," I began, hurriedly, "I'm disturbed. I seem to have gotten off on the wrong foot in your class. Nobody understands me." Johnny looked puzzled. That wasn't the way he planned it. I hurried on. "Now, take today. There wasn't any ice—I wanted to help so . . ." Johnny grinned uncomfortably, but let me finish. He fiddled about his desk a bit before we started back. At the door of the lab he stopped.

186

"Try to do a little better," he said. "And remember, *I* understand you. Perfectly!"

German was different. The lessons of Fräulein Wertz were never like this, so I appealed to Ma Bloom, who knew more languages than a Ph.D. Three nights a week, she translated and I wrote. My marks began to change. Now I was flunking. There is an inherent similarity between German and Yiddish, but the instructor wasn't interested in similarities.

Soon after Christmas, I began to get very tired. Everything was an effort. Past performance alone brought me through basketball season, and I finished volleyball scarcely able to raise my hands above my head. Thoroughly alarmed I went to the infirmary, and was told I had pleurisy. It was crazy. I felt fine, had lost weight, but that was good; now I could cross my legs, wrapping them around each other the way Opal did when she sat in Lucy's high chair; but I was tired, always tired. No more physical education, the nurse had said; but if I couldn't run and play any more, what was the good of remaining in school? The Dean urged me to finish out the year by spending my gym periods on a cot in the rest room. It was spring again, time for Pesach. In a few days track practice would begin, with its fast cinder paths, spiked shoes, soft jumping pits, fragile wood hurdles, the sharp crack of the starter's gun—and me flat on my posterior. I wrote to Pop, not that I was ill, but that I wanted to come home for Easter.

Opal and Lucy cried when I left. I had no physical pain, but the pain of parting, of leaving the school I had learned to love, was a pain far deeper than the scars on my lungs.

Traveling towards Mandan, I began to worry about going home. What could I tell Pop? How could I convince him I was sick? Maybe if I had a cold, it would look better, so I got off at every stop and walked up and down the platform without a coat, trying to catch a good, deep cold. When the train stopped at Bismarck that night, Sue got on. She looked at me sharply, but there was disappointment in her eyes, and I wondered why. A few minutes later we pulled into Mandan. Pop was there, but

187

he walked past me, not recognizing me until he saw Sue, then he looked at me, too, but he wasn't disappointed; he seemed relieved.

"Where'd you come from?" He scowled at Sue.

"Oh, I just happened to get on the same train," she lied.

"Well, what *is* the matter with you," Pop asked.

"Yes," said Sue. "We thought you were pregnant!"

By noon the next day, I was sweating it out in a pneumonia jacket at the Mandan Hospital. For days my temperature stayed above the hundred mark, my knees looked like dime store door-knobs on my flabby legs, my skin was dry and ashy. I couldn't sleep at night for watching the empty bed in my room, white and ghostly in the moonlight. I'd think about the people who died in hospitals, who had died in the other bed, in my bed, and I'd ring for the nurse, and she'd find me more wet from fear than from fever.

Pop came to see me when he could, for it was a long walk up the steep hill to the hospital. When he couldn't make it, Elsie Wagner came, Elsie and the minister and all the people I knew. I felt fine—better, I thought, than the doctor who listened to my lungs and tapped my big knees with a brass hammer. I wasn't tired any more, only weak and skinny and bloodless, but still they said I needed more rest, and that I could do at home. Uncle John and Ann offered to take me to Bismarck with them so I could get more sunshine and care, but I would not go.

All day long friends came to the store, bringing soup, home-made jelly, and flowers. The nurses from the hospital came, and so did the principal and the shorthand teacher, the choir leader, the manager of the Red Owl, and the Reverend's wife. Even people who had never come to our store before came now, came often.

Pop had his hands full with me and the store and Elsie. Playing nurse, Elsie fed me heavy pancakes hot from the hotel and kept my bed tidy. Elsie was used to making beds. Every evening she and her brothers came over and fought with me, so I let my fingernails grow to long, pointed daggers so I could

188

better defend myself. Pop told the doctor, but he said let us alone, let us fight, maybe that was what I needed. He didn't have much faith in his medicine either. Well, we threw pillows and tussled and sang until Mrs. Wagner came to take them home, and I grew stronger for it. Secretly Elsie helped me out of bed and taught me to walk again, and one day, when Pop was out, helped me to the top of the hotel roof to sun. I was back in bed a week when Elsie, satisfying a long-suppressed desire, cut off all of my hair. Looking like a bald-headed zombi, I arose from my deathbed and went to the barber's shop, cured of pleurisy and Elsie.

As soon as I was strong enough to travel, the Dahl sisters, Madge and Margie, who were spending the summer alone on their homestead, invited me to join them. The farm was forty miles away, near Fort Clark, an inland town, whose only communication with the outside world was a motor van that delivered farm machinery, mail, and people, space permitting. When I reached the little town there was no one to meet me, so I wandered up the street until I came to a house with a sign in the window proclaiming it a library. The library was a small parlor with rows of books lining two of the walls. A tall, lean woman came from the kitchen and stood in the doorway.

"How do you do," I said.

"Howdy." She was neither hostile nor friendly, but tight-lipped and silent, like mountain women in *Esquire*.

"Just looking over some of your books. Friends were to meet me, but they didn't come."

"Oh."

"You don't know anybody who could drive me out to the Dahl place, do you?"

"No."

"Nice books you have here." I picked up a chemistry text which looked vaguely familiar. The woman came a step closer.

"You like books?"

"Yes. I write, too," I said recklessly.

"Books?"

"No. Newspaper articles and poetry. Not paid things," I hastened to add. (The town wasn't *that* far inland.) "Most of it was for the university paper."

The woman perked up instantly. "You go to the university?"

"Yes, I did . . ."

"Clem! O Clem!" she called. "Clem, that's my son. He's going up there this fall." A tall youth came in from the kitchen. He stared at me, then smiled. "Clem, this girl's been to the university. You can ask her all them questions you been wantin' to know."

"Gee!" His eyes lit up with excitement, and the questions tumbled out.

Half an hour later I was sitting beside the woman in the back seat of a seven-passenger car, Clem driving and still asking questions.

Mamma had a question, too. "Say, miss," she said abruptly. "What are you anyway—an Indian?"

About two miles out of town Madge and Margie came galloping towards us, leading an extra horse for me. Clem and his mother would accept no money for the ride, and my respect for education increased.

After the first burst of conversation, the sisters and I lapsed into prairie silence. It was good to be astride a horse again, to be riding over the sage and the dry buffalo grass in the warm summer twilight. Far away in the purple distance the dark sky was closing down upon the hot earth, shutting out the tired light. Fires sprang out of the ground, little spots of flame dotting the country to the north of us as burning surface coal mines became visible. Like Indian ceremonial fires, they were, and I could almost see the red men dancing about the blaze, copper bodies bending, hatchets shining in the eerie light.

By the time we reached the farm, total darkness had come— a warm, friendly darkness, pregnant with tiny stars that pierced the sable canopy millions and millions of miles overhead. Madge made a quick wood fire in the range and prepared supper, while

Margie and I put the horses up. We sat down to eat at a little oilclothed table in the kitchen. A big white miller flew around and around the kerosene lamp, and there were the pungent odors of boiling coffee, of burning wood, and I had a strange feeling of having been there before, a vague, familiar feeling, a whimsical, nostalgic sensibility of another being in another world.

"You're home," said Madge. "Do as you please, go to bed when you want, get up when you wish, eat what we have. We don't talk much, Marg and I."

Silence was no stranger to me. Those were happy, peaceful, healing days; days in which I found my strength, got back my zest for living. There I saw my first spring, its clear, cold water spouting from the pebbles; went bullberry picking down in the sharp ravines; and in the early evening watched coyotes come boldly up to the brink of the hill and give their plaintive howl. Madge and I slept downstairs under homemade patch quilts, for it was chilly once the sun was down. Sometimes we talked far into the night, saying the things we had felt during the day, confiding to each other our hopes and ambitions. "I want to travel," she would say. "I want to see the world, to know people." And we'd dream about the West and about the East and the wonderful lands across the sea.

When I returned to Mandan, a patch quilt was creative, a glass of jelly beautiful. So I made a patch quilt on the sewing machine in one afternoon, a lumpy, grotesque thing, with blue serge and silk, organdie and flannel, side by side; and with Elsie I picked berries and made a glass and a half of jelly and ate it up the same day. The quiet charm of the country, too, was gone.

I nearly had a relapse when Mr. Beck, health masseur, came to town. He set up business with a bathtub, furniture from our store—and a lot of supersalesmanship. I made three signs for him, earning my first—and last—dollar in the field of commercial art. Pop and Mr. Beck became very good friends. Together they joined the chamber of commerce and attended church suppers, and somewhere during a lull in a meeting or a meal Pop and Mr. Beck struck a bargain, and I was exchanged for a furniture bill. For six agonizing weeks, he cracked my vertebrae, snapped my neck, pulled my joints apart, then salted me down and sat me over a tub of boiling water to evaporate. When the bill was liquidated, I returned to the Dahl farm to recuperate. I never knowingly sold furniture to a member of the healing profession again.

In the fall Madge went to Fargo to college, and Margie and Elsie returned to high school. The spot on my lung was gone now, but the doctor had bad news for me: I could never run again . . . . I pushed the past two years behind me, closed them out of my consciousness, but there was a void so big I couldn't go around it, so deep I couldn't wade through it, so high I couldn't see over it; so I tried to build another castle, to shape a new future, one without college, without athletics.

Winter dragged on, and I spent long hours at the library reading. Came the new minister, a soft man, a somber man, apologetic. In his very first sermon he said something about the "poor darky slaves," and I followed him home. Over the packing boxes in the living room we talked. He was dreadfully sorry; he had meant no harm, hadn't been conscious of saying it. So I defended my race for the first time—and my opponent was a man of God.

Having few duties in the store and unable to find work outside, I sought the doubtful companionship of Mrs. James, one of two colored women in town. She regaled me with tales of Chicago and Montana, of her life when she was young, when she worked in the sporting houses as maid—she said. There were years she never mentioned, about which I never asked. The Jameses sold home brew from their back door and went on drinking orgies in their little shack; but when I was there Mrs. James shooed the customers away and hid her cigarettes. She talked of exciting things, of daring people, and I clung to her every word. She didn't want me to be like her. "Always do right," she'd say. "Don't trust no man too far. You take what I say, child, 'cause I know; I've done everything they is to do, and look at me now. A old woman; ain't got nothin' to look forward to but a grave in potter's field. You go on back to school and learn to be somebody, so you won't have to work in no whorehouse or white folk's kitchen."

After a lot of dickering on the farm note, the bank made a final settlement of two hundred dollars, which Pop and I divided. The old restlessness, encouraged by the money, returned. I'd go to Chicago this time, to a big city where there were thousands of people and thousands of jobs and one more person wouldn't matter, wouldn't be noticed. I wrote to the Y.W.C.A.—the colored Y.W.C.A.—and early in March packed my trunk and again rode away in the night.

Chicago!

My eyes grew big and my heart pounded as the yellow cab weaved in and out of the maelstrom of traffic, turned into Michigan Avenue, and started south. A huge double-deck bus staggered around a corner, top-heavy and clumsy. I saw a colored man. Four white men in a long black car shot past. Gangsters! They had to be gangsters. Chicago was full of them. A colored woman, another colored man. The crowds and the traffic slowly decreased. All around me now were colored people, lots and lots of colored people, so many that I stared when I saw a white person. Here was North Dakota and St. Paul twenty minutes apart.

The cab stopped in front of a Jewish temple.

"Lady," the driver said, pushing his cap back and scratching his head, "I can't find no South Parkway. Should be along here somewhere."

"Are you lost?" I asked weakly.

"No, I'm not, but if I don't find South Parkway, lady, you are." He turned off the meter and drove around the block until he came to a drugstore. "I'll ask in here." He came out grinning. "We were on it all the time. South Parkway is Grand Boulevard. They ought to change their signs."

A few minutes later I was again approaching the doors of

193

a Y.W.C.A. I wouldn't be turned away this time: if the *W* meant white in Grand Forks, the *C* could mean colored in Chicago. I was taken to the matron, an attractive woman, dignified and cultured, with a trace of the South in her voice. She asked where I was from.

"How did you get way up there? Isn't it awfully cold?"

The same questions I heard in St. Paul, the same questions I was to hear again and again. The matron asked other questions, too: did I have a job, how long did I intend to stay, did I know anyone in Chicago, did I have sufficient funds to sustain me until I found work. She sounded like Tom.

It was late afternoon by the time I unpacked and put my things in my side of the dresser, in my end of the closet. As I sat at the window looking down upon the unending caravan of traffic moving down the boulevard like gray molten lava, sat watching colored people hurrying by, there was a knock at my door, and the girl across the hall entered.

"Hello," she said. "Would you like to go down to dinner with me?"

I told her I would, I certainly would, so she sat down on the window seat and asked where I was from—and I had to go all over that again. She was a slender, yellow girl with a fine voice like spun honey—Southern honey. She told me she came from Georgia, was taking a stenographic course at Crane, that it was easier to get work if you finished from a Chicago school.

I was grateful to her for taking me down to dinner, for I dreaded meeting the others. They had to like me here; it couldn't be another St. Paul, I couldn't keep on going farther away, seeking companionship, finding rebuff. I stayed close to the girl, hoping they wouldn't notice me. The dining room was gay with little yellow tables and bright curtains. Gracefully the matron presided over the meal and the forty-two sedate young ladies. There was an undercurrent of gaiety and fun that I was too new to feel, too bewildered and absorbed to notice.

Many of the girls were pretty and expensively dressed, no two exactly alike. Some were dark with a black-brown velvetness,

194

two were white-skinned with gray eyes and auburn hair. In between were all shades of brown, all textures of hair, all kinds of features. They were intelligent, well-mannered girls, with good schooling and from good homes. As they talked, I felt remote, apart, conscious of the difference between their backgrounds and mine, wavering between the shame of not having and the pride of being able to do without.

Like myself, they were new to Chicago, coming from all over the United States, even from Africa and the West Indies, seeking better jobs and further education in the big city. Most of them were still in their teens, away from home for the first time, bewildered and a little awed. It was perhaps this common bond that quickened friendships, for in time they forgave me for having come from North Dakota, and took me in.

Chicago was a city of splendor and squalor, excitement and disappointment. Grimy apartment buildings hugged the streets, elevated trains looked down upon back-door poverty, rain-drenched and wretched. I saw city slums, black slums, black poverty, and black prosperity side by side, for the streets of the Black Belt were dotted with Negro business houses, from imposing banks to greasy lunch counters, and in between were the white-owned food stores, foul with the smell of rotting vegetables and live poultry; white-owned clothing stores displaying cheap, gaudy merchandise, inviting credit.

At night the streets sprang to life as the lights along the rialto blazed a path where black folks walked lightly. Blues poured from open doors, thumped from drugstore jukeboxes. There were the smells again: barbecue, fried shrimp, creole dishes, and a new thing from the stockyards. Peddlers plied the streets, beggars squatted on busy corners begging and cursing, people filled the buildings and stores, ran over into already crowded streets.

Negro churches were endless. No matter what the faith—and there were nearly as many as there were churches—ceremonies were usually long, collections numerous, choirs robed, some even capped. Emotion ruled the sermons. With all the

195

various faiths and picturesque names, staid Episcopalians and shouting store-fronters sought the same God; for some it took but an hour, for others all day. The music was a thing apart, incomparably beautiful.

At the Y the atmosphere was cultural. Girls dressed for formals and practiced for recitals. Every night, somewhere there were concerts and classes, clubs and lectures, always some place to go that cost money, so my funds dwindled rapidly, and with them went some of the glitter and glamor of Chicago. It became increasingly difficult to write Pop and admit failure to find work, to explain that it cost a dime to use the laundry, a nickel to make a phone call, a nickel for carfare to seek work. For three weeks I visited employment offices and answered advertisements with no results, so when a call came to the Y for a temporary stenographer in a law office, I took it, knowing I shouldn't have, and it wasn't long before my employer knew it, too.

The office was in an ancient red-brick building deep in the stone-and-mortar canyons of the Loop, where elevated trains rumbled past unwashed windows, where the light of day never entered. The lawyer was a little black man, nervous and irritable over his candidacy for something in the coming election. The first day I did nothing but answer the phone. The second day he called me into his office to take a letter to an Illinois senator, requesting jobs for the two white men waiting. Somewhere between the salutation and the second paragraph, Gregg failed me. As I shifted into a combination of longhand and shorthand, the lawyer increased his speed, the room became smaller, hotter, his words blurred.

"What's the matter?" he screamed. "Can't you take shorthand?"

I burned with humiliation. He raced on to the end and motioned me away. In the outer office I sat before the typewriter, trying to recall what he had said, trying to reconstruct the letter, but it was no use. The lawyer came to the door frowning, and I began to type furiously, something about a job. The machine jumped spaces, the *e* stuck, and I wished to heaven I was back in Thompson's secondhand store.

When the lawyer read the letter, he swore and threw it back on my desk on his way out. All the rest of the day I worked on it, putting it together again and again, bit by bit, piecing together cold dictation. When I went home that night I left a reasonable facsimile on his desk. The next morning it was gone, but so was the trash in the wastepaper basket.

During the remainder of the week I saw my employer but twice: once when he dropped a ten dollar bill on the floor, and again when the detective came to see about three hundred dollars the lawyer said was missing from the vault. Returning the ten dollars spoke well for me, but I was still on the spot. The detective took my name and address, and for days I lived in terror lest the matron put me out or the police come for me with handcuffs and leg irons.

On my last day I found my pay in an envelope on the desk. At five o'clock I covered up the typewriter and locked the door without ever seeing the lawyer again, without ever knowing what became of the money or the election—without caring.

When the Y received a call for a girl to work in a magazine office, I said I'd take it—if there was no dictation. For a while there wasn't. Mr. Moore's office was a large, cold room on the second floor of a social agency. Mr. Moore was a quiet young man, a dreamer and a veteran of World War I, with two decorations and fourteen incisions. For the next three months, at ten dollars a week, I learned how to run a magazine on hope, patience, and a very worn shoestring; to proofread and write advertising copy—and keep warm by burning unsold magazines in an old fireplace. For the first time I read books written by Negroes, and when Mr. Moore learned of my interest in writing I earned an extra dollar for each book I reviewed. It was during the height of the Negro renaissance in literature, in the late twenties, when Claude McKay, Langston Hughes, Rudolph Fisher, and others were at their creative best. W. E. B. Du Bois' *The Dark Princess* impressed me more than did any of the other books, for never before had I read of black people beautified, Negroes exalted.

Much of his writing was over my head, but I liked the feel of it. His words sang, giving off a haunting cadence, a mystic something that set him on a separate hill.

Besides book reviews, I wrote the histories of familiar hymns and an occasional editorial. When I began writing features, I discovered the field of fine arts, of priceless treasures to enjoy free for the asking, far away from the noise and smoke and grime. For a whole day each week I browsed around, gathering material, reading the yellowed pages of a facsimile of the Gutenberg Bible at the Newberry library, or spent an afternoon with an Irish guard studying the exhibit of Chinese purgatory at the Field Museum; days full with discovery, ecstatic with the fruition of prose. The ten dollars Mr. Moore paid me did not meet my expenses, small though they were. It would have been more remunerative to enter the domestic field, as did many of the other girls, but I liked my job and was learning more about writing than I could ever have learned in school. If I moved to a cheaper place, I could keep my job, but by then the Y and the girls were as much a part of my life as the university had been. I thought I could never give them up, but suddenly without warning my new life ended.

A telegram from Uncle John said that my father was very ill, and that I should come home at once. I didn't have the price of a ticket. The next two days I lived in a daze, waiting for the money that would take me to him, hoping he would not die, but he was seventy-two. I hadn't realized before that my father was an old man.

The assignment for the week was a story on the animals at Lincoln Park. From cage to cage I wandered looking at them, but always thinking of Father. I watched a coyote in his artificial home behind iron bars, walking back and forth on a stone floor, never giving up, ever seeking escape from his man-made prison. I wondered what it was that I had sought to escape, running back and forth from prairie to city, trying to find myself and my people, only to lose my father: not seeing the forest for the trees.

It was a long ride home. A North Dakotan, neighbor of

Senator Frazier, shared the seat with me as far as St. Paul, and we talked of crops and of drought, for it was midsummer there, and already Chicago was a thousand miles ago. A porter adjusted my chair for the night, but I could not sleep; he brought my breakfast in the morning, but I could not eat. The train sped through Minnesota into North Dakota, through Fargo, Valley City, Jamestown, sped over the flat, dry prairies, hot and crisp in the July sun; over miles and miles of prairie, cracked sloughs and coulees, treeless plains stretching on and on, fields of grain parched and dying in the merciless heat.

Dying as must be my father.

It was twilight when the train stopped at Bismarck. Uncle John was there, tight-lipped, grayer. I wanted to ask him if it was too late, but I could not talk. We got into his battered old car and drove down Main Street out of the town, drove over the black, muddy river and into the flickering lights of Mandan. I tried again.

"Is he still alive?"

"Yes. They operated yesterday, but he's unconscious yet."

We rode on in silence.

The hospital seemed tiny, toylike, after Chicago skyscrapers. The silence was oppressive. We went up the narrow corridor to my old room, stood beside the same bed, and all the old fears of death returned. My father opened his eyes when I touched him, and for a brief moment the veil lifted.

"My baby, My baby!" he whispered through fevered lips. "You come to me at last." His thin, yellow fingers clutched my hand, his eyes closed, and he slept again.

Ann was there. For four days she had been there with him, refusing to leave, refusing to sleep. White Ann and Father, friends at last.

All night we sat beside his bed, waiting. Came gray dawn, cold and lonely. Again I stood by helplessly watching the other part of me die. The breathing grew louder, the pulse weaker. I went to the window and looked out over the quiet town toward the bluffs by the river, gray and forbidding now. Above, the sky was pale and clear. Even my white clouds failed me. I turned toward the bed. Ann and John stood on either side of him, holding his hand.

There was no room for me there.

Alone I stood by the window and prayed for my father to die.

12) SECONDHAND GIRL

Alone, this time, I stood at the grave. Dry dust. Death.
Emptiness. Then a merciful numbness crept over me, stifling
unwept tears. Between two deaths I stood at prairie eventide; the
last symbol of family lay lifeless at my feet. Gone, too, were the
bonds and obligations, and in their stead a bereftness, a desolate
freedom. My life now was my own choosing, and there could be
no more coming home.

Far away from great cities and kitchens, from great people
and politics, my father died. Chief Jergeson was one of his pall-
bearers, and the manager of the Red Owl sang his song. His new
faith buried him, and small-town bankers and foreign farmers
wept at his bier. My father was dead.

The store was a sepulcher. Every chair, every dresser was
the ghost of him, his handwriting in the ledger, his battered
straw hat behind the door, food in the icebox. Slowly the numb-

ness succumbed to fear. I set up new living quarters in one of the two front rooms, carefully avoiding the old things, welcoming the sunshine that streamed in through the big bay window, the comforting sound of people walking past the open door— from July to November the door stood open—an escape from the fear of death, from emptiness. I dared not close the door.

Nightmared nights followed long, hot days. Elsie stayed with me until bedtime, and when she was gone I'd turn out the light and raise the shade and lie with eyes to the screen door, watching an old man pace the sidewalk back and forth from store to hotel; watching until, weary and exhausted, I'd drop off to troubled sleep.

I had to conquer my fear. Funeral and hospital bills had to be paid. My father left no other debts, left no material wealth save a few dollars in the bank and a store full of furniture. Dick was never located, and Tom and Harry could not come, so I reopened the store and began paying off the bills. It was the least I could do for Pop.

The whole town rallied around me. The store was given free plugs by the local radio announcer; a furniture man, my nearest competitor, sent customers; and Tim Murphy, Pop's driver, stopped in twice a day to do the delivering, for suddenly business picked up in the middle of a dull season. I had learned how to move heavy pieces of furniture with a two-by-four; there wasn't much I couldn't do by myself, but the men of the neighborhood were ready to help me. Returning from his vacation, the minister hurried in to apologize for being away during the funeral, for letting me down again; but in those dull days of forgetting, his church was very close to me. My father's faith had its reward. On Sundays Uncle John spent the day repairing, arranging, and sometimes supplementing my stock from his store. When Ann couldn't come, she sent food and gifts.

For months after Father's death, men and women, many of them strangers to me, came to pay their bills, sometimes waking me up to give me their money. Some were unable to speak English, some came empty-handed asking for more time. "I no pay you now," they would say. "No got money, but I pay next time. Yah? You papa, he trust me. He say you no got, you come tell me, and I no bother you. You papa, he understand, he was a gute man!" My father's trust was not violated; not one bill went unpaid.

Gradually my fears subsided, but there were still noises in the night to which I could not become reconciled: aching, groaning noises of a senile building, settling into slow decay. I got a kitten, something alive to absorb the noises. Satan was a ball of blackness, and smart. I taught her to jump through hoops, and it wasn't long before she was high diving from the top of the clothes rack on the heads of unsuspecting customers. Every afternoon, a little after four, she climbed up into the front window and waited for children to shadowbox with her on their way home from school, and long after night sounds ceased, Satan made sounds of her own—light, feathery sounds as she frolicked around the room and over my bed. As she grew larger, more mischievous, sleeping became a hazard. Claws outstretched, she leaped at anything that moved; toes, fingers, eyes—they were all one to Satan. But her aliveness crowded out the void of death, and I was glad.

My neighbors, too, protected me and helped me to forget. Erma Robinski and Fanny Weaver came by at least once a day to see how I was getting along, came bearing hot food and delicacies, things they knew I couldn't prepare, ordinarily wouldn't eat. If I wasn't moving about by midmorning, they were pounding on the back door. On Saturday nights, when strangers and drunks were in town, one or the other stayed with me until closing time. After school there was always Elsie and Patty, Morton's stenographer, who took to dropping in after work each night. When all five of us got together, the store again rang with fun and laughter. So we formed a little club, the five of us, to talk and play cards and roast weiners in the kiln I had built in the backyard.

I was a little disturbed about the cards. We never had a deck in the house while Pop was alive. I saw no harm in our playing, yet preachers railed against them, calling them instruments of the devil, pathways to hell. I didn't know what our minister's views were on the subject, but I managed not to have our parties on Thursdays, and he might never have known about my deck of cards if the rolltop desk hadn't stuck while I was playing solitaire. My customers readily adjusted to the new order of things in Thompson's secondhand store. Those who didn't join in the game insisted I finish my hand before attending to their wants. The bell on the front door was sometimes all that greeted them, and there were times when they were confronted with a sign saying, "Follow the Rope." The rope, tied to the door knob, led to the hotel or the construction company, and I was at the end.

On summer evenings I'd go out the back and across the alley to Erma's to sit on her porch and talk. One night, while she watered the lawn, I was bemoaning life in general, not seriously, just talking to hear myself. When she put away the hose, she came over to the step and sat down beside me.

"Well, what are you going to do about it?" she asked, amused.

"I don't have to live," I said dramatically. "There's always suicide."

Erma jumped up, facing me. "If I ever hear you say that again, I'll slap hell out of you! The idea, a kid like you talking like that!"

"I was just fooling," I said, startled.

She sat down. "You'd better be!"

Erma Robinski cared what I said and thought, what I did. Fanny did, too; I knew that now. The laughing and cussing, the casual dropping-by, the food—all was part of a plan, a plan to which the church, the chamber of commerce, and all Pop's customers subscribed. I had more supervision and discipline than ever.

After the nightmares ceased to haunt my slumber, and Satan, on the brink of adult cathood, assumed a little more dignity, a little less deviltry—came the rumrunners. When the booze truck began making regular runs from Canada, the more devout customers held their vigil on Main Street, and sometimes in front of the store. The truck came as far as First Avenue, then turned and went up the alley to Ab's place. Ab's wife wouldn't let them hang around there, so they waited at Main. The truck didn't get in until well after one, and by then the men were usually so drunk from the bottles held back from the last load that they couldn't recognize Ab when they saw him.

One night about eight of them crowded around the store, talking and singing. Some leaned against the big window, two sat on the sidewalk, their backs against the door of my room, so close I could smell the liquor, could reach out from my bed and touch them through the screen. Soon their drunken conversation became obscene and profane. They demanded women as well as liquor. I was frightened. The door was hooked, but the thin screen was already straining with their weight. If I tried to remove the stop and close the inside door, or phone the police, they would hear me and remember I was alone. Since the beginning of the night carolers, I had been sleeping with Pop's revolver under my pillow, so, with gun in hand, I stood beside the door, ready to defend myself. The men began to argue. Satan, watching the shining muzzle in my hand, crouched and sprang. A shot rang out. When I opened my eyes I was still standing beside the door, the gun at my feet. Main Street was deserted. Two days later, Satan crawled out from under a washstand, meek and hungry. I was never bothered with rumrunners again.

After New Year's, business and the temperature dropped to zero. The mercury didn't stop there; it plunged down until it reached forty-five below, making Mandan the coldest spot in the U.S.A. In Pittsburgh and Minneapolis, Harry and Tom read the papers and sent their condolences, while Satan and I huddled in the corner behind the heater, dodging the icy blasts that whistled under the doors and rocked the brittle building. After a few days the storm subsided, bringing the temperature up, but business did not improve, for it was the dull season that follows

205

the holidays. Instead of putting part of the profits back into stock and setting aside some for days like these, I had given it all to my creditors. Day after day passed without a single sale. By the middle of the month, I didn't have enough money in the bank to pay the rent, so I wrote to Tom for the help he had promised. More days went by, and still no sales. At last Tom's letter arrived with a ten-dollar bill. I looked at the money a long time, then put it in another envelope and returned it. My bank balance now was less than a dollar; my rent was twenty-five.

When Uncle John came over that Sunday, I told him I had eaten my dinner, that business was fair. I was doing all right. The next day I went to the butcher's shop and got scraps for Satan, but Satan didn't like scraps, so I washed them off, cut up two potatoes, and made stew. I didn't like stew. There were still two days before rent was due; with one good sale I could make it. In all the time Pop had the store he hadn't been a day late with his rent; it was a kind of religion with him. With me it was an obsession. I began rearranging furniture, polishing it up, and made a big sign for the oak buffet with a marked-down price, as they do in city stores. The buffet was my best piece. Fanny came in while I was working and saw the sign, but said nothing. She tried to play with Satan, but the cat looked at her and mewed plaintively.

"What the hell's the matter with you?" Fanny took Satan in her arms. "You act like you're starved to death."

"I fed her. She wouldn't eat."

Fanny felt Satan's flat sides. Funny how a cat can get very fat or very thin in such a short time. Fanny didn't stay long. In a little while Erma came through the back door with a covered dish.

"Here," she pushed it towards me. "Take this damned thing before I drop it. Don't ask me what it is; just something new I cooked up, and my husband won't eat it, so I'm shoving it off on you."

"All this?"

"What you can't eat give to Satan. I've got to go, left something on the stove." She pulled her coat over her head and went out the door.

That night I cried myself to sleep.

When I awoke, the cold winter sun was shining through the window. I jumped out of bed and shook down the fire, opened up the drafts, and got back into bed. A truck stopped outside the store, and a farmer got out and knocked on the door. Hurriedly I got into my robe and let him in. He bought the oak buffet.

There were more tough days before the winter was over—days when I hadn't enough money in the bank to cover my checks—but each time a miracle was performed, a sale made. I learned to pray that winter, but I think I prayed more to my father than to our Father, for somehow it seemed that Pop was still taking care of the store. With spring housecleaning, business looked up again, and by the end of May the last bill was paid.

My job was done.

Now that I was free to return to the city much of the desire was gone. If I failed now, there was no one to fall back upon, no one to send to for money, not even Tom, for it was a year before I was to hear from him again. Harry sent five dollars now and then, but girls and new cars usually kept him broke. Uncle John joined with the townspeople in trying to persuade me to stay in business, but it was spring again, a time to dream.

I saw little of Elsie when she began dating. Sometimes I went riding with her crowd; occasionally a railroad man took me to a show. The Jameses were gone, and most of the old high school gang had either married or moved away, leaving older people my chief companions. I began to rely more and more upon the older people who watched over me, believed in me, reminded me I could now return to school. To some I was a revelation, like the business man who, judging ten million Negroes he had never seen by ten he had, thought all colored women were prostitutes and marveled that I wasn't.

The church picnic was one of the highlights of summer. All the Methodists and a good many Lutherans and Catholics gathered in the grove along the railroad tracks for the outing.

Like other young people, Joseph Kolenski and I paired off for the afternoon. I had known Joseph since early winter, when he joined the Epworth League. He made an ideal partner, full of outdoor songs and games that he had learned in summer camps in Wisconsin. When the picnic was over and the minister started us on the way home, Joseph and I were in one of the cars that got lost from the others and ended up at the bend in the Little Heart.

The next time I saw Joseph was at the store. In an effort to raise money to send delegates to the Young People's Conference, a committee from the Epworth League met with me to plan a carnival—the minister having vetoed my idea of a mock divorce. When one of the deacons came for his two daughters, the others began to leave, too; but not Joseph. He sat sprawled out in a chair, perfectly at home. The deacon looked at Joseph and sat down, too. We talked some more, and the deacon started again; still Joseph did not move.

"Are you going now, Joseph?" he asked pointedly. It was getting late. "I'll drop you off if you like; we're going your way."

"No thanks." Joseph got himself a glass of water and sat down again, one leg over the arm of a chair. "I've got my car. Don't tell me you didn't see that pink and gray limousine out front?"

I went to the door with the deacon and the girls, not knowing what to say. The girls looked back at Joseph as if they wanted to stay, too. I left the front door open and the store lights on. When I returned to my room, Joseph was grinning.

"The old boy sure hated to leave, didn't he, honey?"

"I can guess what he's thinking," I said.

"Let him think. I can say good-night to my girl without the whole town for an audience, can't I?"

I stood in the doorway between my room and the store, not saying anything. "You're not scared of me, are you?" Joseph stopped grinning. A car came down the street, slowed down in front of the store like it was going to stop, then drove on. "That's the deacon," said Joseph. "He just had to come back and see."

When the sound of the car died away, Joseph stood up. I waited for him at the door. "Don't you worry, kid. I wouldn't hurt you." He gave me a quick kiss and left. A long time after his old Ford clattered away, I stood in the door, but the deacon didn't return.

I went to sleep thinking of Joseph, and I was thinking of him when I awoke in the morning. The phone rang, and I knew who it was before I took down the receiver. "Good morning, darling. I just called to say good morning."

From then on—until I left Mandan—we avoided each other. I liked Joseph, and I knew he liked me, but Joseph was a white boy and I was black. Our side of the Thompson family didn't believe in miscegenation.

When the last piece of furniture was sold and my things packed, Uncle John came for Satan and me, and for the last time, I closed the door on Thompson's secondhand store and rode out of Mandan over the mighty Missouri and back to Bismarck.

All that fall and winter I worked for my uncle, living with him and Aunt Ann in the basement of their big new store. John had added a line of new furniture from the wholesale houses in the Twin Cities, and had built up a large repair trade. At odd moments he taught me much about woodcraft, about refinishing and upholstering.

I liked working with wood: liked the feel of it, liked to smell its clean out-of-door fragrance; liked the beauty of its grain. It was like hunting for a buried treasure to scrape down through the many coats of paint to find the rich beauty of the naked wood asleep beneath: a beauty neither paint nor varnish could destroy.

Entering a trade magazine contest, I submitted a name for a new coil spring, and won twenty-five dollars. I was paid another dollar for a poem describing the spring. My interest in furniture increased. Again I began to invent, not showers and cars, but ways in which to improve furniture. The drawings I sent a Twin City bedding house resembled blueprints only in the blueness of the ink from my fountain pen, but with all their crudeness, the company accepted one of the suggestions, offering me a choice of the bed or its wholesale equivalent, fifteen dollars. I took the money. *The National Furniture Digest* later carried a full-page advertisement of the "innovation," one of the company's best sellers.

With the money I treated myself to a trip to Grand Forks. The old hurt was gone now; I could return to visit my friends.

Staying with the Walkers didn't give me much access to the Jordan family, so I waylaid Muriel one afternoon on her way downtown. "Still at the U?" I asked.

"No. I quit soon after you did. My old man said he couldn't afford it, and you know I didn't have any money—but I'm going back this fall."

"You've got money now?"

"Don't need it." Muriel looked wise.

"Come on, what's your story?"

"Well, you look like a nice little girl," she teased, "so I'll let you in on a secret. There's a young minister down at First Methodist, a Dr. Riley. Big, redheaded guy, Phi Beta Kappa, Ph.D., and a string of other things. He preaches at Second Avenue Sunday afternoons—that's where I met him—and he's all hepped up about Negroes and education."

"Why?"

"Darned if I know. Just thinks we need educating, I guess. Believes in helping the underdog—even in this town. Well, he's getting the ladies of his church to finance me through college. Can you beat that?"

We stopped walking. "Is that true, Muriel? Is he really going to do that?"

"That's what he says. I can't believe it myself. All the years we've been in this town nobody's ever given a rap whether we lived or died, let alone got an education. Then all of a sudden, out of a clear sky, here comes Santy Claus, leaving his ritzy congregation to come down here across the tracks to help poor us."

"I'd like to go back to school." There, I had said it. I'd been

210

wanting to say it for a long time, but I had been afraid.

"Then you come to church Sunday, and I'll introduce you to him," said Muriel. "Maybe he'll help you, too."

I sat on the Jordans' side that morning, because anything that had to do with the new minister was justified in the eyes of the Walkers. Dr. Riley was all Muriel had said, a forceful, dynamic man with a shock of curly red hair that bobbed up and down as he preached. The closer we came to the end of the sermon, the more fantastic the idea became, the more I wanted to escape. After benediction he came directly to us, smiling a nice smile, shaking a powerful hand. He didn't waste words, just told me to come to his office the next day, and he'd see what could be done.

Dr. Riley sat behind a large, luxurious desk, his sharp eyes watching me, seeing through me as I answered his questions. Questions that began with: "How did you happen to come to North Dakota?" When he had finished with the questions, he leaned back in his chair and smiled.

"I think we can find a way to get you back in school. We'll need one or two people to help with the work at our house; it's too much for Susan—ten rooms and our four-year-old son— besides, she'll be getting her master's next year. Susan's an artist," he said proudly.

"Yes, sir," I said politely, more concerned about the ten rooms than her art.

"Why don't you stay now? The second semester is only a couple of weeks old."

"Oh, no, I couldn't."

"Why not?"

"I'm working for my uncle. I promised to come back."

"Muriel tells me you came here on money you won. Tell me about it." When I had finished he stroked his chin meditatively. "I hear you were quite an athlete and somewhat of a writer."

"I can't run any more. I'd like to write, only I'm not sure just how much of a future there is in it. For me."

211

Dr. Riley snorted. "What do you mean 'for you?' Why not for you? Think it over. If you want to stay on now, we'll make a place for you; if not, come back in the fall and live with us." He stood and held out his hand. "In the meantime, write to me."

"But what should I write about?" I asked, puzzled.

"About anything, I don't care what, just so you keep in touch with me. Promise?"

"I'll write."

"And you will come back?"

I hesitated. "What if I haven't the money?"

"Now, you just let me worry about that. We'll see that you are taken care of. Don't you trust me?"

"Yes," I grinned, "but I'd still like to know where the money's coming from."

Clasping his hands behind him and looking piously towards the ceiling, Dr. Riley swayed up and down on his toes and began to chant: "And again I say unto you, ask and it shall be given you, seek and ye shall find." He was grinning when he opened the door. He could tell from the expression on my face that I thought he had lost his mind. I had no intention of coming back.

I stayed with the Evanses until spring trying to decide what to do, which way to go. I wrote to Dr. Riley, pointing out the dubious glories of the secondhand business, and gave him a hiss-by-hiss account of the battle between a bull snake and a rattler that was raging in the window of the undertaker's parlor next door. All at once an education seemed awfully important; I wanted to go back to school, to study this time, so I went again to St. Paul, not to make friends and influence colored people, but to see if I could stand alone, to get a job and save enough money to pay my own way back to college.

Lee was married to a musician and living in a place of her own, so I roomed with her and Fred, sleeping on a narrow davenport and cooking my own meals, for two and a half dollars a week. Without much difficulty I got a poor-paying three-day-a-week job as typist on the *Bugle,* a colored Minneapolis weekly.

Soon I was writing features and advertising copy as well as straight news. My ten-dollar salary came in tidbits, came late, and at times, came not at all, so I took every odd job I could find, from baby-sitter to collecting back subscriptions. When a friend of Lee's employer was looking for a girl to help her move, I took that, too.

Mrs. Bently, a pretty Englishwoman, showed me the dishes and barrels, told me where to find food when I got hungry, paid me, put on her white hat and gloves, and went on about her business. You can't betray a trust like that, so I worked like a fool. When Mrs. Bently and her two boys were settled in their new apartment, I continued to work for her every other day from nine to two for a dollar a day and carfare. Even when she drove me home, I got carfare.

It was my first job as maid, and I was as ignorant as I was awkward. She had to show me how to operate the vacuum cleaner, and then it terrified me. The corners of the soft orientals were sucked into the nozzle, and the smaller rugs slid over the slick floors or rumpled up like brown and red caterpillars, so when she wasn't home I took the throw rugs out on the back porch and shook the dust out of them.

Then there was the business of eating. I knew maids ate in the kitchen, but I wasn't sure how one went about it. While I set their table in the dining room, Mrs. Bently put a dainty cloth on the enameled table under the kitchen window, set it with the same dishes and silverware they used and took three of the pink roses from her centerpiece and placed them in a vase on my table. She didn't say anything, but I knew she was trying to make me feel at ease. Before I took the food to the dining room, she served my plate and poured my coffee. There was no jumping up and down during my meal; if anything was omitted from her table, she sent one of the boys for it. After the first day I set my own table, and there were always flowers and pretty linen.

Having lived in India for several years, the Bentlys had collected an unholy amount of curios. The living room was crowded with miniatures, knickknacks, whatnots, inlaid tables, teakwood stands, and ivory elephants. Everywhere elephants. A large table in the center of the room was filled with pachyderms of every size and color, elephants to be admired—and dusted. Over her sewing basket, the madam talked of England and India, and as she talked, the elephants came to life, the teakwood tables again held dainty teacups, the big lion-head rug roared in the jungles. And over her sewing basket she talked of her boys and their military school, but never a word about Mr. Bently. When she asked about my writing ambition, it was more than polite interest. Carefully she read the *Bugle,* praising and criticizing my articles. She wasn't aware of it, but she was batting on Dr. Riley's side, and I was glad.

I liked working for Mrs. Bently. There was a quiet luxury in her home, a security, a freedom from want up there on the hill behind the ancient oaks that was new in my experience. Hers was an Old World culture unlike the foreign peasantry at home. This I could admire, but never touch; the other I could share.

Soon after I came to St. Paul, I telephoned the bedding company and received a most cordial invitation to visit them and see the plant. Their man Johnson was eager to meet me, very eager. I had never seen my brainchild, so weeks later, on my way from an assignment for the *Bugle,* I stopped in. There was a long wait. When Mr. Johnson did appear, he was a changed man. Coolly he said hello, perfunctorily he showed me the bed, quickly I left. I didn't care who lay in my bed, I didn't think customers cared who made it, but apparently Mr. Johnson did.

With two jobs and collecting, I hadn't much time to miss the social side of the city. Living with Lee threw me into closer contact with the younger set than I had been before, but I still made few friends. Sometimes Lee and I went with Fred to the roadhouses on the outskirts of the two towns where his orchestra was playing and sat outside in the Ford, watching the white people drive up in big cars, their women gorgeously gowned. We'd sit in the warm night air listening to soft music, eating sandwiches the boys brought us between numbers, wishing we could see what it was like inside. Even when the jewelled ladies staggered out laughing and cursing, we still wished we could see what it was like inside.

I seldom went to the many affairs that were held in the neighborhood, but when the carnival came to the vacant lot behind Lee's house, the sound of the merry-go-round reminded me of the rodeo at Mandan, and Lee had little trouble persuading me to go with her. We were drinking pop and talking to a group of her friends when someone came up behind me and placed her hands over my eyes.

"Guess," said a woman's voice. "Guess, goddamn you!" The hands dropped from my eyes, and two arms went around my neck. "Thompson!" half-crying, half-laughing. "Oh, Thompson, am I glad to see you." Before I could speak, Opal pulled me over to her companion. "Thompson, this is Scotty." Scotty was colored. "Scotty, this is my cousin. I haven't seen her in years. You don't mind if we go off in a corner and talk, do you, honey?"

"Certainly not," he said. "I'll be waiting in the car. Take your time."

I was bursting with questions. Gertrude had written me about Opal running away, leaving Sol and Lucy, but even Gertrude didn't know she was in St. Paul. We found a little table at a refreshment stand and sat down.

"Don't look so startled," she giggled. "I'm colored."

"You're what?"

"Colored, sugar, just like you."

"But why?"

Opal's thin, nervous fingers closed tightly over my wrist. "I left Sol and came here nearly a year ago. The Forks was too dead for me—so was Sol and his goddamned fish! I knew Ma'd take care of Lucy—she was over there all the time anyway. Hell, Thompson, I'm still young; I want some fun out of life. I've always liked colored people, you know that. Once when I was a little snot, when we lived in New York, I ran away and lived with a colored woman for a week before they found me. I cried and fought like hell when Ma took me home. So I am back with colored people."

"Does he know, this Scotty?"

"Hell, no! I told you I'm passing. I work in a colored restaurant and live with a colored family."

"You working in a restaurant?"

"Yes, Thompson, ain't that rich! Me, Opal Block—by the way, I'm a single gal, and my name is Opal Brown—see that you remember. Yeah, me who was too weak to do my own housework, slinging hash eight hours a day and liking it."

"They think you're colored, too?"

"Sure they do. Didn't you notice my Southern accent? I don't swear so much, either. Scotty's breaking me of that."

"And where did you meet Scotty?"

"He's a friend of the people I live with."

"How did you get in with them?"

"Oh, I was walking by and liked the looks of the house, so I went up to the door and gave them a song and dance about being a stranger here and wanting to get in with the right kind of people. Oh, kid, they're wonderful to me—and Scotty! Thompson, I'm happier than I've ever been in my whole life."

"Don't you miss Lucy?"

Tears crowded into her big brown eyes. For a moment she looked old and haggard. "Of course I do. No use lying to you, Thompson, but she's better off without me; Ma'll take good care of her."

After a while we went over to the car, and Scotty drove us around Como Park until midnight. We talked on and on. She was hungry for news of home. I didn't see how Scotty could help catching on from the things she said.

I saw Opal several times after that. Her secret was safe with me. A white woman passing for a Negro—who'd believe me anyway?

Came September, and my savings were still insufficient. Dr. Riley's offer seemed more plausible, more desirable. Returning to school was the only tangible thing I had to look forward to, the only promise of a future. Again I wrote to him, and this time I knew that I would go if he still wanted me. On a penny postal card came my answer:

Susan and I are looking forward to your arrival. Registration begins next week. Expect you on the 10:20 Monday.

Richard Riley

I was happier than I had been for a long time. Firm ground again beneath my feet, again I had a way to go. Back in North Dakota prairie skies and a new home awaited me.

A home and a college education.

13) THE LIFE OF RILEYS

The parsonage was an old house and big, set well back on a spacious lawn in a quiet, tree-covered section of Grand Forks that I had never seen. As Dr. Riley and I came up the walk, a little tousle-headed boy ran out to meet us.

"Jan, this is Era Bell, who has come to live with us."

The boy sidled up to me and smiled shyly.

"Hello, Jan." I held out my hand, but he shied away and ran ahead to open the door.

We entered a capacious hall, cut off from the rest of the house by huge sliding doors.

"Oh, Susan," called Dr. Riley, "come down here. I've got Era Bell."

A small, plump woman came bounding down the stairs. There was first surprise, then relief in her pretty round face. "Well, well," she said, holding out a soft, limp hand. "So here you are." Her voice was nervous and high-pitched, like little tinkling bells. "We've been looking for you, haven't we, Jan?" She put an arm around the boy as he clung to her, watching. "She's just a little girl, Richard; you didn't tell me she was little. I thought . . ."

"Well, aren't you going to ask her in? She must be hungry; she's been riding all night."

"Yes, of course, of course." Susan Riley laughed her nervous little laugh.

"I'm not hungry," I protested, "but I would like to wash up a bit before I go out to register."

"But you're not dirty; you look nice. You look very nice." Her dark eyes were serious and appraising. I began to wonder what *had* she expected: so far I was neither large nor dirty— black, she meant. I didn't know then that she was afraid of Negroes, that she had fought bitterly against my coming, that Professor Crandall, a hangover from my freshman days, had told her I was a big, black woman who would dominate her home, intimidate her child.

Registration took up most of the day. As I again stood in line in the gymnasium, I tried not to notice the crossbars and the baskets for this time there was no physical education on my schedule. Having barely enough money to cover tuition, let alone books and carfare, I postponed the visit to the treasurer's office, awaiting a move from the right reverend. So far he had said nothing.

When I returned to the parsonage that evening, I was sent to the living room to await dinner and get acquainted with Jan. The child had undergone rigid training since morning, and his whole attitude was one of protective kindness as he hovered around me, his big brown eyes serious and concerned; no longer a child, but a little old man, grave with the responsibility of caring for a black girl in a white world.

"Don't you worry." He patted my hand. "They'll have dinner ready soon."

"How old are you?" I asked.

219

"Five. How old are you?"

"Twenty-four."

He wasn't impressed. "You haven't got a mother and father, have you?"

"No."

"That's all right. You live with us now. You can be my little sister, and I'll let you have my mother and father so you won't get lonesome."

"Wait a minute," I said. "Which one of us is twenty-four?"

Though dreading the first meal, I was distinctly relieved when we were called to dinner. I had read about precocious children, but I had never hoped to live with one. Jan's solicitude embarrassed me. In an effort to make a quick conversion, his mother, appealing to his keen sense of justice, had described me as a poor little orphan who couldn't help being what I was. It was effective far beyond her expectations.

The boy led me by the hand into the dining room, where I was introduced to Glen, Dr. Riley's brother, who had come up from Ohio, mostly to play football. With loud protests from Jan I was seated between the two brothers. The meal went badly. Dr. Riley served the plates, heaping them high, with a fine disregard for my personal wishes, while Susan tried to quiet Jan, who had gone into a tantrum about a glass of milk. There was more food on my plate than I could possibly eat, and some—like the fried green tomatoes—I had never seen before.

In the middle of the meal, Dr. Riley suddenly threw down his knife and fork and jumped up from the table.

"What's the matter, Richard? What happened, dear?" Susan started towards him.

"Sit down, will you!" He roared.

"Well, dear, what's the matter? Is it your wisdom tooth again?"

Dr. Riley stamped over to the corner of the room grumbling, his red curls shaking as he pawed the floor like an enraged bull.

Taking his cue, little Jan jumped from his chair and began stamping around the room yelling, "Sit down, you! Sit down!"

Susan was in a dither. She fluttered from one to the other, trying to soothe them, to ease the tension. I looked around for a means of escape. Glen nudged my foot under the table and winked. When Susan went to the kitchen for the dessert, Dr. Riley returned to the table, followed by Jan. A big bowl of brown Betty was placed before me, steaming hot and delicious. I pecked nervously at the pudding, wondering what would happen next. When Richard Riley spoke again, not a trace of anger remained. I could hardly believe my ears.

"You'd better eat all of it, Era Bell. It will probably be the last dessert you'll ever see on this table."

"Richard!" Susan beamed her relief. "Don't try to frighten the poor child. You know we always have dessert."

Frighten me, she said. The man had blown his top, the kid had marched in his own picket line, and now she tells him not to frighten me about a dish of pudding.

"This is only a front," he continued, grinning broadly. "We'll live on soup and water for the rest of the week to make up for it."

"Richard!" said Susan half-reproachfully.

"Yes," echoed little Jan. "We'll probably live on soup and water the rest of the week, Era Bell."

I offered to help with the dishes.

"No, no," said Susan. "You go in the front room with Richard and sit down. Glen and I'll do dishes. You must be tired after such a trying day."

"You'll have plenty of time to help." Dr. Riley led the way into the big room. "Get a book out of the bookcase and read." He lit a fire in the grate and sat down to his evening paper. I wanted to go to my room, where I could think, but instead I dutifully looked through the rows of books—profound, scholarly tomes, about as enticing as a census report. Shutting my eyes, I reached at random and got the *Decline and Fall of the Roman Empire*.

Dr. Riley peered over his newspaper. "Do you like history?"

"No," I said truthfully, "but there isn't much choice."

He snickered and dived behind his paper.

221

When the whole family was assembled in the living room, Dr. Riley took several typewritten lists from the mantel and passed them around. "Now, these are work schedules," he began. "Each member of this household has been given certain specific duties to perform, allowing sufficient time for study and relaxation. We've tried to be fair in allocating the work, so that no one will suffer undue hardships." He stood with his back to the fire and continued: "The house will be run as follows: it shall be my solemn duty to cook the breakfast—and heaven help you if you don't like pancakes." Little Jan clutched his blank piece of paper and laughed at his father's joke. "On Fridays I shall keep Jan and prepare lunch. Susan and Glen will be responsible for the other meals and the dishes, with care of Jan on the days designated. Era Bell will do the laundry on Friday, clean the house Saturday, and iron and mend as indicated on her schedule." My heart sank. "No, Era Bell," he said, sensing my feelings, "that isn't as bad as it sounds. We have a nice electric washing machine, and we even bought a mangle for you."

"Richard," Susan put in nervously, "don't you think that's a little heavy for her?"

"Well, merciful heavens, woman! That's the way you wanted it; those are your terms . . ."

"All right, dear, all right. We can help her some. Glen can help with the tubs." She shot a quick glance in my direction. "I didn't know she was so small. You aren't much taller than Jan, are you? Stand up, Jan, honey, and see which one of you is the taller."

"Oh, for heaven's sake, Susan!" Storm clouds began to gather.

"Daddy, don't get angry." Jan ran to his father.

"Daddy isn't angry, are you, Daddy? Come on everybody, let's sing." Susan sat down at the piano and began to play. "Come on, Era Bell; you, too, Glen, before Richard drowns me out."

222

So we stood around the piano and sang—the cooks, the dishwashers, and the cleaning woman.

For a long time that night I lay awake in my room over the kitchen, wondering what to do. Not a word had been said about money. Maybe he wasn't going to do anything, after all. I wanted to run away, but I had no other place to go; I felt cut off from the world, trapped. Eventually I dropped off to sleep to dream about a washing machine as big as a house with a little boy sitting on a scrub bucket feeding encyclopedias through the wringer, while I was slowly being sucked into the rolling jaws of a red-hot mangle.

When I awoke, Jan was tickling my chin. "Wake up, little Era Bell, or you'll be late for breakfast."

"Jan, where are you?" Susan stuck her head in the door. "Good morning. Did my young son awaken you?"

"No," I lied. "Good morning."

She pulled the boy away.

When I went downstairs, I found Richard Riley standing at the stove, pancake turner in one hand, a book in the other. "Good morning!" he boomed.

"Hi!" said Glen, winking at the stack of cakes.

Jan ran to me, slipping his arm about my waist, proud that he could reach it. Susan fluttered into the kitchen. "Jan has certainly taken a shine to you." She seemed pleased.

The little kitchen table was crowded but peaceful as the five of us sat down to our cakes—big, thick things covered with milk gravy. Feebly I protested about the gravy, but to no avail, so I forced myself to eat, and it was surprisingly good. When we finished, Dr. Riley pushed back his chair and stood up.

"Come into the library, Era Bell. I would have a word with thee." I followed him into the big, friendly room at the rear of the house. "I suppose you've been wondering what you were going to use for money?"

"Well, yes," I admitted.

"Didn't I tell you I'd take care of everything? The good

223

ladies of the guild have decided—after a little persuasion—to adopt you as their experiment in Christian living. Working on the theory that charity begins nearer home, they aren't going over to Africa or India for their heathen this year; they are going to start right here in Grand Forks—and, sister, you're it." He grinned over his glasses. "They are going to give you a hundred-dollar scholarship to cover tuition and books. If there is any deficit, Susan and I will make it up. Your expenses shouldn't be very much. You'll find pencils, paper, and ink in my office, and be sure to make use of these books. Feel free to use the type-writer. You type, don't you?"

"Yes, some."

"Good. There'll be plenty of typing for you to do on Susan's thesis. And don't worry about the work. If you find it's too much, say so, and we'll take some of it off of you. Now get your bill, and I'll take it when I go out this afternoon."

I spent the next two days pressing suits—piles of big black and gray ministerial suits that had been waiting for me since midsummer. It was Sunday before I got away and across the tracks to Grove Street. I stopped at the Blooms' to see Lucy, then hurried on to the big yellow house on the corner.

"How do you like Mrs. Riley?" asked Mrs. Walker, before I had a chance to sit down.

"She's nice. Nervous, but, so far, awfully nice."

Gertrude whistled. "Am I glad to hear that!"

"Yes," said Mrs. Walker. "We were worried."

"But why?"

"Reverend Riley is a fine man," said Mrs. Walker fervently. "He's a wonderful Christian man, and we all love him, but we didn't know how she'd act towards you. She's not used to colored folks. He told us she wasn't."

"Yes, hon," said Gertrude. "When we heard you were going to live there, we didn't know what to do; we didn't want to tell you—to prejudice you against her before you got there—and we were afraid not to warn you."

"If she's nice and treats you all right, just forget what we

224

said, and you'll get along," advised Jim Walker. "Do your work well and behave yourself, and anybody will respect you. You *make* her like you."

"Jim's right," said the woman. "You go on and make good. They're giving you a wonderful opportunity to get a college education. Not every girl, white or black, has that opportunity. I hear he's even putting that Jordan girl back in school, and he's going to fix some way to help Gertrude with her voice."

"Oh, Gertrude!" I exclaimed. "That's wonderful. Tell me about it."

"I don't know, I've still got to see it, but he's talked somebody into giving me free voice lessons for a year. I don't understand it, honest to God I don't."

I went from the Walkers' to the Jordans' boldly.

"What white ladies are mothering you?" asked Muriel.

"The Guild. Have you figured it out yet—why he's doing it, I mean?"

"No, but it isn't a gag, and it isn't easy. He's already lost some of his friends and a lot of his congregation. He never told me—he wouldn't—but somebody that belongs to his church told us that when the Second Avenue kids sang over there Sunday some of his members got up and walked out. For good!"

"It takes a big man, Muriel."

"Plenty big, so the least we can do is go out there to that university and get down under the books. We've got to show these peckerwoods we're worth fighting for."

I didn't mind washing and ironing and scrubbing—even gravy on my pancakes—after that. It really wasn't so bad, the washing. Glen helped with the tubs, and Susan did the rinsing when the Reverend's white shirts began to come out pink. The ironing was fun with a mangle; everything went through, even the stiff collars and the seven pink shirts.

Jan and I were inseparable. From the time he crawled into my bed in the morning until I tucked him in at night, he or the thought of him was with me. Sometimes he cried when I left him to go to school, and when I came home he ran to meet me, throwing his arms around my neck, kissing my cheek, patting my hand. At first Susan objected to the kissing. She did not want to share with me her son's love and affection. She did not want him to share my germs. She tried to stop him, without telling him why; but in a child there are no nice distinctions, no prejudices of color.

"Don't kiss me, Jan," I told him, pushing him gently away.

"But don't you want me to love you?"

"Your mother doesn't want you to kiss me."

"Why?"

"I don't know."

Susan Riley said nothing.

The next day we were in the library with Richard and Susan when again Jan's arms were around my neck. "May I kiss you now?"

"Yes," I said. "I won't stop you any more."

Richard looked at his wife.

"I'll always love you," said Jan. "Even after we get married."

The heart of Susan could no longer encircle one without the other, so it grew large enough for both of us, and Jan and I had her, too.

Everything Jan shared with me gladly.

"We don't want him to be selfish," Susan told me, "so you'll have to be a sister to him. When he offers you something, you take it."

I shared other things with him, too. When I said "dickens," he'd look solemn. "You shouldn't say that," he'd admonish. "It isn't a good word." Sometimes when he talked incessantly, every other word a "Why," I tried answering with an "Uh-huh" and a "Huh-uh," but it didn't work; he didn't know what I was talking about.

One Friday noon when Richard, Jan, and I were eating lunch, Jan asked where he came from. Expecting the old stork gag, I continued to eat, undisturbed.

"Where did you come from?" Richard Riley pushed back his plate. "A long time ago your mother and I met, and we fell

226

in love. Subsequently we were married, and out of that union you were born. You know, Jan, you were once a little egg."

"An egg, Daddy?"

"Yes, Son. Drink your milk and I'll tell you about it. In every man and woman . . ."

I stood up. "Excuse me, please."

"Sit down, Era Bell."

"But my washing. The water's hot."

"Sit down. I don't believe you've heard this story either."

I hadn't. It was an interesting story, the way he told it, the physiology and facts about the conception and birth of a child. Jan took in every word just as he did when his father explained a locomotive or a Methodist conference.

Jan's only comment was another query. "Daddy," he asked hopefully, "can't you and Mother get married again and have Era Bell born to us?"

The home life which meant so much to me was sometimes a trial to Glen, who was as happy and carefree as the hills of his native Ohio, and not too susceptible to housework. And brother Richard was strict. Little by little I filled in for Glen, helping with the salad, setting the table, and firing the furnace. In the Sunday morning bedlam which preceded church, I washed and dressed Jan, cleared the breakfast table—anything to keep from going to church with the family. After they were gone, I'd break my promise to Susan by doing the dishes and starting dinner. You can't live in a house you call home and work on a schedule. Soon Dr. Riley was involved in the Friday wash, and on Saturdays Glen scrubbed while I typed Susan's thesis. It was our house now, not theirs; we, not I.

On winter nights we made peanut butter fudge or popcorn balls and sang songs around the piano. Summer and winter we took long walks through the little park at sunset. Through Susan's artistic eyes I saw rare landscapes and fresh color, and from her musical fingers came the splendor and cadence of Bach and Wagner. At school I delved into Bible philosophy, and in it found a new respect for the Old World and a modern God, one

without a chariot, without slippers of gold. In geology, the rocks
Pop and the boys despised became my friends, and in them I
read the ancient language of the fossils. But between science and
the learned God was space. In the lowly God—the God of my
fathers—there was no space, no gaps, for the lowly God was
omnipotent.

New worlds, these, unfolding before me, worlds like cav-
erns, so vast that each was a lifetime, and I must live again and
again to explore each cavern, to travel each separate vista.

Life at the parsonage wasn't all music and poetry, however,
for the good minister, even without the wisdom tooth, still had
his Irish temper, and moments of serenity often preceded the
storm. With encouragement from the Rileys I began to write
again, entering journalism classes as enthusiastically as I ever
entered the gymnasium. Life with the Rileys made good copy
for my reporting class. A description of the Reverend's one-man
boycott on the local bread companies was posted in the journalism room, and after another piece, a rather colorful account of
his breaking up the plates at a church supper, my writing ability
spread beyond the classroom—and some of the Riley reputation
with it.

A Christmas I had almost forgotten came in on the wings
of carols and the story of the Christ child, pure white with snow
and poignantly sweet and spiritual. With Jan I watched its coming, because of Jan I caught again its true meaning. Bearing, by
command, no gifts except a toy for the boy, I joined my new
family around the twinkling tree on Christmas morning, singing
"Joy to the World," while the smell of roast turkey mingled with
that of evergreen, and mincemeat pies simmered on the window-
sill, for we were being host to all the college students Dr. Riley
could find who hadn't been able to go home, who hadn't been
invited out.

In less than a month after that happy gathering, the Riley
family was on its way to Ohio, and I was alone in the big house.
Glen had renounced formal education at the end of the first
semester, thoroughly convinced there was more joy and less dish-

228

washing back home in Ohio. He hadn't been gone a week when Susan's father was taken seriously ill. Hearing the news, Professor Crandall hurried to the parsonage with words of consolation. When he left, Dr. Riley came into the library, smiling.

"Brother Crandall is worried about you, Era Bell."

"Worried about me. Why?"

"Yes, Richard, why should he be worried about her?"

"Well, I don't know what kind of reputation I have around here, but it seems the dear brother feels it's his Christian duty to warn me that if you and Jan go home, I shouldn't be left alone with Era Bell."

"Heavenly days!" exclaimed Susan. "What does he want us to do with her?"

"Send her away, take her out of school. Shoot her." Dr. Riley was smiling, but my house was tumbling down.

"That old busybody! Richard, what did you tell him? He knows she hasn't any other home. He's never approved . . ."

"Now, Susan, never mind that." The smile left his face. "Do you think I'm a complete idiot? Don't worry, Era Bell," he said kindly. "Nothing is going to happen to you."

When I came home a few nights later there was no Jan to meet me; the parsonage was silent and ghostly in the early winter twilight. On the kitchen table was a note propped against the sugar bowl:

> Dear Era Bell,
>
> Susan's father died this morning. We are taking the noon train. Get Muriel or Gertrude to stay with you until we return. You will find money in the envelope on my desk in the study, and I have made arrangements with the grocery store to let you have whatever you want. Take care of things until we return.
>
> Richard and Susan

Below, in a crooked scrawling hand, was printed: "I love you. Jan."

On the right side of the tracks, spring brought green velvet lawns and long hedges; it brought robins and bluebirds, iris buds and lilacs, but no sage, no buffalo grass and purple crocuses. I wandered leisurely through the campus, over to the powerhouse, and crossed the tracks to the old back road where the prairie grass was soft and warm, sweet and warm. From the stadium came the familiar crack of the starter's gun, the sharp impact of spikes against cinders. Without thinking, without knowing, I began to run. Faster, faster I ran. Suddenly my legs folded beneath me, spongy and useless. I sank in the warm, green road. Cold sweat stood out on my body, my breath came in long, dry gasps, and my heart beat like a leashed tom-tom. For a long time I sat doubled over in the road, waiting for the weakness to pass. And I knew that I could never run again.

All spring there was an air of expectancy, of hushed excitement in our house that had nothing to do with Susan's thesis, though, Lord knows, *it* was excitement enough! A swift exchange of letters and telegrams preceded Richard's trip to Iowa, then more correspondence and pictures of him, pictures of Susan and Jan. We were at the breakfast table when he came in with the letter, and I could tell by his face the news was good, the waiting and hoping at an end.

"This is it, Susan!" he beamed.

"Oh, Richard. Darling!"

I got up to leave. "Sit down, Era Bell. This concerns you, too. By the way, how'd you like to return to Iowa?"

"Quit teasing, Richard, and tell us all about it." Susan was bubbling and bobbing with excitement.

"Well, you are now gazing upon the new President of Morningside College."

"Oh," I said, and wondered what was keeping Brother Crandall.

"For your benefit, Era Bell," President Riley continued, "Morningside is a Methodist school in Sioux City, Iowa, where you are going to finish."

"Me?"

230

"Yes, you. I told the committee if they took us they'd have to take you, too. That's why we turned down the other school."

"We didn't want it anyway," said Susan. "I wouldn't like to live in the South."

When school was out in June, the whole family went to work on the thesis, reducing household duties to a minimum and discarding all regular routines except Jan's meals. Dr. Riley spent most of the summer in Sioux City, driving home weekends to help with the survey. Sometimes we worked all night long, tabulating findings and compiling statistics.

As I typed, I learned of Rembrandt, master of lights and shadows; of the two English painters, Gainsborough and Reynolds, who loved children; about Raphael and his immortal Madonnas; Father Carot, from whose brush spring leaped eternal. And I learned that Whistler's "Mother" was a portrait and not a gag; that the rural homes of North Dakota had more space and respect for the picture "Indian on Horseback" than for the works of the masters; that a framed marriage license was more true to their life than P. Gauguin and all his vivid colors.

When Jan became restless, I took him to the wading pool in the park nearby. The park was beautiful and restful after constant typing, but I didn't enjoy it long. The children stared, but said little until a new boy came to the pool. He walked up to Jan, commanding and belligerent.

"Who is she?" He pointed at me. "Does she live at your house? Where does she sleep? Does she eat with you?"

"Jan, don't pay any attention to him," I said. "Play with the other children."

"Don't listen to her. She's black. Black!" the boy shouted.

The other children stood by, watching.

"Come, Jan, let's go over to the swings," I said.

"Shut up, nigger! Nigger you!" the boy taunted.

I took Jan from the pool wailing and protesting, but I couldn't take him home like that, so we walked and walked, and I talked about other things until he was too tired to protest or remember. I didn't tell the Rileys about the boy at the park, but

231

I tried to get out of going back. Dr. Riley, I think, suspected something was wrong, for he went with us one afternoon—the only afternoon the boy wasn't there.

In August, when the thesis was completed, Jan and Susan left for Ohio, and I began to pack. Dr. Riley returned from Sioux City, made final arrangements for moving, and we drove out of North Dakota, through South Dakota, and into Iowa, leaving gas station attendants bug-eyed and puzzled, wondering what kind of slavery could this be: white or black?

14) PRESIDENT'S DAUGHTER

All Morningside knew the new President was a family man, but when Dr. Riley and I pulled up to the dormitory on three flats at two in the morning, the prim Missouri matron, still groggy with sleep, wasn't quite prepared for what she saw. I was led to the last room in the farthest wing of the almost-deserted building, and I had a feeling the lady wasn't going to sleep much more that night. In the rush of last-minute packing, things were thrown into suitcases with little regard for ownership, so rather than further endanger the Riley reputation, I slept in a size 52 nightshirt and wondered how Prexy was making out at the other end of the building in pale pink jersey.

The matron waylaid me the next morning, cool, still shaken, but smiling. After breakfast, I was to go to the President's office she said, and for the time being I would make my home at the dorm.

233

The few buildings that comprised Morningside College stood like old etchings on the picturesque campus, partly concealed by overhanging trees, latticed over with moss and climbing vines. The main building, housing the President's office, was mellow with age. Dr. Riley's secretary, Grace, and the faculty members he introduced me to were warm like the building, sturdy like the trees. I knew I was going to like Morningside College.

Across the campus, through a white trellis gate that opened into the back garden, was the President's home. It was unbelievably beautiful. The walk led past a tiny goldfish pond, covered with lily pads, through a vine-covered arbor, past a marble birdbath, and up to the big stucco house. To the left of the walk, against a high hedge that separated the garden from Morningside Church, was a large rose arbor. Shrubbery almost hid the tile patio, that ran the full length of the house on the east, and a vast, rolling lawn led up to the wide steps in front. The house itself, once a showplace of Sioux City, was the most beautiful house I had ever entered, and it was to be my home.

By the time Susan and Jan arrived, we had the furniture arranged and the house in order. Two boys—Cecil, a fat divinity student, and Reggie, an English youth—took up residence in the basement and became a working part of the household. From the day of the President's inauguration—when they held up the ceremony until I got back from town with a pair of striped pants —until two years later, when Prexy handed me a diploma, there was never a dull moment.

I made my debut with the students the night of the inaugural, when nearly a hundred of them gathered on the front lawn, yelling for Dr. Riley. He had had a busy day, so I went out on the front porch to convey his greetings and regrets. They gave a couple of yells for dear old Prexy and dear old Morningside, then did what they could with my name.

"Why don't you join us?" the leader asked.

"Okay," I said, and a few minutes later was the only dark link in a howling, writhing chain of dancers that snaked in and out of the business section of the sedate community, coming conveniently to a halt in a confectionary store. I hadn't a cent with me, but somebody, I never knew who, paid for my sundae.

Sioux City got its official glimpse of the presidential family at the first night football game, in the downtown stadium. The two boys and I fell in behind the three Rileys, as they walked across the field, in the full glare of the big lights. The college band played, the audience arose, and cameras clicked all around us . . . . I wonder whatever became of those pictures?

Dr. Riley released himself from his breakfast chore, and Susan's duties as President's wife were definitely on the teacup side. Cecil was cook, Reggie, the downstairs maid. Besides the laundry, I had complete charge of Jan, now an unwilling first grader, and did the family shopping—with an entourage. Ronny Foster, a student, drove me downtown every Saturday, in return for keeping his coupé in our garage. While he parked the car, I faced the curious but smiling eyes of clerk and customer, as I walked through the stores. Jan clung tightly to my arm. Some asked if the boy was mine, he was so devoted, but most of them took me to be the nursemaid until Ronny joined us. Ronny looked like Clark Gable used to look. With Jan swinging along happily between us, as we went about our shopping, conjecture was rampant.

Most of Morningside's six hundred students were "p.k.'s" (preachers' kids), from all over Iowa and adjoining states. I soon found favor in the eyes of both teachers and students, and I don't think it was due entirely to the influence of the President, although that certainly helped. Soon after school started, I was invited to my first night hike. It was pitch dark when I joined the group, and I learned to know them first by their voices as they talked and laughed, then through the warmth of their hands as they pulled me through deep leaves, up hills, over fences. When the campfire lighted up our faces, we were very good friends.

There were no other colored students at the school, but they had seen colored people; I was no enigma to them. Their curiosity concerned the new President: could he really make muffins, and did he swear when he was angry?

The Methodist Ladies' Guild scholarship did not extend to Iowa, but my tuition was happily absorbed and forgotten in the President's back salary. As no journalism was offered at Morningside, I changed my major to social science, renewed my faint attacks on German, and settled down to enjoy to the fullest the leniency and patient sufferance of a Christian faculty. Living at the home of the President certainly had its points.

Gradually I slipped back into athletics, slowly feeling out my strength. To attend all the various practices, I had to include Jan. Put to him in the right way, he became an enthusiastic champion of female sports (especially this female's) and mascot of the Women's Athletic Association. Jan rooted and coached from the sidelines, sat quietly on my lap through tedious board meetings, interceded when we needed the college car for overnight trips to Stone Park. And neighbors mused as we passed by in the golden autumn sunset; walking home from the hockey field, arm in arm, almost an even height now, bare white legs, bare brown legs, the President's son and the President's daughter.

Cecil's cooking went from inadequate to impossible as the tempo of entertaining increased, and the third time the pressure cooker blew up, pasting beans all over the kitchen ceiling, Dr. Riley exploded with it. Kay, a tall, dark-haired freshman, came to our house to live and wrestle with the beans. She hadn't been with us long before she came to my room and sat down on the twin bed opposite me.

"Gee," she said. "How'd you rate this pretty room?"

"Asked for it."

"They think a lot of you, don't they?"

"I don't know."

"You've been with them all your life, haven't you?"

"Heavens, no! Who told you that?"

"Oh, everybody. People just take it for granted, I guess. Say," said Kay, jumping over beside me. "Why can't I move in here with you? You've got an extra bed, and it would be lots more fun together. That is," she hesitated, "if you'd want me."

236

"Sure. It's okay by me."

"Let's move now!" Kay had me by the arm. "Come on, help me lug my stuff over. Know what?" she asked, as she hung her things in my closet. "I was awfully afraid you wouldn't want me."

"Know what?" I answered. "I was awfully afraid you wouldn't ask me."

Long after we went to bed, Kay and I lay awake talking, moonlight bright as day shining in our room, soft night breezes blowing across our faces. She told me her dream of singing in the Morningside a cappella choir, of studying with the Metropolitan Opera. Climbing the heights with her, I would be a famous author and sit in a special box to hear her sing, and she would have a special seat at my lectures, and we'd take our vacations together, sailing the blue Mediterranean from the shores of Tripoli to the Isle of Capri. And thus did two Iowa girls drift off to sleep in one room, to dream the golden dreams of youth in one world, blind to the barriers outside our door: the one not knowing her power of white, the other suspecting, but forgetting, for castles are shining things, and in the blinding sun at the top of the hill color is neither black nor white.

The more help we had, the less semblance of order existed, for neither Cecil nor Reggie were entirely "housebroken." When the Rileys were out to dinner or away on speaking engagements, the President's home was a madhouse. Reggie stood in the butler's pantry with a vegetable dish, catching the baked potatoes as Cecil threw them from the kitchen, and those he didn't catch he had to eat, and those Cecil threw too hard sometimes went through the dish. The mortality rate on dishes was terrific, and the dish towels didn't do so well either, because the boys had all the ends frayed from snapping them at Kay and me. Jan, who preferred to stay with us, joined in the shenanigans and ate food he wouldn't touch when his parents were home. On warm fall nights, Kay and I would slip on our robes and sneak down to the garden to walk in the bright moonlight or sit in the shadows of the arbor, eating the sweet black grapes or the mulberries from the trees behind Science Hall. Sometimes, we'd sniff down the clothes chute for the odor of food and surprise the boys in their secret midnight snacks.

There was fun, too, when the folks were home. Dr. Riley gave a Halloween party for the faculty that ended all parties and nearly brought about the early retirement of some of the more ancient guests. From the corn-shucked game room in the attic to the devil's den in the basement came weird groans and eerie shrieks. Each member of the household manned a horror station. Mine was the manhole cover behind the house, where I stood in my witch's costume, serving to all those able to stumble outside Belshazzar's brew, a concoction of boiled vinegar, red pepper, cream of tartar, and castor oil. It was a long time before Dr. Riley coaxed another faculty member into the house. And on New Year's Day the staid citizens of Sioux City rubbed their eyes anew, when they saw Prexy and his dinner guests sliding down Dormitory Hill with the students.

Spring brought the ebony-feathered martins to their green and white house in the garden, and when the little green buds began to appear on the tree by my window, birds I had never seen before chattered and sang. The whole yard became alive: fruit trees burst into soft, sweet blossoms; flowers sprang out of the rich Iowa soil, forming a variegated border along the walks; pink bramble roses crawled over the trellis and clung to the sides of the arbors; honeysuckle vines peeked over the top of the low porch walls; and dark green fern and pale white sweet peas hid demurely in the shadow and dampness of the house, while the fragrance of the full-bosomed peonies filled the air. When the spring lethargy became unbearable, when one could no longer study, no longer think, the whole student body and faculty (God bless 'em!) deserted the classrooms and hiked to Floyd Monument on the hill. And that was Hobo Day.

Pealing out its hymns on the fresh morning air, the carillon high in the belfry of the ivy-covered church heralded each Sunday, gathering the people of Sioux City and the house of Riley to quiet worship. After our early Sunday dinner, came lazy after-

238

noons, or a long ride in the country, supper along a quiet road, under a shady tree. And there was always time to stop and enjoy the glory of a sunset over the river and the beauty of a lush green valley.

There were also early-morning student hikes to a nearby farm, midnight hikes through the woods, and poetry hikes on an afternoon, when we stopped high upon a hill to lie down on the warm grass, gazing into the blue, blue yonder, to my drifting clouds—comforting now, not beckoning. I loved the poetry hikes. Each girl recited a favorite poem, lying there, and the poems talked to each other. With our backs to the earth, our eyes on the heavens, poetry came alive up there on a hill, and once more was aroused in me the overwhelming urge to create, to write.

That summer Kay went home, both boys took summer pastorates in the country, and Susan and Jan again spent the summer in Ohio. Dr. Riley was out of town most of the time, making speeches or raising money for the school, but when he was home we entertained everybody at Morningside. Sometimes I accompanied him on short trips, driving while he read or reading to him while he drove. We visited little towns and attended church picnics and suppers. If people questioned, I did not hear them, for there were always preachers' sons and daughters I already knew or soon met.

The trips and the outings were fine, but there were times when Dr. Riley became domestic, and I wondered why I ever gave up the secondhand business. When his proclivities took the form of cooking or baking, it wasn't quite so disastrous, but when he decided to can tomatoes and string beans, it was catastrophic. Somehow his beans never stayed canned. Periodic explosions in the storeroom proclaimed each emancipation. For weeks they would foam and seethe within their glass prisons; then with a mighty boom, they would emerge with the top of the jar, and we had beans for dinner—beans that tasted a bit tangy in spite of a pinch of sodium bicarbonate.

Sometimes, after a hectic two or three days at home, Dr.

Riley would pack his bag, I'd drive him to the station, and the house, the car, and the next week or ten days were all mine. One evening a summer student came by to see him. When I told him the President was out of town, the boy sat down on the porch and began to talk about school.

"Don't you get lonesome for colored people?" he asked abruptly.

"I used to," I said, remembering St. Paul and Chicago.

"But what are you going to do with your life—when you finish school, I mean?"

"Oh, I don't know. Get a job, I guess—if I can find one."

"You know," he said, "I used to hate Negroes."

"Hate them! Why?"

"I don't know. Just because they were Negroes, I guess. Other people hated them; my folks hated them."

There was a moment of silence. I had known him for some time. He was a handsome boy, tall, blonde, friendly. One couldn't help liking him. I took a deep breath. "Do you still hate them?"

"Oh, no. Not anymore. You see, I had never known a Negro then. When I was a senior in high school, there was a colored boy in my class. Maybe you know him—Dick Haynes, a great football player—well, he was swell, just like anybody else. Say," he said, "did you ever think about getting married?"

It was getting dark, and the car was still outside in the driveway. I stood up. "I'd better put the car away. There aren't any lights in the garage."

He arose, too. "I'll go with you." As we got into the car, the boy continued, "But what will you do when you are ready to marry?"

"Well, get married, that's all." I stepped on the starter.

"You'll have to marry a white man, won't you?"

I killed the engine. "Why?"

"Well, where will you find a colored man to marry, one that is educated like you?"

I let the car coast down the hill and into the garage. We got out and closed the doors and locked them. Little stars twinkled in the darkening sky as we walked towards the house.

"Have you ever been in a big city?" I asked.

"Sure. I went to New York once."

"Didn't you see any colored people there?"

"Yes. I think so. There were porters on the train and at the hotel where we stopped. There were some Negroes on the streets, too."

"Well, a lot of those porters you saw on the train were college men, working to make money to finish their education, and a whole lot more you didn't see are educated, are professional people with jobs and offices like the people you know. Right here in Sioux City there is a doctor, a dentist, and a lawyer; all of them and their wives are college people."

"Honestly?"

"Sure." I leaned against the rose arbor. "My problem isn't where I'll find an educated colored man," I said, watching the stars and the crescent moon, "but where will an educated colored man find me?"

School hadn't been open a week when Kay had an attack of appendicitis and was rushed to the hospital. After the operation she went home, but she was not strong enough to return to school, to make the trip with the a cappella choir, to finish the castles we started. So we sadly returned to Cecil's cooking, and if he prepared his summer sermons like he did our meals, heaven by now is full of ulcerated angels.

I spent most of my senior year making a survey of the local colored people, a project which took me to strange and interesting places, including an interview with the mayor, legitimate excursions into Negro night life, and a suspended sentence at the city jail. The latter was unpremeditated. On my first trip to the jail, to interview the matron, the elevator operator stopped the car between the second and third floors, and with a meaningful wink, said, "Well, sister, what you in for?"

On my second trip to the jail, the operator said a polite

241

"Good morning," and let me off at the matron's floor. I walked the rest of the way to my destination, because this time I had a date with the judge, and it wasn't about a survey. I had a ticket for double parking, and in a few minutes I would be behind bars. It wasn't exactly a secret, this brush with the law, for Dr. Riley had given me a going-away party the night before, with at least twenty students toasting me with lemonade and wishing me a pleasant weekend. That morning I left a sad-eyed Susan and a tearful Jan. They implored the President to use his influence on the judge, but he said no, it would be a valuable experience; and I said yes, the rest would do me good.

As I joined the line in front of the judge, I wasn't quite so sure. His Honor was handing out fines and sentences with happy abandon and unnecessary generosity. Stories far better than mine were being torn to shreds, as his anger mounted. All too soon, my time arrived.

"Next!" he shouted. "Double parking at Fourth and Pierce. Guilty?"

"Yes."

"Three dollars and costs."

"But I couldn't help it, I—I . . ."

"Five and costs. Next."

I stepped aside and waited. What kind of a democracy was this? When the last person had been fined and sentenced, the judge turned to me. "Well, what are you waiting for?" he demanded brusquely.

"May I use your phone, please?"

"What for?"

"I want to phone the college for someone to come get the car—before I get a ticket for over-parking."

He looked puzzled. "I'm staying here," I explained. "I haven't got five dollars."

"Do you attend Morningside?"

"Yes, sir."

"Um," he mused. "And what are you going to be when you get out?"

242

"Out of where? Here?"

He changed the subject.

"Don't you know you're not supposed to leave a car un-attended and double-parked downtown?"

"I didn't. I left a girl in it, while I went to the store, but she got cold and got out."

"Oh," he said. "And who is this girl?"

"Sigrid Carlson. She's from Minneapolis; she doesn't know any better."

"Ah! Then it's her fault, not yours. And just where is this Sigrid person? I would like to see her."

"Oh, she's gone back to Minneapolis."

"Didn't stay long, did she?"

"No."

"Well, I'll raise that fine to ten dollars and give you a two weeks' suspended sentence."

Not knowing whether that was good or bad, I thanked him and made for the door. "I'd still like to see that Sigrid," was his parting shot, and I had a feeling he knew I was lying. I even had a feeling he had known I was coming.

Within the college, my being a Negro mattered little to students and faculty, but it sometimes interfered with outside patterns of segregation. Like the time our Women's Athletic Association gave a splash party at the Y.W.C.A. pool downtown. I had heard the Y didn't allow Negroes to use their pool, but being a member of the committee that planned it, I couldn't very well back out without an explanation. All of the board members and Jan, with two of his little friends, rode down in the car with me.

The other girls were given lockers together, but I was told I'd get mine later. When we reached the pool, a class of small children were hurried out of the water and into their clothes.

"Is this the group from Morningside College?" The swimming teacher eyed me dubiously.

"Yes," answered one of our girls.

243

"And the boys?"

"I'm Jan Riley," Jan spoke up. "My daddy is President of the college."

"They are with me," I said.

"Oh." Her attitude changed. "You just come with me, dear."

I left Jan with his friends on the bleachers and followed her as she led the way to her dressing room. "Just have a seat," she offered. "I'll be back right away." After all of the children were gone and the doors securely locked, she returned. "You can dress right here." She was flustered and apologetic.

"Era Bell, come on in. What's keeping you?" Jan called impatiently.

When I came out to the pool, all of the girls were in the water. "What happened?" they asked. "What kept you so long?"

"Can you swim, dear?" the instructor asked quickly.

"Not very well." I was beginning to suspect I shouldn't have come. Before I left, I was sure.

Assigning three good swimmers to stay with me to keep me from drowning, she personally saw to it that I participated in all their horrible games. I, who could not swim, dived into ten feet of water, turned somersaults, and crawled around on the rough bottom of the pool, in a soggy daze. I had the reassuring feeling one has about the hero of a movie: no matter what happens, he won't die. I knew only that I would not drown.

"So you went swimming today?" commented Dr. Riley that night. Jan had talked incessantly about it all through dinner.

"Yes. In the Y pool."

"Isn't that interesting!" He grinned. "Did you experience any difficulties?"

"Yes. They wouldn't let me drown."

"Of course not, silly. Do you think they want the whole town to know you were in their precious pool?"

I had heard that about Brown Lake, too, that they wouldn't rent boats to Negroes. So, when a bunch of my college friends suggested we drive out to the lake, I didn't say anything for or against it. As we approached the entrance to the park, the first thing I saw was a sign on the wooden arch over the gate which read, "NO JEWISH TRADE SOLICITED."

I blinked. I had never seen anything like that before. "Give me your money," I volunteered, "and I'll get the boats."

The woman at the boathouse smiled and said it was a nice evening for a ride. As we paddled around over the dark surface of the water, singing camp songs and hymns, I pondered over a Christian pool that didn't admit Negroes and a private lake that didn't admit Jews, and remembering the pool at Bismarck, wondered what there was about water—a purifier—that made people's hearts so unclean.

Word of my survey got around, and for a while I was much in demand as a speaker. Aside from bits of statistical data about the colored population of Sioux City, and my brief sojourns in Chicago and St. Paul, I knew very little about "my people." From the minister at Morningside Church I learned of the poet Paul Laurence Dunbar, and from our basketball team, just returned from Texas, I learned, with the other students, that Southern dialect is more regional than racial. The ancient civilizations of the "Dark Continent," its art and its culture, in my school books, were attributed to the Egyptians and other Africans, mistakenly classified as white. My ancestors were savages with rings in their noses, with thick skulls and kinky hair; they were cannibals who boiled Englishmen in iron pots and traded tons of priceless ivory for handfuls of dime store beads. One book even said Negroes smelled like goats. I asked Dr. Riley about that one—they say sometimes even your best friend won't tell you—but from what he said, I gathered that people who wrote books weren't always bright. So with a background of Norwegians, Swedes, Germans, Jews, and Irishmen, I stood before my audiences and talked about Negroes, and I hope they forgave me.

It was part of the Riley philosophy that everything is possible—even without money, so when *The Green Pastures* came to Omaha, half a day's ride away, I had an urge to see "De

245

Lawd"—an urge, two classes, and fifty cents. The urge won. I went to Omaha, had a good time, and kept my fifty cents. First, I talked Dr. Riley's secretary Grace into going, together, we interested Chuck Adams in our project; he had a new car and the same classes. Then Grace's aunt wanted to go, too, so I invited Susan. One of the classes we were cutting was Dr. Riley's own "Religion and Life," but he said he wasn't going to compete with Marc Connelly's fame or fish fries, so he excused Grace, dismissed Chuck and me, and even took Jan off our hands.

We had a wonderful trip. Each had the delicious feeling of slipping away from something. Grace's aunt hadn't been to a show in years; Susan, sans both child and husband, was gayer than I had ever seen her. I was proud of Susan, proud of the gentle woman, who having conquered her own prejudice, was able to rise above the prejudices of others.

After the show we went backstage to meet Richard B. Harrison, the man who played God. In his tiny dressing room, his long white hair encircling a kindly yellow face, his massive shoulders relaxed, he looked even more like God than he did on the stage.

The last days of college were full and exciting ones. I was writing a column for the school paper, belonged to several campus clubs (Morningside didn't have sororities), won my sweater, and was secretary of an honorary sociological fraternity. But my prospects of graduating were, for a time, threatened by my old allergy, German—the one exception to the Riley theory that all things are possible. So I chucked it. When the President was informed, I found myself in a special class, with seven other linguistic delinquents, deep in the throes of fourth-year Latin. It was a far cry from high school Caesar to Ovid, but I went about it with much the same degree of misunderstanding, and the gap went unnoticed.

Susan and Richard said they would help me; they'd take turns assisting me with my homework, but after the first week, Susan developed headaches, and Richard went out cheerfully to

246

raise money for the college.

"You know you don't have to collect every night," Susan admonished. "You're just trying to get out of helping Era Bell with her Latin."

"Are *you* still at it?" he countered.

"Richard," she said, "it's hopeless, but what can we do? She's got to graduate."

Dr. Riley grinned. "Well, we can always invite her professor over for dinner."

The professor became a fixture at our table, and Brother Ovid came out of the wilderness, jumping.

Graduation week was full to overflowing. The traditional Junior-Senior Lawn Party held in our garden was even more beautiful than the year before. Girls, in long pastel dresses, moved gracefully among the June flowers, boys grouped together, uncomfortable and shy, a tea table stood in the rose arbor, its silver service glistening in the sunlight. In my new organdy dress, I sat at the window of the upstair's sun porch for a long time, looking down on my classmates, on the hedge, the trellis, and the goldfish pond, fixing them in my memory; saddened because my school-day happiness was at an end.

Followed the Senior Tea, the Indian ceremonial at the dorm—when we were made blood brothers of the tribe of the Sioux, my Cherokee notwithstanding—picnics, parties, the Mother-Daughter Banquet, with Susan the prettiest mother present, and at last Commencement, with house guests in every spare bed and company at every meal. President Hutchins, of the University of Chicago, delivered the main address.

In cap and gown I slipped almost unnoticed into the senior procession, as it rounded the corner of the hedge, on its way to the church. I didn't hear much of what President Hutchins said, for my mind was divided between our last tablecloth, now drying—I hoped—on the line, and keeping Susan's voluminous gown from disclosing my bare legs. The speech over, Dr. Riley stood behind the pulpit, straight and solemn, in his cap and gown, the vivid doctor's scarf thrown over his broad shoulders.

One by one he handed out the diplomas. When he called my name, I clutched the gown tightly and went carefully forward. With the morning sun streaming through the stained glass windows, with the pipe organ playing softly, I stood at last before my friend. The moment I had waited for, had worked for, for the last three years had come. I was being graduated, so help me!

"Ask," said Dr. Riley, smiling, "and ye shall receive." He handed me the scroll, shook my hand.

"Is Hutchins staying for dinner?" I whispered. Susan had told me to find out.

"No, and don't worry," he whispered back. "Just leave it to me. I'll take care of it."

And he did. He always did.

Two fellowships I sought failed to materialize. Through Senator Frazier's intercession, Howard University offered me part-time work, which would defray living expenses; but I did not feel that I could again ask financial aid from the Rileys, so I gave up the idea of graduate study and began looking for a job. By the time Susan and Jan returned from Ohio in early September, I had made up my mind to return to Chicago again. If I couldn't find work in three weeks, I promised, I'd return to Morningside.

Leaving Jan was the hardest. Arm in arm we walked for the last time in the warm Iowa sunshine, through the campus, over to the little park we walked, while I explained to him why I must go away. I painted for him a wonderful future, of jobs I hoped to find, money I hoped to make, and things I would send him. Both of our hearts grew lighter, and the sorrow of parting slowly gave way to the excitement of a new adventure.

So I rode away from Sioux City that night, away from the love and shelter, the kindness and democracy of the Rileys, eager and anxious; hating and fearing no one, confident now that I could make my way among the peoples of the world, black or white.

15) CHICAGO, HERE I COME!

Hordes of people poured into Chicago in 1933 to see the World's Fair, but I came seeking work and a home among my people. This time the big city held neither glitter nor glamor for me. No longer was I awed by the girls at the Y, where again I found lodging, for all my thoughts and energies went into the finding of a job.

The first week I exhausted the list of names Dr. Riley had given me and made the rounds of the various social agencies without results, for I had neither Chicago training, field case-work experience, nor political affiliation. The University of Chicago offered a part-time working arrangement that would enable me to get the needed field work, but they weren't too insistent. Colored girls, the lady inferred, were not very reliable.

At the University's Settlement House I met Mary Mc-Dowell, ill and almost inactive. She took me upstairs to her rooms and, though she had no place for me on her staff, gave me something bigger than a job. She restored my self-confidence, confirmed my ideals, told me no obstacle was too great, nothing came too easily.

The second week, I made the rounds of the colored business houses and newspaper offices, beginning with the *Chicago Defender*. Representing myself as more of a former contributor than I had been, I managed to get an appointment with Robert S. Abbott himself. When I arrived at the sumptuous Abbott home, I was shown into a beautiful room, richly and lavishly appointed. A short, dark man, clad in a silk bathrobe, came slowly down the stairs and into the room. He glanced at the gold clock on the mantel.

"You're on time," he said, breathing heavily. "Had you been a minute late, I would not have seen you."

Thus began my conversation with the man who was founder and publisher of the largest Negro newspaper in the world, a man who was known on two continents, who fought the prejudices and hates of the white man, glorified the heritage and color of the black man, yet married two women so fair that even Negroes questioned their racial origin.

Mr. Abbott, old and ill, was no longer able to leave his home. With bitterness he told me how his trust in others had been betrayed, of the need for loyal, intelligent young men and women to carry on in his place, yet he knew the note he was giving me to take to his office would do no good, that his recommendation no longer carried weight.

My old friend, Mr. Moore, was back in the hospital having another operation, and his magazine no longer existed. The other papers, smaller and poorer, were willing to take me on a percentage basis only.

The three weeks were up, and I was still looking, searching, walking the streets, but I refused to give up and go home. Sometimes I paired off with one of the girls at the Y, and together we answered ads, waited hopefully in employment offices for jobs to come in: factory, housework, any kind of job now. There were growing hordes of us seeking employment. Those who had jobs were tight-lipped, mysterious, refusing to talk about their jobs, and when they did talk they lied, saying they worked where they could not, making wages they did not.

Finally I inserted an ad for domestic work in a daily paper. Two of the three inquirers lost interest when they learned I was colored. The third, a West Side woman desperately in need of help, hired me. I lasted only a week. Besides cleaning, ironing, personal laundry, washing windows, and scrubbing floors, there was the curling of an ungrateful little girl's very straight hair, and lugging two-ton Junior to the bathroom all through the night to keep him from drowning in bed. As soon as the house was all clean and shining, my employer paid me off and said she was sorry, I wouldn't do.

Followed more hunting and searching for a job. I paid precious money to the numerous little employment agencies that dotted the streets and was sent to places I was afraid to enter, places where jobs never existed. Now and then, I got odd jobs—a little typing, bussing dishes at the Loop Y. By scrimping, by walking until the soles of my pumps were thin and the heels worn down to nubs, I managed to live. Every letter from Susan was a plea to come home, but always there was another job in sight, another promise or hope for the morrow. We weren't allowed to cook in the Y, so many of us, whose resources were too low to afford even the nominal Y meals, sneaked crackers and cheese, even milk, into our rooms or pooled our food and cooked it on the laundry stove in the basement. For some of us, that was the only hot food we had, unless we were lucky enough to get work in a restaurant or private home.

Three months after I arrived in Chicago, I was making the rounds of the social agencies when a colored nurse caught up with me as I left her building.

"Are you looking for work?" she asked.

"Yes." The little flutter of hope and expectancy that formerly came with those words had long since died, after countless disappointments.

251

"You may not care for this kind of work . . ."

"Oh, I don't mind," I said quickly. "I'll do anything that's honest. I'm not touchy."

"My supervisor is looking for a girl. It isn't all housework; you clean and answer phones in her husband's office half the day, then help at home the other half."

"I'd like to try it. When can I see her?"

The woman took a slip of paper from her purse and wrote down a name and address. "Here," she said. "Go tonight. I'll tell her you're coming."

I had a temporary job making sandwiches that afternoon, in a little restaurant on Drexel Boulevard, but spent the remainder of the morning still looking for work. So many promises had failed, I dared not stop. At two o'clock, I was standing behind a little table trimming slices of bread, spreading, cutting sandwiches, trying to ignore the loud laughter and smart talk about me.

"Um umph!" said a colored busboy. "Baby, ain't you ever gonna smile at your sweet papa?"

The others laughed.

A white woman came up and stood beside me, watching. "You'll have to go faster than that, girl. Here, let me show you." She took the knife from my hand and began spreading the bread like an automaton. "There!" She threw down the knife. "Now let's see you get some speed on you!"

"Don't mind that ole white woman," said the busboy. "She hollers at everybody; she don't mean nothin'. I'll help you soon's I get them dishes out."

Together we finished the sandwiches on time, and I reported to the woman for my pay.

"Didja eat?" she asked.

"No."

"Go back in the kitchen and make Al give you some dinner. Tell him I said so. Be back here tomorrow, same time." She handed me a dollar bill without looking up.

Dr. and Mrs. Nelson lived in a small apartment over the

252

line in the white section of the South Side, about eight blocks from his dental office. I was nervous when I entered the house, but my nervousness left me as the tall, pale woman, sitting there in her housedress, talked quietly as she sewed.

"Can you cook?" she asked.

"Oh, yes," I answered glibly.

"How do you prepare baked beans?" She never took her eyes off the sewing.

"That depends upon how you like them. Everybody," I said hastily, "cooks differently. Just tell me how you like your beans, and I'll try to do them your way."

A slow smile spread over her face. "Can you bake pies?"

"No." She wasn't going to tie me up with that one.

"If you're quick to catch on and willing to learn, it's better than knowing too well." She asked me about myself and the Rileys; she, too, wanted to know how on earth I got way up there in North Dakota. She was a little surprised about my schooling. "Maybe you won't be satisfied with this kind of work," she said uneasily.

"For three months I've tried to get the other kind," I admitted. "I couldn't. I've got to work, and I've done housework before. I'm not ashamed to work with my hands."

When I left Mrs. Nelson, I had a job at seven dollars a week, two meals, and no Sundays. Remembering what the woman at the university had said about colored girls, I stopped at a drugstore and called the restaurant.

To save carfare, I moved from the Y to a private home, within walking distance of the Nelsons'. Now that I had a steady job, I began to look around me and evaluate the world in which I found myself. Comparing it with white standards, weighing it on white scales, I found it wanting; found myself hating the common Negro who had recently migrated from the South without benefit of freedom or education, who, having never had rights of his own, lacked respect for the rights of others. I hated his loud, coarse manners, loathed his flashy clothes and ostentatious display of superficial wealth. Yet by his

253

standards, all of us were judged; for his actions, all condemned and imprisoned in a black ghetto, separated from all of the other peoples of the city by covenants of prejudice and segregation. Little wonder my new landlady "passed."

When I moved to the Burton home, I thought Mr. Burton was white. Mrs. Burton, also very fair, had an undeniably Southern accent, their neat three-story flat was on a border street, and their janitor was a foreigner. Mrs. Burton was a corset saleswoman in a Loop department store, and her husband was foreman in a gear manufacturing plant. I had unwittingly moved into a society of borderline people, Negroes who pass for white on the job, for economic reasons, but remain colored socially.

"Sometimes," complained Mrs. Burton, "those poor white crackers say some of the meanest things about colored customers, talk to them like dogs. It just makes me boil!"

"What do you do?" I asked.

"What can I do? Sit there and take it or lose my job."

"Don't they ever wonder about you, your accent and address?"

"No. There are lots of Southern white folks in Chicago, and this address could be white or colored. Negroes just started moving out this way about five years ago. When we bought this place, there wasn't another Negro on the street, but, good God! Look at it now!"

I began to feel uneasy, to feel a color line within the color line, boundaries within black boundaries: the bigger the city, the smaller the world.

Mrs. Nelson was a patient woman. She came through the more disastrous days of my apprenticeship still calm and smiling. It began with the white collars and cuffs of her blue uniforms, which before long met the same fate as Dr. Riley's shirts. Next I plunged headlong into an orgy of household destruction. There was a certain amount of antique delicacy about the Nelson furniture, which contributed to the growing number of broken table legs and chair rounds. Nor did the office escape. My employers didn't say much, but in time I became alarmed. Mrs. Nelson's hundred-year-old plates still formed a quaint blue and white border around the dining room wall, and two giant teapots sat invitingly near the edge of a high shelf. I made a bargain.

"From now on," I told her, "I'll replace everything I break. Maybe it will cure me."

"You don't need to do that," she said. "We know you don't do it on purpose."

"No, but I do it, and I want to pay you."

I placed the wrong lid on a little glass pitcher, and it went down the neck and out through the bottom. That was four ninety-eight. When Mrs. Nelson paid me that Saturday night, she counted out eight one-dollar bills. "We've decided to give you a raise," she said.

That summer, when the Nelsons went away on their vacation, I moved into the apartment in violation of the restrictive covenant and to the horror of the landlady on the floor above. And when the three Rileys stopped to spend a night with me on their way back from Ohio, the poor landlady nearly had apoplexy.

It was like old times, being with the Rileys again. We trudged the halls of art galleries and museums and drove along the lake front, where white sailboats tossed about on the blue-green waves under a bright blue sky, and for a while I was back in the boundless white world, where all gates were open, all the fences down; for with these, my friends, I entered doors and sat at tables without the fear and the shadow of discrimination. It was a temptation to go home with the Rileys, but I chose to stay in my new black world, feeling that somewhere I could find a happy side, that between the white and the black there must be a common ground.

Before the Nelsons returned, one of the city application forms I had filled out bore fruit, and I became a summer instructor at a colored playground, three days a week, thirty-six dollars a month. Hour upon hour, I stood in the hot sun refereeing boys' softball games and putting down minor riots. Brooklyn isn't the only place where people take their baseball on the fistic

255

side. Applying girls' rules to a boys' game soon precipitated a crisis—wherein I found an unexpected champion and a new thing called race loyalty. I called three outs, but the retiring side wouldn't retire. There had been some fast double play during the innings that I neither recognized nor followed through, because it developed into a free-for-all.

"Aw hell, woman!" said a big, tough-looking boy. "Why don't you go home, before you gits hurt!"

"Good Gawd!" His buddy came up to me swinging his bat half-teasingly. "What you talkin' 'bout? Is you crazy?"

Just then a thin, shifty-eyed youth, in a loud jersey sweater and light gray pants rolled well above his ankles, walked up to the mound where I stood. The boys parted like magic. All arguing ceased.

"Teacher said you out, didn't she?" His voice was low and hissing, his red-brown eyes narrowed. The boys stirred uneasily. He caught one by the arm, hardly moving a muscle as he did so. His long, sharp fingers dug into the bare flesh; the boy winced. "Didn't she?" he repeated between his teeth.

"Yes, Slippery, sho, sho!"

"Teacher say you out, you out!" Slowly he released the boy's arm.

"Thanks, Slippery," I said gratefully.

His lip curled at one corner. I couldn't tell whether it was a smile or a smirk. He walked over behind home plate and stood until play was resumed, then disappeared as mysteriously as he had come.

It wasn't long before I called a ball a strike and started another battle. The boy who had threatened me at first now came to my aid. "You heard what the lady said," he bellowed.

"Yeah, man!"

"She say it's a ball, it's a ball, see, and I don't want no black lip!"

"You right, son, right as hell! You all been belly-achin' 'bout them peckerwood teachers, ain't you? Well, she one of us, and from now on what she say goes!" He lunged towards the leader

256

of the protesting side, his bat drawn.

I never had any more trouble. When my refereeing got too bad, they let me play, and no matter how badly I played, I always scored. When a male instructor was added, I began training a girls' track team for the city playground meet and also a group of dancers to represent our park at the Chicago World's Fair.

On the day of the meet, my team had dwindled down to one girl, and I had to loan her carfare and tennis shoes before she could attend. We didn't set any records. Through no fault of my own, the dancers were good. As one little girl said, "Teacher, you ain't got a bit of rhythm—you can't even snap your fingers." She was quite right. I put down rebellions and attended to minor details, while they worked out their own routines, a bit on the nightclub side, but original. One of the details was costumes. The girls couldn't afford them and the park didn't have them, so we settled for nice clean gym suits. At the last moment, the piano player resigned, and to those who may have witnessed the tap number without music, we, too, were sorry.

When the playground season ended, I could snap my fingers, and, more than that, I got my old job back, had a postal savings account, and a little more knowledge and understanding of my people.

One night in a store-front church, I got another kind of understanding. I had gone to the church to observe religious emotionalism and to hear the spirituals my father used to sing —and the new Negro hates, wants to forget. On the platform were four female shout-singers, swaying, swinging singers, with voices like steamrollers and voices like angels: a big husky one with whiskers on her chin, a little slick-haired one with a mellow voice, a fat light one, working so hard at her music making, and a six-footer with the muscles of a stevedore. As the latter stepped out from the others, the timidity dropped from her expression, powerful arms reached out, and a voice like thunder rolled up from the valley of her soul. Still singing, she led them down from the pulpit, marching, strutting like a general. She had the audience in the palm of her hand, and she knew it. Lord, how that big woman could sing!

I had come to be entertained, but there was nothing amusing about these people now. Their blood flowed in my veins, their color, their features were mine, but not their God, for theirs was a faith beyond anything I had ever experienced. They were singing again, those four women, singing now a song of triumph.

When they sang "Holy!" the whole congregation was lifted to its feet. Some held up their hands and screamed, some stood mute, some cried. I sat tense and tight, trapped in the hard shell of my white folks' religion. All around me they cried, "Holy!" Their tearstained faces said, "Holy!" The eloquent black hands said, "Holy!" The tremulous lips cried, "Holy!" Even the pipe organ shouted, moaned, got down on its knees, and cried, "Holy! Holy unto the Lord!"

Mrs. Nelson had been right. I could not be content with housework. All through the winter, I watched the ads for jobs, filled out application blanks, and continued to make the rounds of social agencies on my day off. I hurried through morning cleaning at the office, so I could practice up on my typing, and I coaxed the doctor into letting me do some of his letters. In the spring, the Illinois Occupational Survey was set up, and I applied for a job as interviewer, giving the Nelsons as reference.

"Probably nothing will ever come of it," I told them. "It isn't that I don't like working here. Both of you have been wonderful to me, and I appreciate it, but I've had interviewing experience on newspapers, and this job pays eighty dollars a month."

"We know," they said. "We'd hate to lose you, of course, but we don't blame you for wanting to better yourself. We knew we couldn't keep you here forever." So they wrote such a good recommendation that I was one of the first hired.

Reporting at a relief station in the heart of the Negro district, I made my way through a block-long line of clients; old people, young people, poor, ragged, silent. They reminded me of that picture in the devil book, of the dying souls marching on to perdition. A staff of seven women, all white, were already at work setting up the program. The supervisor was nice, but the others, especially the three older women, resented me. At noon, they cleared off a table and began to eat their lunch.

"Won't you join us?" asked the supervisor.

"Thanks," I said, "but I didn't bring my lunch. I'll eat out."

"Oh, come on. The food around here's lousy. I've got more than I can eat, if you don't mind thick bread." She handed me a sandwich and a banana.

The others began to talk among themselves. "I hear they're going to be putting on more people."

"If they do, I hope they have the good taste to hire people who belong here."

"Yes. I was born in Chicago, myself."

"I'm from the East, but I've lived here long enough to call it home."

They glared at me. "Where are you from, the South?"

"No," I said.

"Where then?"

"Iowa and North Dakota."

"North Dakota! Aren't you a long way from home? What did you do before you came here?"

"Attended school."

"High school?"

"No, college."

There was an awkward pause. Immediately, I was sorry, for I was fast learning that mentioning a degree during a depression was like waving a red flag in front of a bull; and a Negro girl with a degree was like waving the bull.

"No wonder you caught on so quick this morning. No wonder you did that filing so fast," said the supervisor. And that didn't help matters any either.

That afternoon I slowed down, trying to pace myself with

259

the others, but before I knew it I was back at my old speed, doubling their production. The women waited, but I didn't talk about college or brag about my work, didn't use "big words," as they had expected, so they began to speak to me, to talk a little. Soon, they, too, were offering me part of their lunch, and by the time the unit was moved to a fieldhouse, all the rancor and animosity were gone.

Relief clients who failed to come in for occupational classification were visited at their homes. It was my first contact with the intimate home life of the city's poor, and I was shocked by the illiteracy of the young as well as the old, the stark poverty in which they lived, the lack of shame and decency manifested in the telling of their stories, and I was touched by their deep appreciation for kindness. There were those whose meekness and humbleness angered me, for I did not know then that this was a thing they had learned in the South—and, more recently, from some of the sharp-tongued Northern caseworkers, so exalted by their power to give or deny that they assumed a position equal to God.

A few of the homes I entered were neat and clean, giving evidence of better days, but the majority of them were less than dungeons: bare, dirty, rat-infested rooms, crowded to overflowing, breeding grounds for crime and disease. Mistaking me for the "relief lady," I was sometimes met by sullen faces, peering through partially closed doors. They hated the relief lady. "Questions, questions, questions!" they cried. "Why don't you let us poor folks alone? We done tole you all 'bout everything. You got it all writ down somewheres!"

As our staff grew, the number of Negro workers increased, and the proprietor of the little Greek restaurant on the corner refused us further service. Not that he cared, he explained, but his white customers were complaining. His white customers were a few employees from a nearby factory and quite a few drunks and loafers. Our white co-workers boycotted the place for a while, but one by one they returned, and we pretended not to notice.

As the work drew to an end, interviewers were laid off and stations combined, until the survey finally closed in late September, two days after I had been made assistant supervisor.

Again I was out of work, but I did not return to the Nelsons'. I had Chicago experience now and seventy-five dollars in postal savings. It was a good feeling, having money; it gave me strength to trudge the streets and fortitude to face closed doors again.

The survey staff had been directed to a federal office on Michigan Avenue, where exams were being held to recruit personnel for the WPA offices then being set up. Of the positions listed, clerk and typist were the only two I qualified for, so I gritted my teeth and took the examinations, hoping (please God), they wouldn't call me on the typist.

October, and I was still walking, still looking, still filling out applications. I moved to a cheaper room, closer inside the Black Belt topographically—and racially. This time, there was no mistaking my landlord and landlady's race. I paid two weeks in advance—just in case they found out I was unemployed. They asked no questions; their rules were simple. "You pays every Saturday morning," the woman told me. "Fifty cents extra for privileges, and don't leave no lights burning."

I couldn't count the roomers. Every morning, I met strange faces coming in and going out; sometimes at night there were noisy parties down the hall and the angry voices of men and women fussing and cursing. I had a feeling I was in the wrong place, but when I moved in, the landlady was showering invectives on a couple who were trying to leave, and I didn't know how I could get away without inviting a similar fate.

Days went by and still no work, so I decided to save money by paying the additional fifty cents and cooking in. "Here is half a dollar," I said. "I would like to use the kitchen."

"Kitchen?" she echoed. "Don't nobody use my kitchen. Hardly room enough in there for me."

"But you told me when I rented the room . . ."

"No, I didn't!" She began to raise her voice. "I ain't never

261

told you nothing about no kitchen. The only thing extra around here is room privileges."

"Room?"

The woman suddenly threw back her head and laughed. "Privileges!" she screamed. "Oh, my God, child! Don't you know what privileges is?" She bent down in another spasm of laughter. "No wonder you around here asking me about my kitchen." She was convulsed again. "Girl, where'd you come from?"

I turned and walked down the hall.

"No need you getting mad. If you want to give up that room, it's all right with me. I can git a dollar more for it anyway, and rent it to someone who'll use it."

That night I moved back to the Y.

I made the rounds again, and even applied for a job as detective at the South Center Department Store, but still no work. Through the Y, I found a real friend in a colored woman who operated a real estate business. She gave me a couple of days' typing each week, she didn't have enough work to keep me busy even then, so she sent me on unnecessary errands and spent a lot of time taking me out to lunch.

"Something will turn up after a while," she'd say. "Keep trying; don't ever give up hope, because I believe in you. You can't let me down."

By November my faith and my money were fast diminishing, so I answered an ad for a maid's job in a penthouse on the Gold Coast. It was afternoon and evening work, which would —if I got it—leave me free in the mornings to help my real estate friend and make the employment agency rounds.

When I approached the building, the uniformed doorman reached for the door, glanced up, saw me, and withdrew his hand. I went in under my own power, but that power dwindled as cold eyes were raised, resentful and hostile, as I walked across the thick carpet of the lobby to the desk.

"What do you want?" demanded the receptionist, sullenly.

"I came to see Mrs. Cole. I have an appointment."

She got the apartment on the phone. "Good morning, Mrs. Cole." Her voice was at once bright and sweet. "There's a —a—colored girl here to see you. Yes, Mrs. Cole. She says she has an appointment. Yes, of course, Mrs. Cole. All rightie, I'll send her right up, Mrs. Cole."

As I waited by the ornamental bronze doors of the elevator, the richness and beauty of the lobby seeped through the film of human coldness. I marveled that there were people wealthy enough to live in such a palace, to call it home. The elevator shot up to the top of the skyscraper; a Filipino boy came forward as I stepped into the hall.

"Come," he said.

He ushered me into a long room that looked very much like a morgue. Each piece of furniture was swathed in white cloth, and the windows were bare of curtains. The boy pulled out a chair for me and disappeared. I sat down, scarcely breathing, afraid to move, watching the pendulum of the huge grandfather clock swing back and forth below the hem of the cloth that covered it. I wanted to leave, but I couldn't just walk out without seeing anybody—they'd think I had stolen something, so I sat back and counted the strokes of the clock.

She was halfway across the room before I saw her, moving in like a tank, she was a huge person, her bust and stomach running together like a man's shirt front, the white top of her sleeveless dress joining the black skirt around her ample hips, her dark hair drawn straight up from her face into a tight knob on top of her head. She stopped fully ten feet away.

"Good morning," I said uncertainly. "I'm the girl who called this morning about the ad."

She lowered herself into a chair without removing her eyes from my face. "Can you wash dishes?" she said, bluntly, defiantly.

"Why, yes," I said, "I think so."

"Humph!" She snorted contemptuously. "I'm very particular about my dishes, about everything. Anyone who can't wash dishes can't work for me. Every pot and pan in my kitchen

263

shines as bright as it did the day I bought it. Pots and pans have to be scoured as well as washed."

I didn't say anything.

"I've never had a Negro work for me," she said reflectively. "I've always had whites and Orientals. My Filipino boy has been with us for years."

I didn't say anything.

"Do you like children?"

"Yes, I do."

Slowly she arose, reached under the white shroud of a tall object, and withdrew a picture of three children. She handed it to me. "These are my children."

I looked at the picture and tried to hide my disappointment —the ad said nothing about children or pots and pans. "They're nice."

She almost snatched the picture out of my hand. "They're remarkable children. We adopted them when they were babies."

I wondered where they were, and how children could live in a place like this. My expression must have reflected my thoughts.

She stood up. "You won't do." Her voice was hard and impatient. She pressed a button inside the door, and the boy appeared. "Show her out of here!" she ordered.

Gladly I left the rich folks' castle, hurried past their potted palms and over their deep-piled carpets, through the great bronze doors. Outside the winter sun shone down upon me; no one could take that away. The hard cement of the sidewalk felt good to my feet, and it, too, was free.

When I returned to my room that night, a long envelope from the Department of Public Works was awaiting me. I tore it open nervously: "If you are still available for work," it said, "please call at this office December 1 for assignment." . . . If I was still available!

That night I had a nightmare, and its name was Mrs. Cole.

I was downtown for my appointment half an hour ahead of time, steeled for another interview and another rebuff.

"Miss Thompson?" inquired the man as he glanced up from a sheaf of papers. "You did well on your exam," he said pleasantly. "Would you accept a job as senior typist at ninety dollars a month?"

I opened my mouth. The man looked at me and grinned. "It's night work, may not last long," he added, holding out the papers. "Here, sign these, all six copies, and report to Mr. Hanson, administrative staff, at four tonight."

So began the temporary job that turned out to be the longest job I ever had. For five years, I worked from one payday to the next amid a wave of layoff rumors and layoffs that weren't rumors. Mr. Hanson introduced me to my supervisor, a jolly woman who presided over four long rows of busy typists. I looked at the big machines with their extra long carriages, looked at the payroll sheets as big as billboards with nothing but numbers, and became a little ill. If there was anything about a typewriter I disliked more than the letters, it was that little row of figures I had so studiously ignored all through school.

The supervisor assigned me to a machine near her desk and gave me a stack of cards to type. I spoiled most of them. "Don't be nervous," she said, patting me on the shoulder. "You'll be all right when you get used to it."

It went better after that. I worked through my rest period to make up for the cards I had spoiled.

At eight o'clock, supper time, the girl next to me smiled. "Would you like to come over and eat with us?" she invited.

I pulled my chair over beside her desk.

"I'm Angela, and this is Helga. We're new, too."

There was a foreign inflection in their voices, and unconsciously I was saying "Yah" again and feeling good inside. They were younger than the other girls, just out of high school, and were the only junior typists in the group. The three of us clung so close together that even the supervisor forgot I was a senior and kept me on cards for a month. Far be it from me to remind her—I needed that job.

During peak periods, typists were loaned to the filing department, but not without protest, for no one wanted to work for the blonde bomb named Silver. The second time I was sent to her, she threw a batch of cards in front of me, more cards than I could file in two nights. I scowled.

"If you don't like it, you know what you can do." She stood there glaring, waiting for me to fight back. Silver liked to fight.

"I came over here to work, didn't I?"

"But you didn't want to."

"If I didn't want to, I wouldn't have come!" That wasn't quite the truth, and both of us knew it.

"Do you mean to tell me you like to file?"

"I'd rather file than type, any day." And that was the truth.

"If you mean that," she said, the hostility gone, "I'll get you transferred over here."

"Let me think it over first." As long as I stayed on cards with Angela and Helga, I was contented, but the day they put me on payrolls I went running to Silver and became a permanent member of her staff.

When I had worked around her long enough to see beneath her hard exterior, I found a lonely little country girl and a friend. The first time I went to her home, I was almost afraid, for she was so wild and free with men in the office I half expected to find a prearranged tryst awaiting me. But in her cozy little apartment was a different Silver, a quiet, subdued girl, hungry for small talk, for knowledge and a place in the world. After dinner, she called in her neighbor, and for a long time the three of us talked about our own hometowns, and I came away marveling at the nice apartments available to white girls for the same price I paid for a shabby little room at the end of a dark hall.

After the first big layoff there were only two colored girls left on our floor, Ellen and I. Ellen Harris was a pretty Chicago girl who went quietly about her duties, bothering no one. It was some time before we became friends, because Ellen was very light, and I wasn't sure she'd like me, but she did. It was white people Ellen didn't care for.

Because of the night work, I had moved from the Y to a room on South Parkway with a couple who proudly boasted of being one of Chicago's first families. They didn't keep roomers, really, but occasionally permitted a paying guest to occupy the extra bedroom. One night I walked in on a party my landlady was giving for some of her distinguished friends.

"Good evening," I said as the guests looked up.

All was silence. As I went down the hall, I heard my landlady explain: "That's the girl who helps me around the house. I'm letting her stay until I can find a maid."

Soon she was asking me for two weeks' rent instead of one. Things weren't going any better for the first families than they were for the last ones. The advances eventually grew into outright loans, but, as long as the amount due did not exceed a month's rent, I didn't mind. However, when the husband and son and the son's wife began eating food from my side of the refrigerator, that was helping around the house too much, so I moved again.

My new home was ideal; the room was clean and reasonable, the landlord and landlady were prosperous and intelligent, but they, like Ellen, didn't like white people. I found that out the day I brought Silver home with me. We were met with a cold, hostile silence, far more eloquent than words. I was surprised at first; somehow I had never thought of Negroes being prejudiced, that they could return hate with hate, and hate with far more justification.

When Gwyn Doyle stopped over that summer, on her way to a vacation in California, I was hard put to know how to spend the day. She was a successful Fargo advertising woman now, but still the same old Gwyn of high school and college days. People stopped to stare, as we embraced on the train platform; they stared as we walked arm in arm through the depot and to the bus. I wanted to take her to a nice cafe in the Loop, but there were many places I couldn't go, and for some peculiar reason I was ashamed for my white friend to know that white

267

Chicago did not completely accept me. As the bus rolled through the Negro section, the stares did not subside. I remembered how Negroes looked at me as I walked down the street with Dr. Riley, looked at me as if I were a prostitute. They couldn't know about Grand Forks, and Morningside, and about Susan and Jan, any more than they could know about Gwyn. I was ashamed for my white friend to know that black Chicago did not completely accept her. Remembering my landlady, I took Gwyn to lunch at a corner drugstore and found a shady knoll in Washington Park, where we could sit on the cool grass and talk, where, under the pure blue sky and the whispering trees, no shadow of race would come between us.

When Gwyn left that night, I walked away from the depot feeling that I was fighting the world alone, standing in a broad chasm between the two races, belonging to neither one.

I got Ellen to take me to her club, and because of her, they asked me to join. Their easy talk and happy, careless fun drove me into a self-conscious silence. None of them came from states where I had lived, nor had they attended my schools. On the overnight club trips to the country, I did much better. I could outrun, outride all of them, and in the heat of competition I forgot my inhibitions, and they began to like me, both the girls and the boys.

It was Esther Kerner, the little Jewish stenographer, who first told me about Marian Anderson. Esther, well-read and broad-minded enough to marry a Scotchman, was amazed when I told her I had never heard of the famous singer. That night I went to her home, and a Jew, a Scotchman, and a Negro sat on the floor and listened to a phonograph record, as Miss Anderson sang. The more the Kerners talked, the more conscious I became of my ignorance of Negroes, and the more anxious they were to help me, so they loaned me books and took me to concerts and lectures, to dance recitals and forums. With them I could talk freely about people and races, for they understood black hate and knew white prejudice, and as I talked with them, the chasm narrowed.

My new-found racism suffered a blow the night Joe Louis was knocked out. In this, his only defeat, when black people all over the world were having heart failure—some dying—I won a dollar and a half. We had to work overtime that night, so, with the permission of the supervisor, I smuggled my radio into the office, and we formed a pool, drawing for rounds. I got round twelve. So did Schmeling.

When our office moved into the Merchandise Mart, at that time the world's largest building, neither the merchandisers nor the twenty-four thousand employees welcomed us. They didn't want their nine miles of corridors cluttered up with WPA and its shovel-leaning clientele. Our department, housed in the warehouse in the rear of the building, was quite devoid of the luxury and splendor that marked the rest of the building. Soon eating places were declared out of bounds during working hours, and new washroom facilities were installed to prevent us from using the big lounge on the second floor, but we still came in the front door. It was in a little shop on an upper floor where Theresa, one of the girls from the office, and I had gone to buy rain capes that I experienced my first class discrimination.

"Where do you work?" asked the clerk?

"WPA," said Theresa.

"We don't sell to people from there," he said.

Theresa couldn't understand. "Why?" she protested. "Isn't our money just as good as anybody else's?"

The man didn't answer.

Theresa couldn't understand a lot of American customs, including prejudice, and I guess that is why I liked her so well. One night we were having dinner at International House when a woman approached our table, garbed in the white robe and headdress of some Far Eastern country. In perfect English, she asked if she might join us. We were delighted.

"We were just wondering," said Theresa, "what nationality you were."

"Certainly. I'm Burmese; my home is in Rangoon. You know," she said, smiling, "I came to your table because I was

269

curious about you. I thought you looked interesting."

Our guest turned out to be the wife of the head of Burmese education, on a two-year study tour of America.

"What do you girls do?" she asked.

"We work for the WPA."

The woman looked interested.

"You're supposed to laugh," I told her.

"Laugh? Why should I laugh?"

"Oh, everybody laughs when you say WPA. It's kind of a joke."

"A joke? A system devised to give jobs to thousands of un-employed people, a joke? Taking people off dole and training them for jobs, so they can make an honest living—you laugh at a government that does that? I don't understand."

We felt kind of foolish. The woman asked many questions and seemed to know more about our country and government than we did, even about the nightclubs on the South Side.

"If you ever go to my country," she said, giving us her card, "please come to see me."

When she left, I began to laugh. "Fat chance we've got of going to India on a WPA salary."

"That isn't very funny," said Theresa.

"No," I sobered. "It isn't."

By Christmas, I was back on the night shift. We had a party Christmas Eve, with cake and ice cream and a slightly plastered Santa Claus. Our supervisor was in the same condition. After the party, he came over to my desk and waved a wobbly finger in my direction. "You know what's gonna happen to you?" he asked.

"No. What?" If he knew anything about the new layoff rumors, now was the time to ask him.

"They're gonna get you," he said, steadying himself against the table. "Yes, shir, get all you cullud folks. Specially smart ones like you. Hitler gonna send a bullet straight over here headed for you. Put you back where you belong."

270

I laid down my work and went on a pass. A long pass.

The day after Christmas, the rumors increased; everybody was nervous and irritable. On New Year's Eve the ax fell, laying off fifty percent of the staff—and Hitler got me. The office was in a turmoil, some of the girls cried, some were angry, a few shrugged their shoulders and tried to joke.

"Be seeing you at the flophouse," shouted Silver.

We laughed a little, trying to hide the hurt.

When we were dismissed, I hurried out of the building and into the cold winter night, not waiting for Ellen. I walked across the bridge and turned down Wacker Drive towards the tall buildings rising up white and ghostly against the dark sky, their lighted windows like thousands of tiny eyes. I stopped to watch a barge slide silently up the black Chicago River. Walking until I came to a theater, I entered and lost myself in a world of make-believe. When I came out, bells were ringing, horns and whistles blowing, all about me people were shouting, "Happy New Year!"

16) MY AMERICA, TOO

Again long days of job seeking, of walking in the rain and snow, of answering ads, inquiring at offices, filing applications. The Chicago Relief Administration gave me first hope, then assurance, of a clerical job at a hundred dollars a month. I waited two weeks, then went back and was told I would be called in a few more days; but days passed, then another week, and still no word, so again I returned.

"Oh," said the lady who had hired me, "didn't we notify you? The funds were withdrawn. We can't possibly use you."

Ellen Harris and Esther Kerner urged me to become certified for relief and placed on a project, but relief was charity— I couldn't accept charity, my pride would not let me. I got a job in a grocery store and stayed just long enough to tell a customer the truth about some spoiled vegetables. A deaf woman in Rogers Park hired me as her companion, but when I came with my suitcase, ready to begin, her husband said that she didn't need anybody, that it was a mistake. Again my real estate friend created jobs for me, helped me mark time.

I was beginning to wonder how much longer I could hold out against certification, when I got a call to return to the Chicago Relief Administrative staff as a junior clerk, same salary. Determined this time to become so indispensable that they would never again lay me off, I worked harder than ever before, volunteering for extra work, assuming responsibility for work left undone, training new employees.

When the furniture show came to the Mart, I went in one noon, while most of the guards were at lunch, and as a representative of Evans' Furniture Store, got as far as the bed with the built-in radio and bed lamps (an idea I had, but never submitted) before the sentry asked for credentials. The urge to design was back. Going to the telephone book, I selected five likely furniture companies and sent them letters requesting an interview. A firm at the Furniture Mart responded immediately, and an interview was arranged, but the sweet little receptionist tipped them off before I had a chance.

"A colored girl," she said meaningly over the phone. "A N-e-g-r-o to see you."

When I got upstairs, my man was so busy he sent an assistant's assistant to tell me they weren't in the market for either designs or designers, meaning me.

Well, there was still journalism. I wondered how it would feel to go to college on my own money, not working for room or board, to take a course because I wanted it, and not because it was required, so I bought a portable typewriter and enrolled in a night class at Northwestern.

The class was composed mostly of older men and women, serious and determined. The instructor was suave, sophisticated, with a studied indifference that fringed on boredom. He would get paid, he taunted, whether we got anything out of the course or not; but there were times when he forgot himself, and the animated discourse which followed explained why they paid him.

I might just as well have been back in North Dakota or Iowa, as far as colored classmates were concerned. A few I met in the halls, saw a few in the library and on the campus, but never got close enough to speak to them; and I got the feeling they wanted it that way, that I could add the barrier of numbers to those of color and class. It was hard enough for one Negro to get along, so, they reasoned, it would be twice as hard for two. There was also a certain amount of pride placed upon the doubtful distinction of being an "only Negro," the thing I came to Chicago to escape. The world was becoming very small indeed. The white students, also conscious of racial patterns, made few overtures, so my little experiment of going to college with money and clothes and a job proved to be the loneliest school days of my life.

Early in the semester, I was called upon to read my article —a rather long feature on the Negro burial associations that had superseded, to some extent, the lodge, and were well near the top of Negro businesses, in spite of their doubtful legal status. I don't think anyone in the room knew what I was talking about, including the instructor, and he took no more chances after that. In the course of our work, we were to visit the Chicago Board of Trade, so I took two hours off one morning and went to fabulous La Salle Street, where I sat in the gallery, fascinated by the tumultuous transactions of the grain world. When I paused in the lobby to see the grain exhibit, an elderly guide joined me.

"Interested in grain?" he asked.

"Yes," I pointed proudly to a phial of North Dakota flax. "I've seen that grow."

Soon we were deep in a discussion on farming. Eventually the conversation got around to what brought me to the grain pit. He beamed when I told him I was going to school, and he asked if I knew the famous Negro dermatologist, Dr. T. K. Lawless. As usual, I didn't, so he told me about him and the work he was doing and bade me follow in his footsteps.

"No matter what you do, do it well, be the best there is, and

274

remember, here in America all things are possible, everyone has the opportunity to become great."

So I paid thirty dollars for a course at a noted university, and an Irish guide, amid the shouts of the grain giants, taught me more in half an hour than the learned professor did in a semester.

There was method in my education: all employees enrolled in tuition schools were exempt from overtime. After each layoff, overtime (without pay) increased, until the grumbling and discontent neared open revolt. Feeling slightly guilty about my two nights off, I got out a little one-page newspaper and surreptitiously passed it around the files. It made them laugh. I wrote another, poking fun at the higher-ups and flattering my best friends, and that one got out of hand. It passed along from one section to another, until it disappeared into the Holy of Holies. Everybody waited breathlessly. When the door opened, the supervisor came out laughing. We relaxed, and my salary continued.

For want of a better name, I called the paper the *Giggle Sheet,* and it soon spread to other departments. One day, the Big Supe came out of her sanctuary and over to my desk.

"You're wasting your time here," she said, unsmiling.

I wondered how she found out. The tall file cabinets formed a secluded recess, in the R-S-T section, of which we had quickly taken aesthetic advantage, producing, to a limited audience, an impressive ballet with the new wheel-bottomed chairs.

"I'm sorry," I said, and hung my head.

"What for?" she demanded. "Anybody who can write like this," she threw the "staff" copy of *Giggle Sheet* on my desk, "hasn't any business filing. You belong on the Writers' Project, where you can develop your talent. I'll see what can be done."

But salaries of certified professional workers, it seemed, were less than I was making, so I continued to file, with less emphasis on ballets and more on writing.

In time, the good people of the Mart prevailed, and most

275

of WPA was moved to a less pretentious warehouse on lower Michigan Avenue. There, *Giggle Sheet* celebrated its first birthday by putting out a yearbook—and came out with a $3.39 surplus, after selling all two hundred copies. The papers I had been typing at home fell so far short of our increased circulation that I went to the Supe and laid my cards and the $3.39 on her desk. The paper should continue, she said, and if I could cover all departments on all four floors, she would provide the mimeographing. The unpaid staff grew, and the free paper became larger, and for the benefit of you taxpayers who might be experiencing belated qualms, the work was done on our own time.

By vacation time, I had saved a travel fund of fifty dollars—enough to go East, for I had to see more of America; rural and urban Midwest were not enough. Traveling by bus, I was able to make the trip East on forty-five dollars, and didn't miss a thing, not even an automat. I stopped in Detroit to see Harry. It was like getting acquainted all over again, and I think Harry suddeny finding a strange sister on his hands, was quite relieved when my stay was over.

As I boarded the bus for Canada, an irascible old woman was having an argument with the driver about her suitcase. Exasperated, the middle-aged man accompanying her moved over to the seat next to me.

"My aunt can make me so angry," he exclaimed. "But I fixed her; I told her I'd sit with you!"

I looked at him.

"She doesn't like colored people," he explained. "She doesn't like anybody but herself."

I raised the window. It was getting stuffy.

"Good!" he said happily. "I like plenty of air. I was afraid you wouldn't want the window up."

I buried myself in a magazine. When the bus picked up speed, the early September breeze whistled through the window. "Now, if that wind is too much for you . . ." he began.

"Oh, no," I said, trying to keep my teeth from chattering. "It's quite all right."

He was silent for a while. The wind blew harder, blew through his thin, grayish hair, until he pulled his coat collar up around his neck. "I'm afraid you'll catch cold in that draft," he said, reaching for the window. It came crashing down on his little finger. Wringing his hand, he jumped up and down in the aisle, threatening to sue the bus company. "Just look at my finger!" he cried, thrusting it under my eyes. "Don't you think it's broken? Can't you see it swelling?"

I couldn't.

Eventually he calmed down, but he never stopped talking until we parted that evening at Niagara Falls. After the inevitable race question was disposed of, he told me about his student days at college and showed me points of interest all along the highway, an old route to him. As we passed a Heinz plant he described seven of their fifty-seven varieties; he knew the exact place where beautiful Lake Superior came into view, and he pointed out tobacco plants, the first I had ever seen. When we stopped for lunch, my friend joined his pouting aunt, who I strongly suspect, held the family purse strings. After lunch, I stood by a post near the bus reading a Canadian newspaper. I saw my friend come out of the lunchroom and disappear behind the buses, then run back to the lunchroom, look inside, and run toward the ladies' rest room—and I wondered what he'd lost in there.

"You can't go off and leave her," he told the driver excitedly, as he came back to search the bus. "I know she's around here somewhere!"

"Can't wait much longer," said the driver. "We're late now."

I looked up at the bus in front of me. It said "Indianapolis." They were looking for me.

In Niagara I picked up a twelve-year-old Italian boy, who took my bags to the other depot and volunteered to show me the way to the Falls. It was a nice walk, after riding all day in a bus, and the kid was full of information. He wouldn't accept pay or even let me treat him—said he was going over anyway. When I came out of the dressing room, all togged out in rubber pajamas, on my way to Cave of the Winds, the kid was still there.

"If you're sure you can find your way back," he said, "I'll be going now."

My seatmate on the bus out of Niagara that night was a young married woman, still bubbling over from her holiday with childhood friends. Before we were well out on the highway, she and I and the couple behind us—an English girl and her Polish husband—were old friends. The other passengers didn't get much sleep that night. We got out for coffee at every stop, we sang songs and heckled the driver, we told stories and laughed at nothing; then early the next morning, in the damp grayness of dawn, the girl slipped out of the bus on the edge of a little Pennsylvania town and was gone. A Boston college boy, returning from a summer with his grandmother in Jersey, soon took her place. These three companions, thoroughly familiar with the East, made my entrance into New York an exciting one. When we arrived at the terminal they put me on a subway for the Harlem Y.W.C.A., and I was on my own.

New York is a wonderful city. I climbed inside the Statue of Liberty, went through the liner *Queen Mary,* waded in the Atlantic Ocean, visited every observation tower, mourned at everybody's tomb, temple, and monument. Few were the things I didn't see, didn't do. New Yorkers, contrary to western propaganda, turned out to be very friendly people. Police went off their beat to direct me, bus drivers were patient while I struggled with their two-man, every-other-corner system, and no one tried to rent me the Brooklyn Bridge. On exclusive Riverside Drive, people were just as human, I found. Approaching a stern-faced, gold-braided colored doorman, in front of the biggest and most luxurious apartment building, I asked if he had any vacancies— something small and cozy for the winter. Bowing low, face solemn, he said in a thick Memphis cockney, "Madam, I am so dreadfully sorry, but we ain't got a thing, don't you know."

"Oh, deah!" I moaned. "Must I return to Harlem?"

"Do, madam," he answered sadly. "Please do!"

When I got to the corner, I looked back and he and his gold

braid were doubled up laughing.

Before I left New York, I had lost five pounds and found Sarah Cohn, my Bismarck friend, now a well-paid secretary who divided her evenings between a private pool, where she was lifeguard, and an orchestra, where she was the only female musician. Sarah had followed through.

The last thing I did in New York was to visit a colored newspaper and apply for a job. I wanted to hear "No," and know it didn't matter.

I spent a day in Washington, D.C., and thought I was deep in the heart of Dixie. While ascending the narrow stairs of the Capitol on my way to the dome, I was caught between two groups of Southern white people who out-accented Amos and Andy, and I thought my lynching time had come.

From Washington into Maryland I went—beautiful Maryland with its green velvet hills and its red clay roads, which I was ready and willing to leave long before I did. At a little bus stop, in the middle of the night, high in the Cumberland Mountains, I was introduced to Jim Crow, Southern style. Everyone got out of the bus for coffee. The other two colored passengers went into the lunchroom ahead of me, but when I entered they were nowhere to be seen. Picking up a wrapped sandwich, I moved on up the line.

The man behind the counter drew my coffee and, nodding to the rear, said, "Back there."

In a corner of the kitchen, partly hidden by a dirty curtain, sat the two colored passengers.

"Back there!" he repeated, pointing to the curtain.

I put the sandwich back on the rack, left the cup of coffee on the counter, and walked out. Alone in the empty bus, anger gave way to fear, and all the awful stories I had heard of the South loomed big and terrible. I had defied a white man: black men and women had been lynched for less. When the bus finally drove away, I breathed a prayer of relief. It was a sour ending to a lovely trip.

New layoff threats were mingled with rumors of complete

279

disbandment of the WPA, as the depression subsided. Many of my white friends returned to private industry. Then began a wave of state and federal civil service examinations, and I took every one, from rooming-house inspector (which required one to draw the inside of a flophouse), to city policewoman, where applicants under five feet didn't get any farther.

I didn't get any farther.

The most difficult exam was an all-day ordeal for physical education instructor, the one thing in which I had had experience. It was a cunningly conceived thing, consisting of a series of rooms wherein sat three silent judges behind tables on which typed directions were neatly tacked. In the first room, for instance, were dance instructions to be executed without music, encouragement, or question. It was definitely not for the self-conscious. Midway through the building, a seven-man board of regents grilled me on world affairs; then came Swedish gymnastics, a one-woman track meet, and finally, a nice big pool of water beneath two high diving boards. There were no written instructions here.

"Put on your bathing suit, swim across the pool and back twice: once on your back and once underwater. Demonstrate the Australian crawl, then rest a few minutes before you start the dives," said a voice from a bathrobe.

I went into the dressing room, continued on out the other end, and across the park, heading straight home.

Still trying, I answered an ad for a female editorial assistant on a well-known theatrical magazine, and was promptly called in for an interview. Again I was thwarted by a receptionist. After a hurried consultation with her superiors, the girl told me to return in half an hour. By then the job was taken, she said.

In a colored paper, I read an item about a girl who was out of town doing publicity work for a religious organization. I had an extra week's annual leave due that spring; so why not try it? The Methodist church sponsored many Negro schools in the South, so I phoned their Rush street publishing house, and they were interested. Taking no more chances with receptionists, I mailed them a little booklet giving seven perfectly wonderful reasons why they should hire me, and won a trial assignment to cover the spring exercises at Philander Smith—all expenses paid!

I was thrilled at the prospect of visiting my first Negro school, but Philander was in Little Rock, and Little Rock was in the South—much farther south than Maryland. Riding a new streamliner out of Chicago, I changed at St. Louis, and was directed to my first Jim Crow car. It was about half the size of a regular coach, and part of that was taken up by the trainmen. But it was clean. I spent some time trying to figure out the man across the aisle—was he a light colored man trying to be friendly or a dark white man trying to be fresh? I finally gave up and turned my attention to the out-of-the-window South, which was equally baffling, for instead of cotton blossoms and magnolia trees, all I could see were vast areas of inundated land and raging torrents caused by the spring rains.

President Jones met the train and drove me to the few small buildings which comprised the college. After exploring the heatless dormitories, I was glad to be housed in the President's home, for it rained steadily for five consecutive days. After plodding through mud and water to visit classes and interview young divinity students, I came back to my room at night and huddled beside the gas heater to type my stories. If this was the sunny South, I thought, give me North Dakota. I couldn't get very close to the students, for in the school was a well-defined dividing line between them and the faculty; and I was now faculty. I even ate with them in a little fenced-in corner of the dining hall, and for some reason—the rain or me—the eight or ten teachers, both white and colored, ate in sullen silence. The food was Southern and atrocious. It was a happy day when I wandered over to the practice cottage and found out about its low prices and good meals, with tea and toast instead of grits and grease. Immediately I deserted the faculty.

I'm afraid the impression I made upon the college was more bad than good. As a guest, I was expected to attend all social functions—something I didn't do at home—so when I went for a walk during a tea given partly in my honor, there was a chill in the Southern air. My second *faux pas* was made at an assembly when I was asked, without warning, to make a half-hour speech on the field of journalism. That was very much like the invitation to swim the length of the park pool; it was over my head, and I knew it. My dress was too short for the high platform, and I knew that, too; but there was no alternative. For twenty minutes, I hid my legs behind the rostrum and sweated blood. When I sat down, a member of the faculty woke up, looked at his watch, and came over to shake my hand.

"This is the first time," he said warmly, "we ever had a speaker who got us out of here ahead of time!"

Much to my relief, the President announced that, unless the weather changed, formals would not be worn for the remaining social events. I didn't have a formal. Came the final day, the day of the big banquet. The morning dawned still cold and rainy, but towards noon the clouds lifted, and the sun broke through, warm and radiant. I rushed downtown to purchase slippers and dress, and those who didn't know about my lack of proper habiliment soon found out, for the girl who did the alterations marched boldly across the campus to the President's home, the dress over her shoulder.

With the change in weather, I took heart and stayed over an extra day to visit Hot Springs with three of the teachers. As we drove through the beautiful Ozarks, I found myself almost liking the South. Seven days, and I had encountered none of the horror and the abuse I had expected; in fact, the clerks in the Little Rock dress shops were more gracious and friendly to me than the average clerk along Chicago's State Street. The same was true of the salesman in the one shoe store I visited, and on the trip to Hot Springs, filling station attendants gave us prompt and courteous service. Of course, aside from that trip and one short afternoon of shopping, I had been so confined within the Negro district I had little opportunity to come into contact with the white South. The railroad station, with its "For Colored" and

"For White" signs above the doors, was a mute reminder of the dual racial system, and the train home was a typical Jim Crow coach, not at all like the modern one on which I had arrived; but a dirty, full-sized coach, close to the engine, close to the smoke and the noise.

And that's all I know about the South.

At last I heard Marian Anderson sing. High up in the back of the theater, Esther and I sat—spellbound, imprisoned in a wall of music, hynotized by the power of a voice which transcended race and color. Never before had I cared for opera, couldn't then understand the many tongues in which she sang, but had I been stone deaf the magnetism and charm of Marian Anderson, standing down there on the huge stage alone, would not have escaped me. Greater still was the miracle of accomplishment, for she, who had reached the highest pinnacle in music, was once a poor little black girl in Philadelphia with one ambition, one voice. Just one in a million.

With each curtain call, we worked our way down from the roof to the main floor, and Marian Anderson was still singing, for they would not let her go.

"Do you want to meet her?" asked Esther, when we got outside.

"Sure, let's," I said.

We walked around to Michigan Avenue, looking for the stage entrance. Halfway up the alley, we met a couple emerging from the theater.

"Could you please tell us where we can find the stage door?" I inquired. "We want to see Miss Anderson."

"Yes, I'd be most happy to," said the bareheaded young man with a charming British accent. "We just left her."

He proceeded to tell us, then walked away, the dark-haired girl clinging to his arm.

"Wasn't he polite?" I said.

Esther stood motionless, mouth open, staring after them.

"Come on, we want to see Marian."

"Era Bell," Esther whispered, "do you know who that was?"

"He did look familiar. Didn't I see him in a WPA show last winter?"

"My God!" screamed Esther. "Oh, my God! That was Lawrence Olivier and Vivian Leigh! They're playing here in *A Midsummer Night's Dream.*"

We never did meet Miss Anderson.

On the third anniversary of the *Giggle Sheet,* now a ten-page paper, I was surprised with two beautiful pieces of airplane luggage—a gift from the administrative staff. Ever since reading Juanita Harrison's *My Great, Wide, Beautiful World,* I had been threatening to go around the world, too. I had literature on European bicycle tours, rates for tramp steamers, catalogs from the universities of Hawaii and Alaska—and now I had the luggage. I had to go somewhere, the gift was a challenge—and a World's Fair was flourishing in San Francisco, where Tom lived. Poor Tom. I'd best not warn him.

Several people in our office had taken the popular, low-priced, all-expense tours, but I believed I could cover as much territory just as cheaply and save myself and the guide a headache about hotels and restaurants, so alone I set out by train to see the West, or as much of it as $200 and seventeen days would permit. Twice I left the shores of America, passed through fifteen states, spent $153, and came home with one day to spare.

I spent my first night in an upper, and by morning I knew full well what was meant by "berth control." After a few sudden stops and starts, I put my clothes in the bed and myself in the hammock. There was also a little embarrassment about climbing Porter Jacob's ladder, especially with Porter Jacob under it. But for complete frustration, try putting on your girdle up there.

Bypassing the Twin Cities, I rode through the pleasant greenness of Minnesota into the bright blue autumn of my Dakota, with its sunburned prairie grasses and fields of threshed grain. Familiar things, the towns, the highways, red elevators, windmills with blades gleaming in the sun, burned firebreaks, discarded railroad ties, grazing stock in endless pastures, and farmers, grouped around the cream cans at tiny stations, waving at the train. And there was the blue sky stretching out to purple bluffs and distant buttes.

At Fargo, Gywn Doyle was waiting for me. Arm in arm, we walked up and down the tracks, and this time there was no strain, no shadow between us. When the train pulled out, I waved good-bye to my friend and retired to the ladies' lounge, where I could sit facing the big window, looking out at God's country. And it was good.

Uncle John, quite gray now, Aunt Ann, less pugnacious, alone and dependent upon each other, greeted me with tears and kisses, stuffed me with big farm helpings of food, and plied me with questions, as we sat in their tiny quarters in the basement of the store. Long after we had gone to bed we talked through the shallow partition that separated our bedrooms, of those who had moved, had married, or had died, and I regaled them with tall tales of the city, sounding not unlike brother Dick.

Heading westward again, I then rode through the bleak but beautiful Bad Lands of the Dakotas, on into the mining country of Montana, where I saw my first mountain in the daytime. Then slowly began the climb up the Rocky Mountains, with their jagged rocks and pine-topped peaks, up, up onto the Continental Divide, then turning, twisting like a huge snake, the train wound its treacherous way down the other side. Onward across streams, through the evergreen-covered mountains of Idaho, we rode, on into the timberlands of Washington, into the golden sunset of the Far West on the edge of the blue Pacific.

People were friendly in the Northwest. I met a young mother and child on their way home from a three-day pack-horse trip through the mountains, a red-haired girl going to her first dude ranch, a man who knew all about Idaho potatoes. The porters were glad to see me, said not many of our people traveled through that part of the country, especially without a pass, and it was nice, mighty nice. To stay within my limited means, I purchased all of my meals from train vendors, and although I had a tourist ticket, I waited each night until eight o'clock to buy my berth from the conductor—and saved several dollars.

In Seattle, I checked my bags in the depot and spent the day sight-seeing in a dense fog, marveling at the big ships and almond-eyed Orientals. Trying to locate the Negro section, I followed a porter until he disappeared into a tavern, leaving me in such a mixture of Japanese, Chinese, and Negroes that I didn't know which way to turn. A little way up the street, I saw a colored woman behind a counter in a dingy little restaurant and entered. The specialty was sea food, and to me it was abominable. At the counter sat three or four swarthy men, slouched over their plates; in the corner a rickety jukebox wailed slow, sad blues. The woman never removed her eyes from my face. I suddenly remembered all the wild stories Mrs. James had told me, of places where people entered and never came out, of the thousands of strange girls who disappeared into vice markets, betrayed by women who pretended to befriend them.

The big woman shuffled over with my dessert. "What's the matter?" She eyed the untouched plate angrily. "Don't you like my food?"

"Oh, yes," I said hastily. "I'm just not very hungry."

"Humph!" she grunted disdainfully and moved away.

Again outside, the dirty street in the gathering dusk was full of ugly shadows. Twice I thought I was being followed; on and on I hurried, afraid to ask directions. When I reached the main part of the city, it was dark and I was tired, so I went to a show to rest and wait until time to catch the boat for British Columbia.

As the big ship steamed out of the harbor and up Puget Sound, I stood at the rail until the lights of the city grew dim, then took a turn about the ship. On the very top deck, I saw a colored boy reading a newspaper. He was surprised to see me, said he was a Chicago boy, lived on Indiana Avenue, but he didn't say where. He was going to an island in the Sound, but he didn't say why. "I'll be seeing you again someday," he promised as I left him, but I had a feeling he never would.

Back in my cozy little cabin, I lay down on my bunk and fell asleep, before I had time to worry about my inability to swim. When I awoke, the boat was motionless, the gray mist of dawn slowly turning pink. By the time I was dressed and on deck, the boat was pulling away from a tiny island, and the boy was gone.

Three hours later, the ship steamed into beautiful Victoria. It was a clear fall day, with just a hint of coolness under the warmth of the bright sun. I came by the customs' officers, past a line of cabs, and up the street to the huge statue of Queen Victoria that guarded the walk in front of the Parliament building. An ancient cabby with an ancient horse and open coach called out to me.

"Right this way, lady, and I'll show you the great city of Victoria."

"How much?"

"Oh, it won't be much. I'll show you all . . ."

"How much?"

"Only two dollars."

"No, thank you," I said. "I'll find it. I've got all day."

He laughed. "You have at that, and a nice day for it, too."

I backed up to take a picture of the Queen. The cabby climbed down from his seat. "Here," he said. "Now you give me the camera, and you stand over beside Her Majesty, and I'll take a picture of both of you."

All day I lived under the British flag, where English bobbies directed miniature cars and numerous bicycles, where women wore knit suits and men tweed knickers. I took a funny little streetcar and rode to the end of the line, where I found a flat, scraggy lake, bordered with dirty gray sand, and in the afternoon I visited the famous Butchart Gardens. And in all of Victoria's forty thousand people, I saw but one Negro. Regretfully, I said good-bye to the cabby and promised to return some day to ride with him.

It was cold on the water. Snow-tipped mountains rose up from the mainland, smoke blue and hazy, with lazy white clouds

287

caught in their rugged crevices. As the sun sank down into the pale gray waves like a great red ball, a girl standing at the rail began to sing "God Bless America." Others stood up to join her, facing the setting sun, their voices swelling with the waves.

I could see her mountains, I knew her prairies well, all around me was the ocean, white with foam. For a brief day I had been away from America, and yet my heart thrilled, my eyes blurred, as I looked out across the water towards my country, my home.

Late that night, I took a train from Seattle and headed down the coast to Portland. There were a lot of things there I wanted to see, but it was only seven in the morning when I finished my breakfast in a little dairy lunchroom, so I took the next train, filled to overflowing with migrant workers, who pulled down the shades, shutting out the view of the sun.

So I got off at the next stop, and again I was sorry, because I found myself stuck for eight hours in a town I had never heard of. Determined to make the most of it, I boarded the only bus in sight, and though the driver warned me there was absolutely nothing of interest to see, I stayed with him until he came to the end of the line—and the beautiful campus of the University of Oregon. I viewed its buildings and flower gardens, entered its modernistic library, then, in loyalty to Susan, went over to the art museum. The building wasn't open, it being between summer and fall semesters, the caretaker said, but he could tell me what it contained. He told me many more things, things about his wife and sons, the years he spent farming in—of all places—North Dakota, of his life in Illinois and Canada. No wonder the coastal states attract so many people from the prairies; there was a spaciousness about them, a fresh wholesomeness that reminded me of North Dakota, and I was glad that I had stopped.

As we crossed the border from Oregon into sunny California, a porter brought me a bottle of fresh orange juice, compliments of the cook, and stayed long enough to show me my first palm tree. I was disappointed. It looked awfully funny without a pot. For miles we traveled through the smelly oil-well

288

country, then followed bodies of water that were not ocean, but stretched endlessly.

At San Francisco, the Travelers Aid gave me the name of a colored girls' home that stood so far above the street the cab driver had to run up the steps and peek at the number before he let me out. Cab fare under such conditions precludes porter service, so I tugged my precious bags up the steep steps and right back down again, for the home was filled. They sent me to a house three blocks away, as the crow flies, but in San Francisco a crow would knock itself out unless it was related to a helicopter. The house was at the bottom of the next valley, a musty old building, with plumbing as old as the Barbary Coast. And just as dangerous.

As soon as my blood pressure receded, I went to Tom's hotel, left word I was in town, and hurried down to the ferry and across the Bay to Treasure Island. To the left loomed Alcatraz, like a huge black monster rising out of the sea, and to the right was the San Francisco Bay Bridge. Somewhere farther out, obscured by the fog, was the famous Golden Gate—said the travel folder. The World's Fair had turned Treasure Island itself into an enchanted fairyland, with rainbow lights and pastel castles growing out of beds of flowers, fantastic and unreal, like something right out of a Walt Disney studio. Regretfully I left the land of make-believe and found my way back to my dreary room.

Tom was waiting for me in the hall, a smiling Tom, glad to see his roving sister. We spent Sunday together, talking of Pop and home and the ten long years since we had parted, and before he left we wrote a letter to Harry, for it was also his birthday. The next day Tom hired a cab, and we rode up and down the perpendicular hills, rode out to Fisherman's Wharf, and through Chinatown, stopping in a cafe where a redheaded girl served raspberry sodas, while a radio played Hawaiian music. But still I didn't see the Golden Gate, saw only the fog that obscured it. At noon Tom left me to go to his job, and I continued on down the coast to the City of the Angels.

For two days I toured Los Angeles, visited famous and fabulous Hollywood, and spent a glorious day at Mr. Wrigley's beautiful Santa Catalina Island, where lazy seals sunned themselves upon rocky shores, where fantastic tropical fish swam in submarine gardens, and real sea horses and flying fishes frolicked in a warm turquoise sea—and hamburgers were twenty-five cents.

On the Island, and on sight-seeing tours especially, I noticed the change in the attitude of my traveling companions, most of whom were from Texas and other parts of the South. They maintained a studied indifference, cold and aloof. Bus drivers alone were my friends, walking and talking with me, breaking the hard white wall of silence. When I returned to the bus from Observatory Hill, I found our driver leaning against the fender watching the thousands of twinkling lights in the city below. We stood there a long time talking about city and country and about people. When the others returned, they stiffened visibly, silent indifference changing to silent contempt, but the driver assisted me into the bus and kept right on talking, and, although he didn't have to, he took me all the way to the other end of town to my hotel.

I was leaving California on my way to Arizona when I saw and recognized my first orange grove, but before I could enjoy the scene we came to the burning Mojave Desert, where Orientals gave way to Indians, palms to Joshua trees, and nothing remained but hot sand and sage and cactus. The nice old Nebraska couple who sat in front of me were also on their way to the Grand Canyon. It was their first vacation together in twenty years. All day long, they fed me figs and grapes from their baskets.

When I awoke in the morning, we were slowly climbing up the pine-covered sides of a mountain, up and up to the Canyon. At first glance, it was just like a big hole in the ground, but as the day wore on, as lights and shadows brought out the colors, it became more prodigious, more awesome. While I was having an egg omelet at the lodge, the caravan started down

Bright Angel Trail. This is a trip where for six dollars you put your torso and your trust on a donkey, and if he ever trips on that rimless path, it's all the more angels to you!

The old couple met me on my way to purchase tickets for the tours and, taking me aside, they told me to take only one trip around the rim and save my money; the other trip was the same thing, they warned, only you see the Canyon from the opposite side. So I saved three dollars and sat two hours, squeezed in between a couple of bulky women, while an Arizona bus driver with a Texas accent told an uncute story about the "nigger porter" who thought the Canyon was a good place to throw old razor blades.

Because of a washout up the line, our train left Williams without a diner. A forty-cent breakfast of orange juice and coffee in the first station restaurant sent me in search of less pretentious surroundings. I can truthfully say I made every dime store lunch counter between Albuquerque and Kansas City. And, by the way, when I got to Kansas City, the depot was jammed with people. They were lined up ten deep along the street outside, and a cordon of police was thrown around the building to keep back the crowds. Cameras clicked, a band played. It was quite a surprise, all those people there to meet my train. It pleased me, and I'm sure it pleased Wendell L. Wilkie.

He got off, too.

I couldn't talk very much about my trip when I returned home. People on WPA weren't supposed to be able to travel, and a trip to California was in the luxury class, certification or no certification, in a compartment or on $153.

The airplane luggage was nearly a year old before I had an opportunity to take an airplane ride, and then I couldn't use it. Silver, like many others, had left our office for a job in a social agency, and she was realizing one of her ambitions by attending night school. When her sociology class chartered a twenty-two-passenger airliner to observe the pattern of the city from the sky, she invited me to go along as one of her guests. Her other guest, a fellow from her office, was as surprised as the instructor was when he saw me. After two hours up and out of this world, it was hard to come down to the lowly level of a streetcar, to get our feet back on the ground. I don't know what happened to the fellow, but Silver and I, hearts still soaring above the clouds, rode out to Jackson Park, got hot dogs, and walked over to the harbor to watch the boats.

"I'm going to be somebody and ride airplanes every day," said Silver. "I'll be damned if I'll be a clerk all my life!"

"What are you going to be?" I asked.

"An actress or a scientist—or something. I want to do big things, to startle the world!" She looked sharply at me. "Well?"

"You know what I'm aiming for? Some day I'll write a book or have a magazine of my own, a funny one."

"Know what?" Silver's gray eyes were shining. In her new job she had found herself; for the first time in her life she had a goal. "This is 1941. By the fall of 1943 my name will be up in lights or headlines. I mean it, Era Bell."

"And I'll have had something accepted for publication— paid acceptance, not contributions."

Many things happened in the next two years, including Pearl Harbor. Silver got her name in headlines all right, even got her picture in the papers, not as a scientist or a star, but as winner of a cow-milking contest at the stock show. By 1943, Silver was dead—she committed suicide, they said, in a sudden fit of despondency.

And I? Well, I was a failure as a paid writer and still alive by Divine Providence, having experienced another of those cycles of calamity that ran the whole gamut from talking myself into an operation to narrowly escaping the Detroit riot; and the only evidence I had to show for my escapes, besides a cute little incision, was a pair of torn jodhpur breeches, mementos of Willow Springs.

I had found the city version of horseback riding, replete with saddles and tight breeches, unsatisfactory, to put it mildly. When one thus attired crosses a teeming Sunday highway on a strange horse, things can happen. An impatient driver miscalculated our speed, and suddenly I found myself entangled in a bumper, four flying hooves, and a pair of stirrups. The driver calmly backed off the horse and went about his Sunday driving.

My job picture took a sudden change for the better in those two years, and I was called on one of the many clerical exams I had taken and was assigned to a civil service job back at the Merchandise Mart. It was a nice office, this time, one with metal furniture and indirect lighting, with venetian blinds and a thirty-eight hour week. All that and air-conditioning! At the end of six months, most of my friends were getting meritorious raises, and if Washington hadn't intervened, I might have gotten one, too.

A letter I thought I was sending to an employee in the State Department of Labor, across the river, got into the wrong mail basket and landed in Washington, the Federal Department of Labor. It took two months to trace it back to me, and by that time I think everybody from Secretary Perkins down to the boys in the mailroom had read my very poetic reasons why such-and-such a labor dispute was delayed by so and so. Whether that had anything to do with it or not, I had to wait six more months for a raise and an apartment.

The place I wanted was in a building recently turned over to Negroes (at double the rent), and its tenants limited to those earning at least three times the rental. Even with the raise, I barely made it, but on the day I moved, I received a telegram to report for duty as an employment service interviewer, at twenty dollars more a month. At last I was free from landlords and landladies. I had a home of my own, a place where all my friends were welcome, both white and black, for although the large numbers of colored workers now in white-collar jobs has brought about a healthy change in public attitudes, there are those in both races who still frown upon mixed friendships.

After ten years' experience in Chicago, with and without jobs, it is a pleasure to be on the other side of the desk, on the giving side instead of the asking. It is exciting, this employment business in Chicago, the crossroads of America. From the East and West, the North and South, they come—rich man, poor man, black man, white; the foreigner, the old-timer, the young, the intellectual, the illiterate—restless, changing jobs, changing skills and locations, seeking new industries and higher salaries.

Sometimes they are a little reluctant to talk to me, because I am a government employee and some people just don't like government employees; because I am a woman, and what does a woman know about an annealer in a foundry? Because I am a Negro.

"I'd tell you what I do," said a powerhouse electrician, "but you wouldn't understand."

"Maybe I would."

"Have you ever seen a generator or a rotary converter?"

"No, but I can soon tell if *you* have." I found the definition of a powerhouse electrician in the *Dictionary of Occupational Titles* and read to him. He wanted to buy the book.

To the Southerner new to the North, it sometimes takes a bit of doing to come to a Negro for an interview.

"You know," said a disheveled, unshaven Okie, "I ain't never seen no cullud folks workin' in offices before."

"Is that so?" I asked out of politeness, not curiosity.

"It's all right, though; I'm not complainin', mind you, but down South, where I come from . . ."

I went on with the interview.

Referral card in hand, he lingered at my desk "This is a good job you give me, and I sure hope I git it. Thank you—Miss."

Some come in griping, complaining about the government, the job, the waiting in line—impatient and hard-to-please people —but after they tell their story, get it off their chests, they can laugh again and, if need be, get into another line. In the struggle for jobs, class, racial, and religious prejudice quickly comes to the fore: college people have difficulty finding jobs in factories, Protestants rail against Jews, Negroes are denied jobs because of color. I have heard an Italian woman say she hated Poles, an

294

Irishman refuse to work for a Jew, but when a white Protestant accused his employer of discrimination, said the Jews and the Negroes (and those were not his terms) got all the good jobs, I thought I had heard everything.

But the public, quick to complain, is just as willing to comply, and sometimes to quite amusing lengths. A thoroughgoing Canadian, seeking employment, came equipped with birth and marriage certificates, first divorce and naturalization papers, recommendations, and Red Cross card. A colored man, feeling the need for proof of dependents, laid his five-month-old baby on the counter and said, "It's mine, lady, and I've got three more at home just as helpless."

Most of the applicants are good-natured, friendly people, eager to see the sunny side. They exhibit pictures of sweethearts and children, bring in poems they have written, letters they have received. A miner from Nevada returned to show me a beautiful diamond ring he bought for his fiancée; a policeman, after his interview, said the only difference between talking to me and going to the priest was absolution; and a woman admitted she had had a little trouble with her last job, but everything was all right now. Her employer was dead. She should know; she killed him.

Cranks, philanthropists, or plain, everyday Americans, I like them all. For every bad one, there are twenty good ones. We can't always find jobs for them, we aren't always successful in getting them to take the jobs we find, but we can give them a kind and sympathetic audience. It is surprising to know how many people in the world are hungry for kindness, to have someone believe in them. And I do believe in them.

When a forelady in a box factory asks, "Isn't it wonderful to live in a country where you can sit down and tell your troubles to someone and have them listen?"

When an old man, a retired engineer, comes up to your desk, saying, "Last night I heard the President's voice He said he needed me. I don't want pay; I want to help my country."

When a young kid comes in to tell you that he's still on the job you gave him, and that his company this very day is being awarded the Navy E. And he's so proud and happy, he tells the little colored girl next in line where she can find a job—the same place where his sister works.

And the employer at the other end of the phone says, "I like you; I like the way you talk. You sound like a real American girl."

When those things are said, I know there is still good in the world, that way down underneath, most Americans are fair; that my people and your people can work together and live together in peace and happiness, if they but have the opportunity to know and understand each other.

The chasm is growing narrower. When it closes, my feet will rest on a united America.